MR. ADAMS'S

Last Crusade

MR. ADAMS'S

Last Crusade

JOHN QUINCY ADAMS'S EXTRAORDINARY
POST-PRESIDENTIAL LIFE IN CONGRESS

JOSEPH WHEELAN

PUBLICAFFAIRS
New York

Published in the United States by PublicAffairs™, a member of the Perseus Books Group.

BOOK DESIGN BY JEFF WILLIAMS

Library of Congress Cataloging-in-Publication Data

Wheelan, Joseph.

Mr. Adams's last crusade : John Quincy Adams's extraordinary post-presidential life in Congress / Joseph Wheelan. — 1st ed.

p. cm.

Includes bibliographical references and index.

ISBN-13: 978-0-7867-2012-5 (hardcover)

ISBN-10: 0-7867-2012-3 (hardcover)

1. Adams, John Quincy, 1767-1848. 2. Adams, John Quincy, 1767-1848—Political and social views. 3. United States. Congress. House—Biography. 4. Legislators—United States—Biography. 5. Presidents—United States—Biography. 6. United States—Politics and government—1815-1861. I. Title.

E377.W47 2008

973.5'5092—dc22

[B]

2007040831

First Edition

10 9 8 7 6 5 4 3 2 1

Contents

Author's Note

American presidents rarely diverge from the ancient example of Cincinnatus, the Roman consul who, after serving as dictator during a national emergency, returned home to his plow. George Washington was the American exemplar of this model of public service, and his successors, for the most part, have adopted the practice of retiring to their home place.

Ex-presidents often become living ghosts of their formerly famous selves. We see them at ceremonial functions, but otherwise they are invisible to us. We picture them in their studies, organizing their papers and spending a couple of hours a day writing their memoirs, or golfing, sailing, or riding horses—indulging in the private pursuits that they often sacrificed while they were busy serving the public.

In my lifetime, presidents Jimmy Carter and Bill Clinton broke with this archetype to devote their post-presidencies to humanitarian and other public causes. Previously, William Howard Taft, president from 1909 to 1913, was appointed to the U.S. Supreme Court in 1921 and served nine years as its chief justice. After losing a third-party bid for the presidency, Theodore Roosevelt explored Brazil's River of Doubt, a place visited (at least figuratively) by all presidents at one time or another. Andrew Johnson, impeached and nearly convicted, was subsequently elected to the Senate but died after serving only four months.

But no ex-president can match the astonishing record of John Quincy Adams. His presidency, generally regarded as a failure, was of only one term's duration—he and his father, John Adams, were the only one-term presidents among the first seven chief executives. Adams appeared destined for anonymous retirement in his native Massachusetts when something serendipitous happened; his friends and neighbors sent him to the House of Representatives. This book focuses on Adams's amazing seventeen years in the House of Representatives. No recent Adams biography, and few of any vintage, has made his congressional career its primary subject; books on the second Adams tend to recount his life as a rising narrative climaxed by his dismal presidency. His congressional career is usually presented as an afterthought. While this book relates Adams's extraordinary early life as a diplomat, son of the Revolution, and secretary of state, his actions during these years and his presidency are here presented as a prelude to his entry into the House of Representatives in December 1831.

Adams entered the House as a freshman congressman at the age of sixty-four, believing that if the people summoned him, he was obligated to obey that summons. This was an antiquated notion that did not fit with the raw political ambition and slash-and-burn politics of the Jackson era. In the seventeen years that followed, Adams largely redeemed his presidential record by becoming Congress's leading champion of the First Amendment right to petition and its first great opponent of slavery. He also became a passionate advocate for the sciences and oversaw the establishment of the Smithsonian Institution, ensuring that James Smithson's generous bequest to the United States was not squandered. Most importantly, Adams became Congress's conscience—a prickly, sarcastic, and highly articulate voice of reason. His allies fondly referred to him as "Old Man Eloquent"; his enemies not so kindly called him the "Madman of Massachusetts," and worse.

Few public figures have been as highly principled or as extraordinarily intelligent as Adams. Few have worked as hard as he.

Adams knew the ropes of the House better than his longer-serving colleagues. He used that knowledge to torment the slave power during the 1830s and 1840s, to condemn the government's cruel removal of eastern Indian tribes, to uphold the right of women to participate in the political process, and to argue against the war of aggression against Mexico.

Why is John Quincy Adams relevant now? Today, we Americans regard our government with weary cynicism and distrust. We need to be reminded that it needn't be this way.

America once produced a fearless, combative, highly principled "man of the whole country" in the person of John Quincy Adams, and she can do it again. We need to listen for his or her clear, reasonable voice amid the din of equivocating, obfuscating, and temporizing politicians. The byword that Adams had engraved on his signet ring is a good enough admonition: We must "Watch."

Prologue

"*And so I am launched again upon
the faithless wave of politics.*"

—Former President John Quincy Adams, upon being
nominated for the 12th Congressional District

SEPTEMBER 18, 1830, BOSTON

The unlikely courtship ritual began with an unsigned paragraph in the *Boston Daily Courier* proposing that John Quincy Adams, eighteen months removed from a disappointing single-term presidency, represent Massachusetts's Plymouth District in Congress.

On this mild late-summer day, the stout, severe-looking scholar, poet, amateur scientist, devout Christian, master diplomat, and sixty-three-year-old son of the Revolution, indifferently attired as usual, traveled to the Worcester home of Congressman John B. Davis for the ritual's next phase.

Well versed in the antiquated gentlemen's politics of George Washington, Thomas Jefferson, and his father, John Adams, John Quincy Adams knew what the summons to Davis's home meant and what his answer would necessarily be. The sixth president's hometown, Quincy, had recently been gerrymandered into the 12th Congressional District (also known as the Plymouth District), now represented by the Reverend Joseph Richardson of Hingham. Members of Richardson's Unitarian congregation had grown impatient with his long absences in Washington over the past three years and were now pressuring him to forego another congressional term so that he could devote more time to church matters.

Richardson's quandary notwithstanding, Adams was certainly not honor-bound to uphold the National Republicans' standard in Congress. No former president had ever returned to elective office, much less Congress. Adams's unhappy tenure as chief executive and the surpassingly vicious 1828 re-election campaign that had supplanted him with the "military chieftain," Andrew Jackson, had surely curdled any vestiges of ambition in him.

At Davis's home, Congressman Richardson, as expected, informed Adams that he had resolved to return to his parish and would not seek a third term. Would Adams consent to run in his place? The office, said Richardson, was not beneath an ex-president; "instead of degrading the individual, [it] would elevate the Representative character."

Adams agreed with Richardson's assessment. "No person can be degraded by serving the people as a Representative of Congress. Nor, in my opinion, would an ex-President of the United States be degraded by serving as a Selectman of his town, if elected thereto by the people." Nevertheless, he was inclined to pass up the invitation because of his advanced age and poor health. "It might depend upon circumstances," he said as he left, leaving the door slightly ajar.

In the parlance of the code observed by Adams, this was tantamount to acceptance. After his defeat by Jackson in 1828, he had been sounded out about serving in the U.S. Senate. His initial reaction had been to decline and "withdraw from all connection with public affairs," but two days' reflection had led him to modify his position to one in which he would "not hold myself at liberty to decline repairing to any station which they [the people] assign me." The people, however, chose someone else.

The old political etiquette that he nearly alone persisted in practicing forbade him to give the slightest indication that he was seeking office. "To say that I would accept would be so near to asking for a vote, that I did not feel disposed to go so far. I wished the people to act spontaneously, at their own discretion." It was this curiously passive attitude, so out of step with the aggressive new politics being practiced at the time, that had enabled the triumvirate of Jackson, Martin Van Buren, and William Crawford and their many allies to sink Adams's "Liberty with Power" agenda and crush his re-election bid in 1828. Accurately reading Adams's willingness to run for Congress, Davis, Richardson, and their friends worked to build support for his candidacy in the Plymouth District, the "Old Colony" where the Pilgrims had landed and settled in the 1620s. Leading citizens came forward to encourage Adams to accept the nomination. A deacon at Adams's church suggested that many citizens wished to see him elected. Others warned that if he declined, "there was no prospect" that another worthy candidate could be found.

The *Boston Daily Courier* carried an extensive story exploring Adams's candidacy, and a favorable editorial ran in the *Hingham Gazette*. "We think him a good rallying point," Solomon Lincoln Jr. wrote to Congressman Davis, "for those who wish to throw off the incubus of Jacksonism, to send an able man to Congress, and at the same time to compliment an abused patriot."

Adams finally yielded, and on October 13, 1830, the National Republicans nominated Adams for the 12th Congressional District. "And so I am launched again upon the faithless wave of politics," the new candidate observed dryly.

Less than two years earlier, the former president, seared by the savagery of the 1828 election, had professed a longing for "the deepest retirement." Adams had known in his bones as early as 1826 that he, as a minority president whose agenda had been trampled by his many adversaries, had scant chance of winning a second term. During the 1828 campaign, both presidential candidates had been outrageously slandered: Adams was accused of procuring young women to seduce the Russian czar, and Jackson of stealing another man's wife. While Adams's supporters depicted Jackson as woefully unqualified for the White House, the well-organized Democrats, led by a military hero with a populist touch, accused Adams of aristocratic aspirations. Unfortunately, Adams played to that misconception by avoiding rallies and remaining silent and above the fray, in the tradition of the "old politics." The Jackson Democrats' most effective weapon against Adams, however, was his purportedly "corrupt bargain" with Henry Clay, which had won him the presidency in 1825.

After being decisively defeated, Adams had been so bitter that he boycotted his successor's inauguration, an uncommonly severe rebuke by a former president. The only other president to do so was his father, John Adams, who refused to attend Thomas Jefferson's inauguration in 1801. In his encyclopedic diary, faithfully kept with few lapses since the age of twelve, John Quincy Adams revealed his dark mood: "The sun of my political life sets in the deepest gloom."

In three decades of matrimony, Louisa Catherine Johnson Adams had accompanied her husband to Prussia, returned with him to Massachusetts and then the nation's capitol, and then journeyed to St. Petersburg, crossing war-ravaged Europe in 1814 to join Adams in Ghent, with their young son Charles, amid Napoleon Bonaparte's "100 Days." During this time, she also gave birth to twelve children, only three of whom survived their first two years.

Nothing had been easy for Louisa. Although her father was American, she was British-born and educated in Europe. These circumstances became a recurrent issue in her life with John Quincy Adams, beginning with her mother-in-law Abigail's negative reaction upon learning of her son's engagement: "I would hope for the love I bear my country that the Siren is at least a *half-blood*." Although Louisa grew to respect her mother-in-law's intelligence and forceful character, they were never close. John Adams, however, was fond of his daughter-in-law.

After her husband won the presidency, the White House years proved to be long and difficult for Louisa. Frequent periods of illness led her to confine herself in her chambers for days at a time. The isolation, lack of exercise, and poor diet made matters worse.

Now, finally out of the Washington pressure cooker, she was dismayed that the respite after thirty years of public life was to be so brief. "There are some silly plans going on here and God only knows in what they will end, but I fear not at all to my taste," she wrote understatedly. If she were going to be "dragged forward" again, "it should be for something respectable and worthy." Evidently, being a congressman's wife was neither. With sarcasm, she observed, "Family is and must ever be a secondary consideration to a zealous patriot."

Their son Charles Francis Adams flatly opposed his father's decision, believing that he had succumbed to the "temporary seductions of popular distinction," against which resistance "is the most solid evidence of greatness." For all that, Charles still regarded his father with admiration, while regretting that he had effectively condemned his family to an exhausting life in the public eye.

John Quincy Adams's eighteen-month hiatus from public life had been a compendium of grief, worry, energetic work on family matters, scholarly indulgence, vengeful composition, and sometimes, boredom. The Adamses had lingered several months in Washington at Meridian House, which they had rented from Commodore David Porter. There, Adams assembled his papers and books in preparation for the trip to the home place in Quincy. He also exhaustively researched and wrote an 84,000-word rebuttal in his ongoing dispute with thirteen prominent New England

"Old Federalists," but he was ultimately persuaded not to publish the scathing diatribe.

Amid the family's transition to private life, shattering news reached them: the death of the oldest of the Adamses' three sons, George Washington Adams, a gentle, high-strung ne'er-do-well with a drinking problem, who, as it turned out, had fathered an illegitimate child by a chambermaid. While en route to Washington to assist in the move to Quincy, the twenty-eight-year-old had become delusional and had vanished from the deck of the steamship *Benjamin Franklin* into Long Island Sound. His body washed up on City Island weeks later. Heartbroken, the Adamses tried to console one another by praying together, but George's death would torment them for years.

Upon reaching Quincy, Adams found the nearly century-old family home of John and Abigail Adams dilapidated and stripped of most of its furniture, as a consequence of the division of John Adams's estate among fourteen heirs after his death in 1826. Aided by his sons John II and Charles, Adams set to work making the mansard-roofed "Big House" habitable again, as it had always been his cherished dream to live there with Louisa. His return to the home place occasioned no welcoming ceremonies or dinner invitations in Boston, whose mayor, Harrison Gray Otis, was the leader of the "13 Confederates" with whom he was feuding. The Boston establishment further signaled its displeasure by dropping Adams as president of the American Academy of Arts and Sciences.

Adams compared the abrupt transition from the busy White House to private life to "an instantaneous flat calm in the midst of a hurricane." He found it disconcerting. "I cannot yet settle my mind to a regular course of future employment," he wrote, but clearly stated his intention "to bury myself in complete retirement, as much so as a nun taking the veil." Oppressed though he was by George's suicide, Adams tackled the daunting job of making the

Big House livable. One satisfying task was unpacking the boxes and trunks that contained his nearly 6,000 books, which he had had shipped from Washington. "No such library exists in the hands of any other individual in the United States, but I have never had the enjoyment of it," he wrote in his diary. He hired tradesmen to build bookshelves throughout the house, to install Franklin stoves for wintertime heating, and to make repairs. Cash-poor, Adams saw his debts climb to $42,000, with $13,000 worth of notes coming due.

From these practical affairs, he turned to organizing his father's papers as a prelude to writing his biography. "I propose to devote henceforth three hours a day to that portion of my business," he vowed. But the writing project was often put aside as Adams occupied himself with his fitness regimen of daily walks and swims and the pleasure that he took in prowling the ancestral Adams acreage that he had cobbled together from his father's heirs.

On the last day of 1829, Adams summarized the year's severe reversals: "The loss of power and of popular favor I could have endured with fortitude, and relief from the slavery of public office . . . But my beloved son! Mysterious heaven! Let me bow in submission to thy will. Let me no longer yield to a desponding or distressful spirit."

No matter how strenuous his efforts—the diary to which he devoted hours every day, the Bible-reading, the poems he wrote, the lengthy correspondence, his public duties—Adams was never satisfied with himself. Although Adams had had a lifetime of extraordinary achievements—serving as minister to the Netherlands, Prussia, Russia, and England; negotiating the Treaty of Ghent, which ended the War of 1812; and serving as a U.S. senator, secretary of state, and U.S. president—he astonishingly observed: "My whole life has been a succession of disappointments. I can scarcely recollect a single instance of success to anything that I ever undertook." Yet he acknowledged, "Fortune, by which I understand Providence, has showered blessings upon me profusely."

NOVEMBER 1830, QUINCY

When his would-be constituents cast their ballots, it was clear that the large majority wanted Adams to represent them in Congress: Adams received 1,817 votes, the Jacksonian Democrat, Arad Thompson, received 373 votes, and William Baylies, the "Old Federalist" candidate, garnered 279 votes. The jubilant Adams acted as though he had just won his first public office. "My election as President of the United States was not half so gratifying to my inmost soul," he gushed. Tempering his joy was the sober realization that his election would force him out of a peaceful retirement and cast him "back again amidst the breakers of the political ocean."

His family's unanimous disapproval of his new public career might have warned him that the path ahead would not be strewn with roses. Louisa announced that she would not accompany him to Washington, where Adams had eagerly proposed to go as soon as possible, though he needn't have returned until March, when he would be sworn in. Louisa had no desire to live again as a Washington politician's wife. She unhappily confessed to their son John II, "My nervous system is too much shaken by long suffering to admit of my again plunging into the very focus of political machination."

Twenty-year-old Charles impertinently suggested to his father that he should have taken up literature instead of politics. When Adams replied, "I must fulfill my destiny," Charles irritably retorted, "I cannot help thinking success would be far more certain, if you rejected the idea of *Destiny* altogether!" Evidently realizing that "destiny" sounded presumptuous, Adams responded more humbly: "I must take blame to myself for all the disasters that befall me."

Adams's five presidential predecessors had all retired from public life after leaving office, but Adams predicted that his example would encourage them to participate in public affairs, even if it meant accepting subordinate offices. It was inconceivable to Adams that he would decline a summons from the people with the excuse that he had already served. His election was no less than a call to duty. As he wrote in his diary, quoting his hero, Cicero: "'Defendi rempublicam adolescens; non deseram senex.'" (I will not desert in my old age the Republic that I defended in my youth.)

MR. ADAMS'S

Last Crusade

Chapter One

Favored Son of the Revolution

---

*"I shall be much mistaken if, in as short a period
as can well be expected, he is not found at
the head of the diplomatic corps."*

—President George Washington on
John Quincy Adams, minister to the Netherlands

JUNE 1791, BOSTON

*I*t had been a discouraging few years for John Quincy
Adams, the vice president's oldest son. His life, previously unfolding in a seamless fabric of opportunity and
achievement, had lost momentum. His precocious childhood amid
the excitement of the Revolution, in Paris by the side of the era's
prime movers—Thomas Jefferson, Benjamin Franklin, and his
father—and in St. Petersburg as a teenage translator, and his Harvard career and law studies had ended anticlimactically with his
semi-employment in a threadbare Boston law practice at age
twenty-three. He had lost his first case, and clients were few; his
scanty income had compelled him to break off courting his first
love. While business was slowly picking up, he often wrote poetry
or read Cicero, Tacitus, Burke, and Hume to pass the time during

the long afternoons in his quiet office. Sometimes he dreamed of being a literary man instead of a lawyer.

But the publication of Thomas Paine's incendiary defense of the French Revolution, *The Rights of Man*, with its attack on the Revolution's great English critic, Edmund Burke, inspired Adams to put pen to paper, and he discovered that he had a gift for polemics. His eleven "Publicola" letters in the *Columbian Centinel* were the monumental turning point of his young life, lighting the way to the public life for which his parents' painstaking guidance and his years abroad had been a long preparation.

Born July 11, 1767, in Braintree, Massachusetts, John Quincy Adams was named for his mother's grandfather, Colonel John Quincy, who was dying as his great-grandson was being baptized. As Adams would later write, "It was the name of one passing from earth to immortality" and thus "a perpetual admonition to do nothing unworthy of it."

Adams's father and his mother, Abigail Smith Adams, were both descended from the earliest settlers of the Massachusetts Bay Colony. They were related to *Mayflower* Compact signer John Alden and Priscilla Mullins of Plymouth Colony, and through John Quincy Adams's paternal grandmother, Susanna Boylston, to Zabdial Boylston, who introduced the smallpox inoculation to North America. The ancestry of the family in England dated to the 1215 Magna Carta, which bears the name and seal of Saer de Quincy. Clearly, John Quincy Adams's consciousness of his ancestors' achievements was a lifelong influence that spurred his ambition.

The Adams farm consisted of 140 acres by the sea at the foot of Penn's Hill and was bequeathed to John Adams by his father, "Deacon John" Adams. In one of the property's two clapboard farmhouses was born John Adams in 1735, and in the other, thirty-two years later, John Quincy Adams entered the world. John Adams later bought a house in town—the "Big House"—where he lived after he retired from public life and where his son and his family lived in the summertime. All three structures survive today as historical sites.

John Quincy, the eldest son, was two years the junior of his sister Abigail, or Nabby. A second sister, Susanna, born in 1769, died a year later. Charles was born in 1770, and Thomas followed Charles in 1772. At age nine, John Quincy routinely rode horseback from Braintree to Boston to post the family's correspondence, sometimes stopping to see his kinsman, Sam Adams. He did not attend the Braintree school, which was closed during the Revolution to save money for the war, but was tutored by his father's law clerk, John Thaxter. By the time he was ten, he had read two volumes of Tobias Smollett's *Complete History of England*, James Thomson's *The Seasons*, and Shakespeare and Alexander Pope. Like his father, he read Lord Henry St. John Bolingbroke, including his popular *Idea of a Patriot King*, making notes in the margin beside his father's. He struggled valiantly with John Milton's *Paradise Lost*, to the point of "the shedding of solitary tears," but did not get through it until he was thirty years old. "I might as well have attempted to read Homer before I had learnt the Greek alphabet," he later observed.

As a young child, Adams had a window seat on the early days of the American Revolution. He strolled with Sam Adams on Boston Commons to look over the British troops there and also saw the Boston militiamen. When a Patriot unit on its way to Lexington briefly camped on the Adams's property, the young John Quincy, tutored by a soldier, learned to perform the manual of arms with a musket. The Adamses also took in Patriot refugees from Boston. On June 17, 1775, John Quincy climbed Penn's Hill with his mother and watched the fighting on Bunker Hill, where more than a half-century later, he would see stonecutters hew granite for the Bunker Hill Memorial. Adams would remember all his life his father's letters from Philadelphia in July 1776 reporting Congress's progress on a resolution for independence.

John and Abigail Adams closely regulated their children's behavior and guided their learning. John Quincy learned early on that one should never waste time, as evidenced by a June 1777 letter the nine-year-old boy wrote to his father. In the letter, obviously prompted or dictated by his mother, he regretfully observed, "My thoughts are running after birds eggs, play and trifles. . . . I am more satisfied with myself when I have applied part of my time to some useful employment than when I have idled it away about trifles and play." Abigail's zealous supervision of her children's moral development may have been prompted by the troubled life of her alcoholic brother, William Smith Jr., who eventually abandoned his family.

On a raw February day in 1778, the ten-year-old John Quincy Adams and his father stepped into a rowboat at his Uncle Norton Quincy's dock. Their feet were covered with hay to keep them warm as they were rowed to the *Boston*, a new frigate bound for France, where John Adams hoped to obtain financial and military aid for the American Revolution.

During the Atlantic crossing—a first for both of them—British warships shadowed the *Boston* for two days before she shook them off. Then, during a storm, lightning struck the mast, stunning three crewmen into unconsciousness. Later in their journey, the *Boston* captured a British privateer after a battle in which a cannonball sailed over young Adams's head and smashed the spanker yard. A few days later, a signal gun accidentally exploded, shattering the leg of a lieutenant. John Adams held the man down while the leg was taken off, but the lieutenant later died and was buried at sea.

In Paris, John Adams learned that Benjamin Franklin and French diplomats had already signed a treaty of alliance binding the nations commercially and in common cause against Great Britain. Congress decided that John Adams was unneeded, and in the summer of 1779, father and son sailed home. A few weeks later, the Continental government asked Adams to return to Europe as a peace commissioner, in the expectation that peace negotiations with Great Britain would soon begin.

John Quincy Adams initially resisted returning to Paris with his father and younger brother, Charles; instead, he wished to fulfill his family's plan for him to attend Andover Academy. But his mother finally convinced him that he would learn more in Europe than he would at Andover.

On November 12, 1779, twelve-year-old John Quincy Adams took his father's advice and commenced the diary that he would indefatigably maintain for the next sixty-eight years, ultimately filling fifty manuscript volumes. His first entry began: "This morning at about 11 o'clock I took leave of my Mamma, my sister, and Brother Tommy, and went to Boston with Mr. [John Jr.] Thaxter to go on board the Frigate the Sensible of 28 twelve Pounders." Five years would pass before young Adams would again see his mother, brother, and sister.

Abigail continued to lecture her son about his comportment, mental occupations, goals, and duties from afar. While John Adams guided his children's practical education, Abigail shaped their characters. Abigail admonished John Quincy to be on guard against "the odious monster"—vice—and to not disgrace his mother or prove himself unworthy of his father. Her letters often were an admixture of Herodotus expounding on the qualities of a great leader and Marcus Aurelius counseling self-sacrifice. John Quincy, she felt, had a duty to excel. "It will be expected of you, my son . . . that your improvements should bear some proportion to your advantages. Nothing is wanting with you but diligence and application, since nature has not been deficient." Abigail also could be a Spartan mother advising her son to triumph or to die in the breach: "For dear as you are to me, I had much rather you should have found your grave in the ocean you have crossed, or any untimely death crop you in your infant years, rather than see you an immoral profligate or a graceless child."

In the summer of 1780, the Adamses moved from Paris to Amsterdam, where John Adams, the new minister to the Netherlands, borrowed money to buy food, arms, and uniforms for the Continental Army.

Then in 1781, Francis Dana, a family friend and diplomat from Boston, asked fourteen-year-old John Quincy Adams to travel with him to St. Petersburg as his translator and secretary. The fourteen months Adams spent in Russia served as his apprenticeship in American diplomacy. When he was not translating the French spoken in the czarina's court for Dana, Adams was roaming Peter the Great's city on the Gulf of Finland and reading David Hume's and Thomas Macaulay's histories of England, Molière's plays, and Adam Smith's *Wealth of Nations*. He translated Cicero, soaked up Russian culture, and indulged in what would become a lifelong passion for buying and collecting books.

Later, he joined his father in Paris, where the teenager formed friendships with two of the preeminent Founding Fathers, Franklin and Jefferson, as they and his father tried to secure trade agreements with the European nations. Young Adams accompanied his father to glittering receptions and frequented the opera. His diary describes attending merry dinners with Franklin, Jefferson, and other diplomats, going to the theater with Franklin, and discussing "animal magnetism" with the inventor diplomat. His more informal relationship with Jefferson was akin to that of young uncle and favorite nephew, and Adams often made notes on some of his far-ranging conversations with Jefferson. In one, Adams wrote, "the blacks, he tells me, are very well treated" in Virginia, where Jefferson owned one hundred slaves. Reminiscing forty years later about those days in Paris, John Adams wrote to Jefferson that John Quincy "appeared to me to be almost as much your boy as mine."

In 1785, Adams returned to America, where he enrolled at Harvard, his father's alma mater, and embarked on a career in law.

The eighteen-year-old was described as well groomed, "rather short and plump," and prone to cock his head, with one eye half-closed and one hand in a pocket, similar to his father's mannerisms. He also wore a sword, which was customary among European gentlemen. Adams graduated second in his class of fifty-one and delivered a commencement oration that urged patriotic self-sacrifice.

John Quincy Adams joined five other law students in the Newburyport office of Theophilus Parsons, one of New England's best attorneys and a future Massachusetts Supreme Court justice. Try though he did, Adams never learned to love the legal profession. Practically every day, Adams found himself wishing that he had chosen another vocation and that he was anywhere but in Newburyport, a town of 5,000 that seemed even smaller for his having recently lived in St. Petersburg, Paris, and Boston. He decided that he wanted to be a literary man, "who can invent, who can create." For diversion, he read voraciously, cultivated a passion for writing poetry, played the flute, and shot birds.

Seeking relief from his solitude and the tedium of his law books, the Puritan from Braintree began going to parties where he danced with pretty young women until the early hours of the morning. At dinners with male companions, Adams and his friends passed the time "smoking and singing," as well as indulging in the young man's pastime of recreational drinking. His remorseful morning-after diary entries reveal the price that he paid for his bacchanalian excesses.

Like young adults in all times, Adams speculated about his future. On his twenty-first birthday, July 11, 1788, he wrote, "I feel sometimes a strong desire to know what my circumstances will be in seven years from this: but I must acknowledge, I believe my happiness would rather be injured than improved by the information."

Worries about the future likely triggered the episodic depression that sometimes, while he was a lawyer-in-training, kept Adams housebound for days, even weeks. Adams's susceptibility to depression was probably hereditary; his biographer Jack Shepherd writes that John Adams and all three of his sons suffered from some degree of depression, as did several later Adams descendants.

Adams's diary entry of December 6, 1787, was his first written acknowledgment of this problem. "I felt a depression of spirits to which I have hitherto been entirely a stranger," he wrote, conceding that while he had felt downhearted before, "the feelings which I now experienced were different from what I ever knew before and such, as I hope I shall never again experience." Sleepless much of that night, he finally fell into a light slumber in which he had "extravagant dreams." Two months later, he reported having been in "low spirits" for the past ten days. "My nerves have got into a disagreeable trim, and I fear I shall be obliged to pay still less attention to books than I have of late."

During a recurrence in the fall of 1788, his severe anxiety prevented him from sleeping, studying, or reading. He was driven to write in his diary, "God of Heavens! . . . take me from this world before I curse the day of my birth." While taking medicine prescribed by the family doctor, Adams took his mother's advice to adopt a routine of "constant exercise"—long walks and bird hunting—and he began to recover. He eventually completed his apprenticeship in the Parsons law office and in 1790 opened a law practice in Boston in a house owned by his father.

During his final year of reading law under Parsons, Adams fell in love with fifteen-year-old Mary Frazier, the second daughter of Moses Frazier of Newburyport. They met at a party, and romance bloomed. In the fall of 1790, soon after Adams moved to Boston, he broached the subject of an informal engagement, to begin when his law practice began to flourish and he no longer needed his parents' financial support. But her parents objected to an informal engagement, insisting on an immediate, formal engagement, to which Abigail Adams was unalterably opposed. She icily wrote, "Common fame reports that you are attached to a young lady. I am sorry that such a report should prevail. . . . Never form connections until you see a prospect of supporting a family."

The relationship ended when Mary announced that Adams must either agree to a formal engagement or break off his courtship. "Final conversation with M.F.," Adams noted tersely in his diary. With cold formality he informed his mother, "I conjure you, my dear Mamma, not to suffer your anxiety on my account to add to any other evils with which you are afflicted" because of "my attachment." When she did not reply, he wrote, "I am perfectly free, and you may rest assured I shall remain so." Mary Frazier remained single for more than a decade and eventually married Daniel Sargent in 1802. She died of consumption a few years later at the age of thirty. Three decades later, Adams was moved to tears at the mention of her name when he happened to see her daughter's headstone.

As his courtship of Mary Frazier was drifting toward the shoals, Adams lost his first legal case, in the Court of Common Pleas—to Harrison Gray Otis, who in years to come would become one of Adams's "Old Federalist" nemeses. In a letter to his father, Adams admitted that his nerves had gotten the better of him in the courtroom. "I was much too agitated to be possessed of proper presence of mind. You may judge of the figure I made." When he realized that his son was downhearted about losing the case and discouraged about his lack of clients, John Adams tried to be optimistic. "Your case is the lot of every youth of your profession. The world cannot be forced. Time must be taken to become known in any situation."

Adams began to attract clients, but not enough to relieve him of his dependence upon his father's monthly checks. He diverted himself with evening strolls to the Boston Mall, next to the Commons, where he sometimes met women for random assignations that occasioned "mortifying reflections" afterward. He and some other young professional men and businessmen friends formed the "Crackbrain Club," what was then called an "interest club." Its chief purpose seemed to be camaraderie, and Adams remained a member until leaving Boston in 1794.

As Adams grew increasingly morose over his lack of success, his parents became concerned that he might relapse into depression. When they invited him to join them in Philadelphia, he leaped at the chance to take a vacation from his dreary life in Boston. During the weeks that he visited his parents, he met President George Washington, cabinet members, and congressmen, and in the evenings he attended the theater.

In Philadelphia, Adams felt the gravitational tug of public service on his innate sense of duty. He also observed with intense interest the early manifestations of an American political party system, of Federalists and Republicans. His sympathies lay with the Federalists. In a letter to his father, he mocked the states' resistance to the government's plans to assume state debts and establish public credit: "The partisans of our State governments are continually on the rack of exertion to contrive every paltry expedient to maintain their importance and to check the operations of the government, which they behold with terror." Adams's blossoming as a political writer was nearly at hand.

In *The Rights of Man*, Thomas Paine, the corset maker and journalist renowned for his Revolutionary War–era pamphlets *Common Sense* and *The Crisis*, described government as a social contract for protecting the individual's "natural rights" of liberty, property, security, and freedom from oppression. In Paine's opinion, a republican government best safeguarded those rights, whose abrogation justified revolution. Paine was living in England when he wrote *Rights* in two parts in 1791 and 1792, as a rebuttal to Edmund Burke's negative *Reflections on the French Revolution*. In passing,

Paine also derogated the English constitution, evidently in the hope that the English people would overthrow their government. Recognizing just this possibility, the English government suppressed Paine's pamphlet. Paine fled to France, while in England he was tried for sedition in absentia.

The publication of *The Rights of Man* in the United States was a sensation, no less so because of its unauthorized endorsement by Secretary of State Thomas Jefferson, who had read an advance copy lent to him by his friend James Madison. In a private note, Jefferson, who admired the French Revolution but not its excesses, had praised the pamphlet as a repudiation of "the political heresies that have sprung up among us"—interpreted as a slap at the political philosophy espoused by John Adams in his recent *Discourses on Davila*.

Public men had to be careful with their candid opinions, for they were likely to read them in cold print. Jefferson had penned the lines in an informal note to the indiscreet brother of the man who was going to reprint *Rights of Man*. Jefferson's veiled refutation of Adams's essay and his flattering words in support of Paine's point of view, "I have no doubt our citizens will rally a second time round the standard of Common Sense," promptly became the pamphlet's introduction and appeared in newspapers around the country.

And then in Boston's *Columbian Centinel* from June 8 to July 27, 1791, there appeared a series of eleven literate, closely reasoned, barbed rebuttals to *Rights of Man* and Jefferson's endorsement, signed by "Publicola." The essays, reprinted nearly everywhere, were an instant sensation. Intensive speculation swirled around the mysterious author; many believed it was Vice President Adams, although the *Centinel* editor punctured this conjecture. It was James Madison who astutely surmised in a letter to Jefferson "that Publicola is probably the manufacture of his [John Adams's] son out of materials furnished by himself. . . . There is more of method also in the arguments, and much less of clumsiness and heaviness in style, that characterize his [John Adams's] writings."

Publicola sarcastically reminded Jefferson, without actually naming the "heresy hunter," that Americans have "a full and entire freedom of opinion" and "have not yet established any infallible criterion of orthodoxy, either in church or state." He suggested that before Paine was enshrined as "the holy father of our political faith, and this pamphlet is to be considered as his Papal Bull," that its contents should first be examined. Paine had written that because there was no written English Constitution, Englishmen were free to overthrow their government. If this were so, wrote Publicola, does this mean, too, that when the United States adopted "common law," "did they adopt nothing at all, because that law cannot be produced in a visible form?" A constitution is not a piece of paper, but "the system of fundamental laws by which the people have consented to be governed." Only when the people "feel an actual deprivation of their equal rights, and see an actual impossibility for their restoration in any other manner" can they "have a right to lay their hands on their swords and appeal to Heaven." England's problems were not due to her constitution or government, but to "the universal venality and corruption which pervade all classes of men in that kingdom." Thus, Paine was wrong in advocating the overthrow of England's government.

Publicola was the new pivot on which John Quincy Adams's immediate future would soon turn. No longer was he known only as John Adams's son; by revealing his talent for polemics, he had impressed the era's most gifted men, the nation's founders. Moreover, he had forcefully asserted principles that contradicted those of his childhood friend, Thomas Jefferson, at the very moment when sides were being chosen for the first political party system. Adams's elders—President George Washington chief among them—now saw the "son of the Revolution" in a new light, as a useful young ally for whom great things lay in store.

Flushed by Publicola's success and by the surprising satisfaction that writing gave him, Adams took up his pen again, writing under the pseudonym "Menander." He challenged Boston's "blue law," which prohibited theatrical performances, after city authorities arrested some actors for violating the puritanical ordinance. Then, writing as "Marcellus," he recommended that America remain neutral in the fighting that had broken out in Europe, because to "advise us to engage voluntarily in the war, is to aim a dagger at the heart of the country." In his pseudonymous clashes with local officials, Adams revealed a slashing, caustic literary style, once writing of Massachusetts Attorney General James Sullivan that "no half-fledged spurless chickling on a dunghill, could strut and crow, and flap her wings, with more insulting exultation." Although Adams was burnishing his reputation as an essayist, he did not want to jeopardize his legal career. "I have sincerely wished rather to remain in the shade than to appear as a politician without any character as a lawyer."

Two years later, Adams's powerful pen played another pivotal role in U.S. history and earned him the gratitude of President George Washington. In 1793, French minister Edmond Charles Genêt arrived in the United States with the mission of winning U.S. support for the French Revolution. Genêt commissioned privateers in Charleston, South Carolina, to attack British vessels, and he attempted to organize U.S. filibusters against Spain's and Britain's North American possessions. When the Washington administration complained about Genêt's actions, the Frenchman threatened to appeal directly to the American people, knowing that many Anti-Federalists, including Secretary of State Jefferson and Virginia Congressman James Madison, supported him. Washington's cabinet demanded that France recall Genêt.

With Treasury Secretary Alexander Hamilton defending Washington's action and Madison defending Genêt—both writing under pseudonyms—John Quincy Adams weighed in on the side of the president. Writing as "Columbus" and then as "Barneveldt," Adams asserted that the president had the authority to dismiss a foreign minister if he were dangerously meddling in U.S. affairs, as was Genêt. "Every public measure of the French Minister, since the profession of his resolution to appeal [to the American people], may be traced to the policy of arming one part of America against the other. . . . If he cannot corrupt the sacred fountain of legislation, he hopes at least to poison some of the streams which flow from it." It was the first of many assertions by Adams in support of presidential prerogative for nationalistic purposes. In seeking the identity of "Columbus," Washington had only to ask his vice president to learn who he was.

Impressed by John Quincy Adams's intellect, his erudition, and his facility as a writer, and grateful for his loyalty to the Washington administration, the president in May 1794 named Adams minister to the Netherlands. It was a remarkably prestigious appointment for a twenty-seven-year-old. The United States had just five missions, in the Netherlands, England, France, Spain, and Portugal. But Adams had grown up in foreign embassies and had learned poise in the presence of royalty. He could fluently speak several languages, including French, Europe's diplomatic lingua franca, and could read Dutch and a half dozen other languages. Adams was initially dismayed by the appointment, which shattered the quiet equipoise he had come to enjoy in Boston as an essayist and lawyer, but his father quickly soothed his misgivings. In a buttery congratulatory letter, the vice president assured him that the appointment was not due to his influence but "the result of the President's own observations and reflections. . . . It will be a proof that sound principles in morals and government are cherished by the executive of the United States, and that study, science and literature are recommendations which will not be overlooked." In September 1794, Adams embarked for the Netherlands with his brother Thomas, who would be his secretary.

Just as Abigail had acted as the Spartan mother during her son's first trip to Europe, John Adams now played the part of the stern father, serving up some spine-stiffening advice: "If you do not rise to the head not only of your profession, but of your country, it will be owing to your own *Laziness, Slovenliness, and Obstinacy.*"

It was established that Adams's chief responsibility in the Netherlands would be to administer, according to a schedule written by
Treasury Secretary Hamilton, the repayment of Dutch loans to the
United States during the Revolutionary War, but that went out the
window the day that Adams reached The Hague. France had invaded the Netherlands.

As all around him Europe boiled with intrigue and armies on
the march, Adams settled into his new, unforeseen role—America's front-row observer, an assignment that suited him perfectly.
To his surprise, Adams discovered that he liked the diplomatic life
very much. He was earning $4,500 a year, and he had time for
reading, writing, walking, conversation, and the theater. "I have
found here exactly what I wanted, and feel myself to be once more
my own man again," he wrote to a friend. To his father, he reported
that the posting was "much preferable to that of eternal expectations in a lawyer's office for business which, when it comes, is
scarcely sufficient to give bread, and procures one more curses than
thanks." He confessed to hoping that he would not have to return
to practicing law again.

In August 1795, Adams sailed to London to exchange ratifica-
tion documents for the new "Treaty of Amity, Commerce and
Navigation" with Great Britain, which would be known in the
United States as the Jay Treaty. While waiting for instructions
from Philadelphia and attempting to avoid scheming British
diplomats who may have thought young Adams more pliable than
his older and more experienced colleagues, Adams became a frequent visitor to the grandly appointed home of the American consul in London, Joshua Johnson. Johnson had first come to England
before the Revolutionary War as the factor of an Annapolis firm.
During the war he had served as a U.S. representative in France,
returning to London afterward as U.S. consul. His brother,
Thomas Johnson, was governor of Maryland. Johnson's friendship,

position, and connections weren't all that brought Adams to his front door; Johnson had seven daughters, three of marriageable age. Adams was especially attracted to the second oldest, Louisa Catherine. Louisa was smart, beautiful, self-confident, and independent, fluent in French, and musically talented. Moreover, like Adams, she enjoyed literature and the theater.

For three months, Adams courted Louisa without revealing his intentions—until Louisa's mother persuaded him to acknowledge his aim of marrying Louisa. Nonetheless, Adams returned to The Hague without setting a wedding date. From America, his mother had been counseling delay, suggesting that Louisa, whom she never mentioned by name, was an insubstantial woman who would plunge him into debt with her feckless spending. "Time will trim the luster of the eye, and wither the bloom of the face," she grimly predicted, advising her son to seek a "more lasting union of friendship," and adding exasperatedly, "I would hope for the love I bear my country that the Siren is at least a *half-blood.*" Irritated by his mother's meddling, Adams wrote back that if he waited for a spouse that suited her, "I would certainly be doomed to perpetual celibacy." Abigail quickly backpedaled. "I consider her already as my daughter," she wrote.

On July 26, 1797, thirty-year-old John Quincy Adams and twenty-two-year-old Louisa Catherine Johnson were married in the Johnsons' Anglican church, "All Hallows Berkyngechirche by the Tower of London." By then, Adams knew that his father-in-law's grand living style concealed ruinous debts; there would be no dowry. "I have done my duty—rigorous, inflexible duty," he dourly noted. In fact, his grudging marriage to Louisa would blossom into a deep, enduring relationship.

Pleasant though Adams's life was at The Hague, he had to concede his presence was pointless, with the Netherlands occupied by France. "At present I am liberally paid for no service at all." President George Washington, however, was pleased with Adams's incisive letters on European developments. "Things appear to me exactly as they do to your son," Washington told John Adams. "Your son must not think of retiring from the walk he is in. . . . I shall be much mistaken if, in as short a period as can well be expected, he is not found at the head of the diplomatic corps." Washington was especially impressed by the "political insight" of a letter from Adams that included the observation, "Above all I wish that we may never have occasion for political connections in Europe." Adams's words influenced the composition of Washington's 1797 "Farewell Address," in which he warned against "foreign entanglements." Washington rewarded Adams by appointing him minister to Portugal at a yearly salary of $9,000, twice what Adams was receiving at The Hague. But before Adams could travel to Lisbon, his father succeeded Washington as president, and he was reassigned to the new Prussian ministry in Berlin.

APRIL 1801, BERLIN

After five miscarriages, Louisa Catherine Adams gave birth on April 12 to their first child, George Washington Adams, although Louisa nearly died from rough handling by the drunken midwife. As a mark of respect toward the U.S. minister's wife, the Prussians banished all traffic from the street where Louisa and John Quincy lived. And each day, a servant from King Frederick William III's court made his way to the Adams's home to inquire about the health of Louisa and the baby. These signs of respect attested to John Quincy Adams's success during three and a half years at the Prussian court.

In Berlin, Adams fully matured as a diplomat, and he savored his lifestyle even more than he had while at The Hague. More importantly, Adams had achieved his principal goals—renewing the United States' expiring ten-year treaty with Prussia; avoiding a U.S. commitment to a coalition of European neutrals in the world war between Great Britain and France, a commitment sure to have incurred Britain's enmity; and filing ruminative dispatches assessing the European situation—while failing only in signing a new treaty with Sweden. Now fluent in German, Adams became one of the first Americans to praise German letters and later was pronounced "the father of German studies in America" by the noted bibliographer Frederick H. Wilkins. Inspired by his newfound love of German literature, Adams devoted his free time to translating Christopher Martin Wieland's romance, *Oberon,* into English. He never intended for it to be published. "I had made it as a school-exercise in learning German," he told Spanish Minister Calderon de la Barca nearly a half-century later when Calderon, who had read it, inquired about it. (Adams's superior translation remained unpublished until 1940, when it was widely praised by modern scholars; it was probably his greatest literary achievement.)

In his dispatches to Philadelphia, Adams in 1798 urged his president father to open negotiations with France, believing the French were ready to end the so-called Quasi-War. The episodic naval war, fought mainly in the West Indies, stemmed from France's attempts to thwart U.S.-British trade by seizing hundreds of American commercial vessels. President Adams had taken his son's advice, which led to the Convention of Mortefontaine and the end of the Quasi-War, but the issue fractured the Federalist Party and thereby ensured Thomas Jefferson's electoral victory in 1800. John Quincy supported his father's principled position in the teeth of fierce partisan attacks and bestowed upon him a compliment that would later define his own outlook: "The man [is] not of any party, but of the whole nation."

Two weeks after his son George's birth, John Quincy Adams received notification from the outgoing secretary of state, John Marshall, that his father, unwilling to grant Jefferson power over his son's fate, had recalled him as one of the last acts of his presidency. On July 12, 1801, the day after Adams's thirty-fourth birthday, he and his family left Prussia. Seven years after embarking on his first mission to the Netherlands, Adams was returning to Philadelphia with solid diplomatic accomplishments, an English-born wife, and a son. The

Federalist Party was out of power, his father had been out of office exactly six months, and Adams himself was now adrift as well.

After his return to America from Prussia in September, John Quincy Adams confronted a momentous question: Should he risk the uncertainties of a political career, or should he re-embark on a legal career that might make him rich but unhappy? At thirty-four, he no longer was a young prodigy. His financial situation was shaky. His brother Charles, a sad alcoholic who had died in his squalid New York rooms in November 1800, had lost several thousand dollars that Adams had entrusted to him in reckless real estate speculations, recommended by their sister Nabby's rakish husband, Colonel William Stephens Smith.

It was clear that Adams's diplomatic career, as much a product of the goodwill of George Washington and his father as of Adams's considerable diplomatic skills, was at an end, at least for as long as Thomas Jefferson occupied the White House. While accompanying Louisa to Washington to visit her postmaster father and her sisters, he had dined with the president. It was, Adams observed, "a chilling affair." With a wife and young son to support, Adams had to somehow earn a living.

As long as there have been "literary men," their prized objective has been a position that earns adequate income but that grants time to write. Public life, Adams reasoned—and he was thinking of the Massachusetts legislature—would accomplish both ends, with the added benefit of giving him visibility that could aid his literary career. But Adams was torn over whether he could serve the public while remaining independent of partisan politics. He confided his divided mind to his diary: "I feel a strong temptation and have great provocation to plunge into political controversy," while acknowledging that partisanship was a basic element of political life. "A politician in the country must be the man of a party. I would fain be the man of my whole country."

Adams would change his mind about serving in the legislature, but these last words—nearly identical to his father's attitude during the storm over his decision to negotiate with France—would serve as his lodestar throughout his long life. He later called it "the principle by which my whole public life has been governed from that day to this."

Elected to the State Senate in April, Adams served without distinction during the Massachusetts legislative sessions that spring and in January 1803. "I was not able either to effect much good, or to prevent much evil." He did manage to display his independent streak, however, and startled his Federalist Party colleagues two days after taking his seat by proposing that Republicans be given proportional representation on the Governor's Council. Fairness required it, he said, but the Federalists buried the idealistic plan.

Needing money, Adams ran for Congress in the fall of 1802—and lost to the Republican incumbent, Dr. William Eustis, by just fifty-nine votes, 1,899–1,840. Then, in March 1803, he was chosen by the state legislature to fill one of Massachusetts's two vacant U.S. Senate seats; former Secretary of State Timothy Pickering was selected for the other. Pickering, a "High Federalist" who had helped defeat John Adams in 1800, made no effort to cooperate with his son.

The Adamses reached Washington on October 20, 1803, just hours after the Senate approved the Louisiana Purchase by a 24–7 vote. All the New England Federalists, including Pickering, voted against it. Adams, however, wholeheartedly supported the purchase of the 828,000 square miles between the Mississippi River and the Rocky Mountains, believing it was a spectacular bargain at $15 million and would keep Napoleon Bonaparte out of North America. Federalists feared the expansion of national power that they believed would come at New England's expense. Adams angered his colleagues by voting for the bonds to complete the purchase. "The Hon. John Quincy Adams will certainly be denounced and excommunicated by his own party," predicted the Republican Worcester *Aegis*. Yet he confounded critics who said he had gone over to the Jefferson administration by opposing bills extending federal authority over the new territory, invoking the principle that it would amount to taxation without representation. He further baffled Federalists by siding with them against the Jefferson administration's impeachment of Supreme Court Justice Samuel Chase and its attempts to buy West Florida and to shrink the Navy.

But Adams's consonance with Federalists on these questions only masked widening cracks in their relationship; at heart, neither Adams nor the Federalists respected one another. Wrote Boston banker Stephen Higginson: "Like a kite without a Tail, he [Adams] will be violent and constant in his attempts to rise . . . and will pitch to one side and the other, as the popular Currents may happen to strike . . ." For his part, Adams regarded the Federalist Party as "a carcase [*sic*] seven years in its grave."

Even more than her husband, Louisa welcomed the move to Washington. In 1805, Louisa was thirty years old with two sons—George, born in 1800, and John, in 1803—to show for seven pregnancies. She was lively and smart, played the pianoforte and harp, wrote and recited poetry, spoke French fluently, and liked to sing, dance, pun, and tell fortunes. Chilly Boston and its Puritan ways had seemed alien to her, whereas Washington, where her father and sisters lived, was warmer and felt like home. Louisa's brother-in-law, Walter Hellens, a prosperous tobacco speculator, invited the Adamses to stay in his large home near Georgetown. After the death of Louisa's father, the generous Hellens also took in Louisa's mother and her younger children.

Every day Adams walked from the Hellens home near Georgetown to the Capitol and back, a five-mile round trip that he made in all weather and that gave him time to think. Because Adams was new to the Senate, his official duties at first utterly consumed him. But he and Louisa dined out often—with Secretary of State James Madison, with the French and British ministers, and sometimes at the President's House with Thomas Jefferson, whose initial chill toward the Adamses had dissipated. "He tells large stories," wrote Adams, clearly fascinated by him. At one dinner, the president claimed to have learned Spanish "with the help of a Don Quixote lent him by Mr. Cabot, and a grammar, in the course of a passage to Europe, on which he was but nineteen days at sea." At another dinner, with Vice President Aaron Burr and Navy Secretary Robert Smith in company, Jefferson claimed to have seen "Fahrenheit's thermometer" record readings of twenty below zero in Paris for six weeks straight, although it was never that cold when Jefferson was there. "He knows better than all this; but he loves to excite wonder," observed Adams. Louisa, however, despised the president, who had removed her father from his District of Columbia postmaster job after defeating her father-in-law. "Everything about him was aristocratic except his person, which was ungainly, ugly and common."

Latter-day Puritan that he was, Adams could never measure up to the high standards that he set for himself; he could only strive every hour of every day for moral and intellectual perfection and to fulfill what for him was a grave civic duty. Each generation, he believed, must do its utmost for the next generation, as payment of its debt to the preceding generation. A day when he did not perform a good deed was a wasted day. He passed on this severe philosophy to his sons: "You should each of you consider yourself as placed here *to act a part*—That is to have some single great end or object to accomplish, towards which all the views and the labours of your existence should steadily be directed."

Chronically dissatisfied with his speaking performances in the Senate, he wrote after an acrimonious debate on a minor bill, "I was, as I always am, *miserably defective* . . ." Following an hour-long speech, he declared that his "defects of elocution are incurable, and amidst so many better speakers, when the debates are to be reported, I never speak without mortification." It was thus ironic that Harvard chose Adams in 1805 as its first Boylston Professor of Rhetoric and Oratory, a chair created by a distant relative's bequest. Yet Adams found one encouraging sign in his otherwise dismal public speaking efforts: "When my feelings are wound up to a high tone, elocution pours itself along with unusual rapidity, and I have passages which would not shame a good speaker. . . ."

In 1805, Adams broke yet again with his fellow New England Federalists, whom he believed were plotting secession. The "Essex Junto," as these Federalists were called, were alarmed by the Jefferson administration's purchase of Louisiana from France and by its friendly relations with Napoleon. Encouraged by Nova Scotia's governor general in their belief—patently wrong—that Jefferson was clandestinely cooperating with Napoleon in a plan to take over Canada and revolutionize America, the "Essex men" became convinced that only England and her navy could stop the purported conspiracy. Many Essex men were the same High Federalists who had turned on Adams's father in 1799 when he negotiated with France and ended the Quasi-War. Adams became convinced that they, with Massachusetts Senator Timothy Pickering as their ringleader, were prepared, if necessary, to secede and form a Northern Confederacy friendly to England. As the Essex men stood in violent opposition to Adams's closely held belief that "the whole continent on [*sic*] North America appears to be destined by Divine Providence to be peopled by one nation," Adams ceased to cooperate politically with them, becoming, as he later described it, "free from the shackles of dependence upon any party." Yet, he was also well aware by the end of 1805 that he was paying a price for his independence: "My political prospects continue declining."

The Federalists grumblingly tolerated Adams's uncooperative-
ness until the summer of 1807, when the British warship HMS
Leopard attacked the U.S. frigate *Chesapeake* just ten miles off Cape
Henry, Virginia. Across the country, the old hatred toward England was rekindled; rallies and town meetings were held everywhere. Making matters worse, British warships anchored inside
the Virginia Capes and fired at passing U.S. vessels. President Jefferson closed all U.S. ports to British ships, as war fever raged
throughout the nation.

Adams, who was teaching rhetoric at Harvard when the attack
occurred, urged Boston Federalists to hold a special town meeting to protest the British action, but they did not. Disgustedly
observing that the Federalist inaction was motivated by a repre-
hensible "private interest" in preserving the lucrative Anglo–New
England trade, Adams committed the unpardonable political sin
of attending a Republican mass meeting at the Massachusetts
State House. He then compounded his transgression by serving
as the lone Federalist on a committee formed to write protest
resolutions. Although Adams later attended a hastily scheduled
Federalist rally at Faneuil Hall—with the Essex men staying
away—and chaired its resolutions committee, the damage had
been done. "J. Phillips told me I should have my head taken off
for apostasy by the federalists," Adams wrote on July 11, his forti-
eth birthday. "My sense of duty shall never yield to the pleasure
of a party."

Adams's affiliation with the Federalists had been hanging by
only a slender thread, and it now snapped under the strain of his
wholehearted support in December 1807 of Jefferson's Embargo
Act, which interdicted all trade with all foreign nations, though it
was really aimed at punishing England. The Embargo was fiercely
opposed by Federalists and throughout New England, as the region was heavily dependent on European commerce. Adams
served with four Republicans on the Senate committee that
drafted and pushed through the Embargo. Timothy Pickering, his
Massachusetts colleague, voted against it. "This measure will cost

you and me our seats," Adams predicted to a fellow committee member, "but private interest must not be put in opposition to public good."

Adams was now a pariah—despised by Federalists, not altogether trusted by Republicans—and he knew even as he labored to push through legislation implementing the embargo that his political career was doomed. "My situation here at this moment is singular and critical," he wrote to his father. "I find myself charged with the duty of originating and conducting measures of the highest interest. I am made a leader without followers."

John Adams, who had proscribed his own defeat in 1800 by alienating the very Federalists who now condemned his son, was unshakably in his son's corner. "Your situation you think critical. I think it is clear, plain, and obvious. You are supported by no party. You have too honest a heart, too independent a mind and too brilliant talents to be sincerely and confidentially treated by any man who is under the influence of party feelings," he wrote to his son. While his course was "the path of justice," he advised John Quincy to return to his professorship and his law practice. "Devote yourself to your profession, and the education of your children."

John Quincy Adams unmistakably showed where his sympathies lay on January 23, 1808, when he attended the Republican Congressional Caucus in Philadelphia. The caucus chose Secretary of State James Madison to be its presidential candidate in the fall. Adams's presence deepened the Federalists' hostility toward him; a Federalist editor described him as "one of those amphibious politicians who lives on both land and water, and occasionally resorts to each, but who finally settles down in the mud." For the first time, but not the last, hate mail came to Adams's desk. "Lucifer, son of the Morning," read a letter signed by "A Federalist," "how hast thou fallen! . . . Oh, Adams, remember who thou art. . . . Awake, arouse in time." Even Abigail thought her son had gone too far in attending the caucus, which "staggered my belief"—to which her son tartly replied, "I could wish to please my country, I could wish to please my parents—but my duty I *must* do."

Adams's abrupt departure from the Senate, occurring with lightning speed months before his term was to end, stunned even him. His father had warned him in January, "Your fate is decided. . . . In the next Congress . . . you will be numbered among the dead." After the fall 1808 election, it was a foregone conclusion that the Massachusetts legislature would send another Federalist to the Senate in Adams's place for the congressional session beginning in March 1809. But on June 5, 1808, the legislature decided to further display its displeasure with Adams by prematurely choosing Adams's successor, James Lloyd Jr., a former Harvard classmate, on a close, 269–240 vote, with Republicans supporting Adams. The legislature then instructed Adams and Pickering to introduce in the U.S. Senate several anti-embargo resolutions adopted by the Massachusetts Senate.

In his letter of resignation dated June 8, Adams wrote that he could not support the Massachusetts resolutions because they required "a sort of opposition to the national administration in which I cannot consistently with my principles concur." Republicans immediately urged him to run as a Republican for the House seat in his congressional district, but Adams declined, as it would have meant running against his friend and kinsman Josiah Quincy. A month later, on his forty-first birthday, Adams wrote, "In the course of the last year I have been called by my duties as a citizen and man to act and to suffer more than at any former period of my life."

Chapter Two

The Road to the Presidency

"I have the duty of a citizen
to obey the call of his country."

—John Quincy Adams,
upon returning to diplomatic service

$\mathcal{J}$ohn Quincy Adams's forced retirement from public life would be brief. Whether from residual spite over the "Publicola" essays, his estrangement from John Adams, or his preoccupation with the problems that beset his last year as president, Thomas Jefferson retired to Monticello without rewarding Adams for his political self-immolation over the Embargo, although other Republicans believed he should have. Jefferson's protégé and successor, James Madison, swiftly atoned for this lapse; on the second day of his presidency, Madison nominated Adams as U.S. minister to Russia.

Adams would make the most of his return to public life, which would carry him to the threshold of the presidency. During eight years as an ambassador in Europe, he would become one of the most important American statesmen of any era. From St. Petersburg and Paris, he witnessed Napoleon Bonaparte's pyrrhic victories in Russia and his phoenix-like rise from exile on Elba. From

Ghent, he helped negotiate the treaty ending America's last war with England. In London, he defined America's role in the world after the War of 1812 and framed her new relationship of equality with England.

In St. Petersburg, Europe's most extravagant court, the Adamses were forced to severely economize in order to live on his $9,000 annual salary and modest expense allowance. They moved nearly every year from one ramshackle lodging place to another. In one vermin-infested dwelling, the bold rats would "drag the braid from the table by my bedside," complained Louisa. In a hotel where the Adamses lived for a year, the walls were so thin that when Louisa and her sister Catherine sang and played the piano, the neighbors would applaud and shout, "Brava, brava!"

When the Franco-Russian war commenced in June 1812, Adams, nearly alone among diplomats in St. Petersburg, accurately predicted that Russia's grand strategy of avoiding decisive battles would defeat the French. "The Fabian system of warfare [named for the Roman general Fabius Maximus who successfully employed it against the invading Hannibal], which succeeded in our Revolutionary War . . . probably was never brought to a severer test; but the modern Alexander [Napoleon, not the czar] may after all be destined like his predecessor to be arrested in his career of domination by the Scythians [Russians]."

While minister to Great Britain from 1815 to 1817, the seasoned diplomat Adams helped reconcile England and the United States for truly the first time since their break forty years earlier. As a true son of the American Revolution, however, he never trusted or loved the English.

Adams, Albert Gallatin, and Henry Clay signed a commercial convention in London with Great Britain that began the process of normalizing trade between the two nations but left for the future the question of trade with the British colonies. The Convention of 1815 would prove enduring and was renewed again and again over the years. Adams also attempted to settle the other outstanding issues remaining between the nations: disarmament on the Great Lakes; impressments; compensation for captured slaves; and fishing rights off Nova Scotia and Newfoundland. Agreements on these issues would eventually result from the discussions he had begun, but would not be completed while Adams was in England. "My special duty at present is to preach peace," Adams wrote to his father in 1816.

Impressed by Adams's international experience and his clean slate politically after years abroad, President James Monroe named him secretary of state in 1817. Adams's vast experience in diplomacy and international relations made him the best-qualified secretary of state in American history, and he did not stint on expending his impressive gifts to their best effect. He worked harder than he ever had before, leaving himself little time for personal pursuits, except for daily Bible reading.

During nearly eight years as secretary of state, Adams did no less than lay the foundations of American foreign policy, while systematizing the State Department. He reorganized the department's financial accounts and filing system, and he began a State Department library. In meticulously written instructions, he trained and set high standards for his diplomats, while demanding that they file numbered reports containing their detailed observations.

Adams enjoyed an excellent working relationship with President Monroe, who was involved to a high degree in making foreign policy. The men respected one another. "They were made for each other," Thomas Jefferson observed. "Adams has a pointed pen; Monroe has judgment enough for both and firmness enough to have *his* judgment control."

Adams had just departed from a second happy reunion with his mother since having returned from Europe when she unexpectedly died in October 1818. News of her death reached the Adamses as they arrived in Washington after a weeks' long stay in Quincy. She was seventy-three and in apparent good health when they had left her. Adams was grief-stricken. Abigail, wrote Adams in anguished diary passages attesting to his devotion to her, "was an angel upon Earth—She was a Minister of blessing to all human beings within her sphere of action. Her heart was the abode of heavenly purity. . . . She was the real personification of female virtue—of piety—of charity, of ever active and never intermitting benevolence—Oh! God! Could she have been spared yet a little longer! . . . Never have I known another human being the perpetual object of whose life was so unremittingly to do good."

Abigail's death was a sad distraction from the thorny problems that occupied Adams in Washington. General Andrew Jackson had lit a powder keg by invading Spanish Florida, from where renegade Indians were launching raids into Georgia and Alabama. Historians cannot agree even today whether Jackson's incursion was warranted, much less authorized by the U.S. government. With 3,000 men, Jackson crushed the Indian forces in the Florida panhandle, captured St. Mark's and Pensacola, and executed a former British officer, Captain Robert Ambrister, and a Scottish trader, Alexander Arbuthnot, for inciting the attacks.

Amid Spain's furious protests, Monroe's cabinet, with the exception of Adams, favored disavowing Jackson's actions; War Secretary John C. Calhoun even proposed court-martialing the general, an action that would later cost him a chance at the presidency. Despite overwhelming public approval of Jackson's actions, Monroe was troubled by the stinging criticism of his administration coming from Congress, and especially from House Speaker Henry Clay, already positioning himself to run for president. But Monroe also believed that disclaiming Jackson's invasion would bolster Spain's resolve to not sell Florida to the United States. Discussions on this subject between Adams and Spanish Minister Don Luis de Onís y Gonzales had been stalemated for months.

During five cabinet meetings held over one week, Adams alone defended Jackson's actions and hawkishly argued for keeping St. Mark's and Pensacola. Jackson did not violate his orders, contended Adams, but Spain did violate its pledge in the 1795 Spanish-American Treaty to suppress Florida Indian aggression against the United States. Moreover, "if the question is dubious, it is better to err on the side of vigor than of weakness—on the side of our own officer, who has rendered the most eminent services to the nation, than on the side of our bitterest enemies, and against him."

Monroe chose the middle course of defending Jackson's actions to Spain, while maintaining that Jackson had acted on his own authority, and offering to return St. Mark's and Pensacola. The question of whether Jackson acted on Monroe's authority would continue to smolder in the coming years; indeed, even today it has not yet been satisfactorily answered.

Jackson's invasion induced Minister Onís to resume negotiations with Adams, who had been warning Onís that Spain must either cede Florida, send troops to restrain the Indians, or witness Florida's occupation by the United States. Their discussions culminated in the Transcontinental Treaty, better known as the Adams-Onís Treaty, signed on February 22, 1819. One of the shining triumphs of Adams's State Department tenure, the treaty ceded Florida to the United States, which in exchange agreed to assume $5 million in U.S. citizens' claims against Spain. The Transcontinental Treaty established the boundary of the Louisiana Purchase: the Sabine River (today's Louisiana-Texas border) north to the Red River, to the Arkansas River, and from there to the 42nd parallel (the northern borders of present-day Utah, Nevada, and California) and west to the Pacific Ocean. Spain and the United States abandoned their claims to the Oregon Territory and Texas, respectively.

The treaty, Adams grandly wrote later in his life, was "the most important incident in my life, and the most successful negotiation ever consummated by the Government of this Union." Adams recognized that Jackson's impetuous actions had made the treaty possible. Before politics made them inveterate enemies, Adams was grateful that Jackson had "rendered such services to this nation that it is impossible for me to contemplate his character or conduct without veneration."

Ever on guard against binding alliances that might cause America to slip back into England's orbit or drag her into future European wars, Adams continually looked for opportunities to assert greater U.S. autonomy. Such an occasion arose when the "Holy Alliance" of Russia, Prussia, and Austria, and later France, joined together to aid King Ferdinand VII of Spain in his attempt to reclaim Spanish colonies in Latin America that had proclaimed their independence during the Napoleonic wars. Revolutionaries had seized Ferdinand in 1820 and established a constitutional monarchy in Spain. At the Congress of Verona in 1822, the Holy Alliance monarchs, ignoring England's strenuous objections, supported French intervention. In 1823, France crushed the revolutionaries and restored Ferdinand to the throne.

George Canning, the British foreign secretary, was determined to preserve England's fledgling commerce with the newly independent Latin American nations and to thwart France. In August 1823, he invited the United States to join England in a declaration that they would brook no European interference in Latin America.

England's offer of a limited alliance between equals was an epochal development that President Monroe found tempting indeed. Besides joining America and England as allies, such an agreement would extend de facto British approval to Monroe's recognition in March 1822 of newly independent Argentina, Peru, Chile, Colombia, and Mexico—the United States being the first nation to do so.

As he had done on other occasions, Monroe quietly consulted Thomas Jefferson and James Madison; both recommended that he accept Canning's proposition. When the president laid Canning's proposal before his cabinet, but without mentioning Jefferson's and Madison's concordance of views, Adams quickly declared his opposition. This was only mildly surprising. In a July 4, 1821, oration before the House of Representatives, the secretary of state had denounced colonialism, saying that America "is the well-wisher to the freedom and independence of all," while cautiously adding that America "goes not abroad, in search of monsters to destroy. . . . She well knows that by once enlisting under other banners than her own . . . she would involve herself beyond the power of extrication, in all the wars of interest and intrigue, of individual avarice, envy, and ambition."

Thus, Adams did not object to Canning's proposition because he believed it was imprudent for America to become involved in Latin America; he was ready enough to oppose European interference there. It was because he did not wish to "have the appearance of pinning ourselves too closely upon [England's] sleeve." Better for America "to avow our principles explicitly to Russia and France than to come in as a cock-boat in the wake of the British man-of-war," Adams wrote. It was important, too, that America preserve her advantage in being the first to recognize the new governments. It was well and good to urge England to act similarly, while taking care "to let her know what we shall ultimately act independently for ourselves."

He also cynically argued that the limited alliance's nonintervention proviso could be invoked against America, to deny her Cuba, Texas, or California if they one day became available—perhaps England's secret purpose. But conversely, a unilateral U.S. declaration against colonization might be used to discourage British designs on Cuba.

Adams urged Monroe to "declare our dissent" from European recolonization and "assert those [principles] upon which our own Government is founded": opposition to all future colonization,

America's continued noninvolvement in Europe's wars, and resistance to any European incursions in North or South America. Monroe took Adams's advice and declined the partnership with England.

The monumental policy born from this debate was framed in Monroe's penultimate annual Message to Congress, on December 2, 1823. Folding it into the annual message was Monroe's idea; Adams had wished to announce the policy in diplomatic dispatches.

In just three paragraphs of his fifty-one-paragraph message to Congress, Monroe outlined the three tenets of the Monroe Doctrine, as it would one day be called. The tenet positing no future colonization was Adams's signal contribution, excerpted by Adams from a letter he had written to Richard Rush, the minister to England, and shared with Monroe, who used it word-for-word: "The American Continents by the free and independent condition which they have assumed and maintain, are henceforth not to be considered as subjects for future Colonization by any European power." Furthermore, said Monroe, any attempt by Europe to reclaim any of the newly independent Latin American states would be regarded as "the manifestation of an unfriendly disposition toward the United States." Finally, the president restated America's settled policy of eschewing involvement in Europe's wars. "It is only when our rights are invaded or seriously menaced that we resent injuries or make preparation for our defense." Reactions in Europe to the Monroe Doctrine ranged from praise to scorn to indifference. In any case, its enduring legacy would turn out to be its declaration of fundamental U.S. foreign policy.

In the last glow of the Era of Good Feelings, as historians would one day describe the period of 1815–1825, no new political party system had yet replaced the moribund Republican and Federalist parties. In this rare atmosphere occurred the miracle of John Quincy Adams's rise as a presidential candidate. Only during such an anomalous age could a self-proclaimed "man of the whole country" such as Adams realistically aspire to the White House. "A man must fulfill his destiny," Adams wrote in his diary.

In the tradition of his predecessors, James Monroe had elected to not seek a third term as president. Seven men vied to succeed Monroe, including three Monroe cabinet members: Adams, War Secretary Calhoun, and Treasury Secretary William Crawford of Georgia, who was recovering from a stroke suffered the previous year. The other candidates were Andrew Jackson, Henry Clay, and two long shots—Vice President Daniel D. Tompkins, and former New York Governor DeWitt Clinton. Of all of them, Adams, who did not yet apprehend the threat posed by Jackson, was wariest of Crawford, "not a worse man than the usual herd of ambitious intriguers . . . but his ambition swallows up his principle."

In hopes of promoting his own candidacy and perhaps persuading Jackson to serve as his vice president, Adams and Louisa held a ball in their home on January 8, 1824, to commemorate the ninth anniversary of Jackson's victory at New Orleans. Nine hundred invitations were sent, and Louisa hired a carpenter to install twelve new pillars beneath the lower floor to support the weight of all the guests. On the night of the ball, Louisa met Jackson at the door and was his escort throughout the evening.

The ball, which was an immense success, was surely cause for later regret, when the Adamses' warm feelings toward Jackson had turned to rancid bitterness.

Chapter Three

An "Agony of Mind"

"No one knows, and few conceive, the agony
of mind that I have suffered from the time that
I was made by circumstances, and not by my volition,
a candidate for the Presidency till I was dismissed
from that station by the failure of my re-election."

—John Quincy Adams

SUNDAY, JANUARY 9, 1825, WASHINGTON

*N*ighttime came early in wintertime Washington. At six o'clock sharp, a distinguished visitor emerged from the chilly gloom and was admitted to John Quincy Adams's home.

House Speaker Henry Clay had finished fourth in the November presidential election, which, for the second time since the founding of the republic, had failed to produce a clear-cut winner. General Andrew Jackson had won a plurality, but not a majority, of the popular and electoral votes. Adams had come in second, while Treasury Secretary William Crawford had edged out Clay in the Electoral College voting.

If he chose to do so, Clay could play the kingmaker and throw his support to any of the three when the House of Representatives, to which now fell the task of electing the next president, voted on February 9. Advocates of all three candidates had heavily lobbied Clay since his return to Washington from his native Kentucky.

As yet uncommitted, Clay was calling on Adams to ascertain whether Adams's principles jibed with his own, but as Adams noted later in his diary, "without any considerations for himself"— evidently meaning that Clay did not seek a quid pro quo.

The men's three-hour discussion concerned matters of national importance. Uncharacteristically for Adams, who usually recorded *everything* in his diary, his account of the meeting was vague about the details other than to observe that Clay had said the time had "now come at which he might be explicit in his communication with me."

Sometime around nine o'clock, as Clay rose to depart, he asserted that "he had no hesitation in saying that his preference would be for me," wrote Adams.

Weeks later, amid murmurs about a "corrupt bargain" having been struck between Adams and Clay that resulted in the House electing Adams as the sixth president, Adams named Clay his secretary of state.

Adams, who had attended two church services before Clay visited him that fateful evening, should have taken to heart the reading that he had heard that morning, Ecclesiastes, 7:23: "I said I will be wise; but it was far from me." The so-called "corrupt bargain" would hound both men for the rest of their lives.

1824, WASHINGTON

During the administrations of the Virginians Thomas Jefferson, James Madison, and James Monroe, the secretary of state was the de facto president-in-waiting. Madison had served Jefferson in that capacity, and Monroe had then served as President Madison's secretary of state. Thus, when President Monroe appointed John Quincy Adams secretary of state in 1817, it was implicitly understood that the second president's son, certainly more qualified to be secretary of state than anyone before and possibly since, had been anointed as Monroe's successor.

By 1824, however, it was clear that Adams would face a galaxy of formidable opponents, including, as noted previously, two fellow cabinet members—War Secretary Calhoun and Treasury Secretary Crawford—as well as eloquent, convivial Henry Clay, Speaker of the House and known as the "Great Compromiser" for helping bring about the Missouri Compromise of 1820, and Senator Andrew Jackson of Tennessee, Indian fighter, hero of New Orleans, and leader of the controversial invasion of Florida.

Adams disapproved of the emerging new way of conducting politics, which he believed wrongly pandered to popular opinion while devaluing principles. Of course, this revolutionary change put Adams at a severe disadvantage, for he fairly bristled with eighteenth-century principles from both sides of the Hamiltonian-Jeffersonian divide, but lacked a common touch. "I well know that I never was and never shall be what is commonly termed a popular man," he observed. This was an understatement coming from one who had once described himself as "a man of reserved, cold, austere, and forbidding manners; my political adversaries say, a gloomy misanthropist, and my personal enemies, an unsocial savage." Nearly overnight, Adams's belief that the president was "the first guardian of the public morals" had been made obsolete by a new political age that would reward the inspiring stump speaker and the backroom coalition-builder.

While Adams never organized a campaign in 1824, he did evince his interest in becoming president and did not passively wait for the office to be given to him. Hoping to win support from western states, he tried without success to recruit Jackson and then Calhoun as his running mate; Calhoun instead consented to run with Jackson and droppped out of the presidential race. Adams dined with small groups of voters and made a point of visiting with people while coming and going from Congress, church services, and the theater. He debunked claims made by Jonathan Russell, a member of the Treaty of Ghent negotiating team with Adams, Clay, and Albert Gallatin (with Crawford, then minister to France, advising the commissioners on European politics), that Adams had been willing to concede to the British Mississippi River navigation rights in exchange for obtaining New England fishing rights off Newfoundland and Nova Scotia. In his scorching, book-length rebuttal, Adams proved that Russell had doctored a key letter, ruining Russell's political career.

The approaching election distracted him at church and at the State Department, and he found himself rising at 3 A.M. to get everything done, and sometimes waking up even earlier, which made him tired all of the time. Yet, he doggedly stuck to his predawn exercise regimen of walking Washington's streets, pushing himself at his 120-steps-per-minute pace—first established in St. Petersburg, where he had also determined his stride to be two feet, seven inches—to cover four miles in an hour. In warm weather, he often swam in the Potomac, in his green goggles and black cap sometimes crossing to the Virginia side—and striving to increase his minutes in the water without touching the bottom or shore to an hour.

There was no outright victor in the November 1824 presidential election; none of the four candidates obtained the 131 electoral votes needed. The "man of the people," as Jackson was known, outpolled everyone, with 153,544 popular votes and 99 electoral votes, followed by Adams, with 108,740 votes, and 84 Electoral College ballots. Clay received 47,136 popular votes and 37 electoral votes. Crawford, splenetic-tempered but a talented speaker, had not fully recovered from his paralyzing stroke of 1823. He received 46,618 popular votes and 41 electoral votes. In the vice presidential race, Calhoun easily crushed all comers.

At this point, Adams might have gracefully conceded to Jackson, whose agenda was then a mystery and who, out of gratitude, might have permitted Adams to remain as secretary of state. But there was never a chance that Adams, having come this far, would tamely concede; to him, the election was a life-and-death matter, no less than a referendum on his entire life. "When I consider that to me alone, of all the candidates before the nation," he wrote, "failure of success would be equivalent to a vote of censure by the nation upon my past services, I cannot dissemble to myself that I have more at stake upon the result than any other individual in the Union."

Under the House of Representatives' rules for selecting a president, each of the 24 states cast one vote—with every state congressional delegation deciding who would get its vote. Thirteen votes were needed to win. The November balloting would have given Jackson 11 states, Adams 7, and Clay and Crawford, 3 apiece. Clay could deliver three key states that had supported him—Kentucky, Ohio, and Missouri—and perhaps help swing other states, thereby deciding the winner.

Clay's "American System" was more in step with Adams's nationalism than with the states' rights advocated by Jackson, Crawford, and Calhoun. Moreover, Clay had protested against Jackson's invasion of Florida in 1819 and disliked Jackson's evident indifference to government solutions and diplomacy. Even before the election, Clay had told Missouri Senator Thomas Hart Benton that he preferred Adams to Jackson.

A few weeks after Clay called on Adams, an unsigned newspaper column in the *Columbian Observer* in Philadelphia alleged, without offering any supporting evidence, that "corruption and bargain" had been the meeting's purpose. Indeed, it is unlikely that two experienced public men would have explicitly agreed to trade Clay's support for a cabinet post. But many people believed it outright; others, including Jackson, were willing to believe it only if Adams won the House election and Clay received a choice appointment. After the *Observer* article was reprinted in the *National Intelligencer* in early February, Clay indignantly challenged the author to a duel if he would declare himself, and he demanded a House investigation. Both Clay's challenge and the inquiry came to nothing.

The House elected Adams on the first ballot with the requisite 13 states' votes, when General Stephen Van Rensselaer, the War of 1812 militia general at the disastrous Battle of Queenston Heights, cast a decisive ballot giving Adams New York after praying hard for divine guidance. Van Rensselaer said afterward that when he finished praying and opened his eyes, he saw an Adams ballot on the floor and, believing its appearance to be providential, promptly put it in the ballot box. Adams also picked up Missouri, Ohio, and Kentucky because Clay, his supporters, and the Kentucky legislature all rallied to him, and he wrested Maryland, Louisiana, and Illinois from Jackson. Old Hickory retained the support of just 7 states after North Carolina abandoned him for Crawford, who won 4 states.

At a White House reception presided over by President Monroe, Jackson and Adams shook hands cordially, and would do so just once more. Soon afterward, Adams invited Clay to become his secretary of state, mulishly disregarding the "corrupt bargain" rumors flying around Washington. Clay, insisted Adams, was quite simply the best person for the position, "due to his talents and services, and to the Western section of the Union, whence he comes, and to the confidence in me manifested by their delegations." Clay accepted, to the lasting regret of both men—especially Clay, who longed to become president but now never would.

The Senate sullenly approved his nomination, 27–10, as resentment among Jackson's supporters and allies metastasized into a settled plan to thwart Adams's purposes and jettison him from the White House in four years. The mad, eloquent, imbibing Senator

John Randolph provoked Clay into challenging him to a duel by comparing the purported scheming of Adams and Clay to the scheming of two disreputable characters in Henry Fielding's *Tom Jones*, "Blifill and Black George . . . the Puritan and the blackleg." The Randolph–Clay duel ended with an exchange of shots and no injury.

Famous for holding grudges, Jackson bitterly observed a week after Adams's election, "The Judas of the West has closed the contract and will receive the thirty pieces of silver." He later added: "The people [have] been cheated. . . . Corruption and intrigues at Washington . . . defeated the will of the people."

By stubbornly appointing Clay in the teeth of tremendous animosity, Adams had handed his adversaries the ideal instrument for accomplishing his downfall: a purported backroom deal that had circumvented the people's will. Four years later, when his public career appeared to be over, Adams was still insisting, "in the presence of our country and of heaven," that there had never been a "corrupt bargain."

MARCH 4, 1825, WASHINGTON

Having pledged in his inauguration speech to observe the credo that "the will of the people is the source, and the happiness of the people the end of all legitimate government upon earth," the sixth president returned to his home on F Street to receive visitors, as the Monroes had not yet vacated the White House. Louisa, who had risen from her sickbed to attend the reception, did not accompany Adams to the inauguration ball. The White House was in such dire need of repairs that the Adamses did not move in until early April, and even then, it had no plumbing or running water.

Adams's philosophy of governance, he would learn to his great frustration, was jarringly out of step with popular sentiment and Congress's agenda. He firmly believed, as Sir Henry St. John Bolingbroke had memorably written, "The good of the people is the ultimate and true end of government." He held the conviction that the president should be a remote, powerful personage—a George Washington, as Adams remembered him. His refusal to dispense patronage and fire disloyal officeholders harkened back to his father's administration and exhibited blindness to the political realities of his tenuous position as a minority president.

In the meantime, Congress was busy whetting its knives to exact revenge for the "stolen" election. Adams ignored the abundant early signs of an organized emerging opposition and neither contemplated nor implemented countermeasures. When his political obtuseness reaped a disastrous harvest, he was unable to act.

Antiquated though he was in many of his beliefs, Adams was nevertheless far ahead of his day with his bold "Liberty with Power" national agenda and his plan to reach out to Latin and South America. Liberty with Power was the administration's signature program for the "greater good." It was a compendium of government-funded canals, roads, and bridges and government-supported education, science, and manufacturing. Sweepingly nationalistic and expansionist—increased trade and the acquisition of the Oregon Territory were among its priorities—Liberty with Power required lots of government capital, which Adams foresaw coming from protective tariffs and public lands sales.

Some of Adams's advisers warned him that he was asking for trouble if he made Liberty with Power the centerpiece of his First Annual Message to Congress on December 6, 1825. Attorney General William Wirt said that although he thought Adams's program was "a noble, spirited thing," Wirt's fellow Virginians would accuse the president of "grasping for power. . . . Patrick Henry's prophecy would be said to have come to pass: that we wanted a great, magnificent Government."

Adams heard out his advisers but did not tone down his message. "The spirit of improvement is abroad upon the earth," he declared. "Liberty is power." He recommended an expedition to explore the Pacific Northwest coast; establishment of "a uniform standard" of weights and measures—a few years earlier, he had written the definitive treatise on the subject—and of a national university and astronomical observatory in Washington, citing the need for "lighthouses of the skies"; the creation of a naval academy; and the formation of a Department of Interior (then part of the State Department). Believing that a plan of internal improvements, as he later put it, "was for this nation the only path to increasing comforts and well-being, to honor, to glory, and finally to the general improvement of the condition of mankind," he proposed canals linking Chesapeake Bay to the Ohio River, and Lake Memphremagog to the Connecticut River, in addition to new roads everywhere. Adams also wished to send ministers to the Congress of Central and South America meeting in 1826 at the Isthmus of Panama.

Jackson supporters in Congress grumbled at Adams's rather highhanded admonition to "not slumber in indolence or fold up our arms and proclaim to the world that we are palsied by the will of our constituents." They read into the president's words the insinuation that he would not hesitate to trample on the people's constitutional rights if he thought he was right and the people were wrong. Wrote Jackson: "I shudder for the consequence—if not checked by the voice of the people, it must end in consolidation, & then in despotism."

In his flattering biography of John Quincy Adams, William Seward, who would later become Abraham Lincoln's secretary of state, hit upon a central truth of Adams's presidency: "The administration of John Quincy Adams blends so intimately with that of Monroe, in which he was chief Minister, that no dividing line can be drawn between them." Adams's policies did suggest a continuation of the nationalist Monroe's—in advocating public works (the

Monroe administration established the Board of Internal Improvements) and protective tariffs, and by supporting the national bank.

But Monroe's program had faltered during his second term—partly because of rivalries over succession, but also due to the growing populism that in 1824 had nearly carried Andrew Jackson to the White House. By obstinately ignoring these harbingers of change, Adams was launching his cherished agenda into a tempest.

The trouble began when Adams nominated two delegates to the Pan-American Conference, whose organizers included the South American revolutionary Simon Bolívar. Adams and Clay hoped to foster "the most cordial feelings of fraternal friendship" and increase commercial trade throughout the Western Hemisphere, a marriage of public and private interests. Delegates planned to discuss abolishing the slave trade; preventing future European colonization of the hemisphere; forestalling European interference in wars between Spain and her former colonies; and recognizing Haiti, governed by ex-slaves for two decades. But disapproving proto-Democrats, among them Martin Van Buren and allies of John Calhoun and William Crawford, feared that American participation might lead to the sort of "entangling alliance" that George Washington and Thomas Jefferson had cautioned against.

From the Hermitage, Andrew Jackson warned, "The moment we engage in confederations or alliances with any nation, we may from that time date the downfall of our republic." But Congress reluctantly approved Richard C. Anderson of Kentucky and John Sergeant of Pennsylvania as commissioners and appropriated $40,000 for their trip, one of Adams's rare triumphs in Congress.

It all came to nothing. Anderson died of yellow fever while en route; Sergeant, hoping to avoid a similar fate, delayed his trip and reached Panama after the conference had adjourned. In a message to Congress, Adams lamented the lost opportunity and indirectly rebuked those who had tried to stop the mission: "Nothing was ever lost by kind treatment. Nothing can be gained by sullen repulses and aspiring pretensions."

❊

The "man of the whole country" was reluctant to display himself to the public other than during his fortnightly levees and New Year's Day receptions, when guests were received in the East Room, which Adams deliberately left unfurnished in the hope that congressmen would be moved to appropriate money for furniture; they were not. At these obligatory receptions, he often seemed gruff and stiff.

Crowds that gathered to see Adams were told to go home and "attend to their private duties." When a throng greeted him at a Philadelphia pier in October 1827, giving three hearty cheers in the hope that he would make an extemporaneous speech, Adams described how he "returned their salutation by a bow, waving the hand, and saying, 'God Bless you all!' There was not the slightest disorder." Indeed, there was not; the disappointed crowd dispersed.

At a Baltimore banquet to commemorate the city's repulse of the British during the War of 1812, Adams offered a toast to "Ebony and Topaz—General Ross's posthumous coat of arms, and the republican militiamen who gave it." Observing the confusion on his listeners' faces, the president attempted to explain that the allusion was to a Voltaire story, "Le Blanc et Le Noir." The puzzlement grew. Evidently no one had read Voltaire's depiction of Ebony as the spirit of evil, and Topaz as the good spirit, transmogrified in Adams's toast to General Robert Ross, whose coat of arms was embellished by the king after Ross's death outside Baltimore, and the "good" American militia. The unwieldy eloquence of the "ex-professor" became yet another easy target for the Democrats' ridicule.

For disastrous public appearances such as these, and for his intellectual superiority, the president was pilloried as an "aristocrat" in a populist era. Yet, at small dinner parties he could be surprisingly animated and urbane, and when he wished, he could impress his guests with his stories and his knowledge of wines.

Adams's principled refusal to use his patronage power further damaged his administration. Rather than build a political apparatus through the wholesale replacement of civil servants with supporters, as his predecessors had done, Adams insisted on only filling vacancies as they occurred—and in keeping employees if they were competent, even if they were political enemies. Adams removed only two jobholders and refused to turn out his disloyal postmaster general, John McLean, for the same reasons that his father had kept on War Secretary Timothy Pickering and Treasury Secretary Oliver Wolcott as they conspired against him with Alexander Hamilton. The presidency, wrote Adams, was not an "electioneering machine." He refused to be a party to making government "a perpetual and unremitting scramble for office. A more pernicious expedient could scarcely be devised."

Adams granted that McLean was "hostile to the Administration," but "as he is an able and efficient officer, I have made every allowance for the peculiarity of his situation, and have not believed him willfully treacherous." Thus, McLean was given free rein to use his considerable patronage power to fill the Postal Service's ranks with enemies of the administration. Later, when McLean's double-dealing became embarrassingly obvious, Adams continued to insist that it would be "extremely impolitic" to remove him, perhaps because McLean was a Methodist minister and Adams did not want to risk alienating Methodists.

Secretary of State Clay exasperatedly observed, "The friends of the Administration have to contend not only against their enemies, but against the Administration itself, which leaves its power in the hands of his own enemies." When Clay tried to compensate by using the State Department as a patronage machine, he only succeeded in opening the administration to charges of favoritism. The congressional opposition wrote a report that insinuated corrupt practices by Adams's administration and with loud fanfare unveiled six bills to curb patronage.

Even more portentous was the situation at the Capitol. Vice President John C. Calhoun—as had Thomas Jefferson, John Adams's vice president—was using his position as Senate president to sabotage the president's Liberty with Power agenda, while aiding the coalition forming around Jackson that would unseat Adams in 1828 (his reward would be another term as vice president, under Jackson). The alliance, which also included former supporters of Calhoun and William Crawford, and the ambitious junior senator from New York, Martin Van Buren, began to cohere even before Adams's inauguration, catalyzed by Clay's appointment as secretary of state. On February 27, 1825, New York Senator Rufus King wrote to his son: "A party is forming itself here to oppose Mr. Adams's administration. South Carolina is its headquarters, and I understand that a Dinner takes place today [at] the Quarters of this Delegation, when General Jackson, Mr. Calhoun . . . and others are to be guests. . . . This first step may serve to combine the malcontents." Within a year, the "malcontents" had become a well-coordinated political opposition.

In the House, Adams alienated Southerners by recommending John W. Taylor of New York for Speaker; Taylor won by just two votes. This might not have been a problem if Adams had wholeheartedly supported the majority leader, the gifted Daniel Webster from Massachusetts. But Adams distrusted Webster and did not do enough to secure his loyalty. As a result, Webster was not as energetic an advocate for Adams's programs as he might have been.

Even with Adams's allies ostensibly in the majority, Congress bottled up the administration's proposed internal improvements, its science and education initiatives, and its protective tariff. Adams did not fight for his programs, believing, as a practitioner of the "old politics," that he had done his part by making recommendations and now could only await Congress's verdict. This was akin to his custom of not seeking public office, but waiting to be "chosen." Unwilling to dirty his hands with the work of building coalitions and compromising, the president averted his eyes and provided little encouragement or advice while cabinet members and congressional leaders labored on his behalf.

In the fall of 1826, the proto-Democrats won majorities in Congress during the midterm elections. Their operatives campaigned in the states, overmatching Adams's field manager, Toby Watkins, who had few connections outside Washington. The person largely responsible for this triumph was Van Buren, who then turned his protean organizing skills to electing Andrew Jackson in two years.

Adams now had the unhappy distinction of being the first president paired with a Congress controlled by his adversaries. He was acutely aware of what this meant for Liberty with Power and his re-election prospects in 1828. It was "a state of things which has never before occurred under the Government of the United States," wrote Adams.

Yet, he took no countermeasures, but only became more fatalistic as his adversaries grew more powerful and confident. Even with Congress controlled by the opposition, the president strangely left it to the legislative body to choose which of his internal improvements to approve. Adams refused to intervene as Congress emasculated his grand program—authorizing canal and river navigation projects in swing states to rally support for Jackson in 1828 and junking the rest. The president finally was compelled to recognize that "the great object of my life therefore, as applied to the administration of the Government of the United States, has failed."

Adams did not, however, hesitate to identify his enemies. There were the ones "bitter as wormwood in their opposition," but who managed to attend his levees and dinners and were "always ready to introduce their friends to the President," and there were the "frequenters of gin lane and beer alley," and "two or three slanderers drunk with faction, though not with alcohol." Adams placed in a class all his own the opposition's point man, the brilliantly erratic Senator John Randolph of Virginia, a man of "besotted violence" and "the image and superscription of a great man stamped upon base metal."

When Adams was informed that William Crawford, still a player in spite of all his setbacks, was being proposed as his running mate in 1828, Adams trenchantly observed that it was "treachery of the deepest dye" and compared Crawford to "one of Milton's fallen angels . . . excepting that Milton has made the devils true to each other."

One of the powers behind Crawford in 1824 had been Martin Van Buren. Van Buren grew up in Kinderhook, New York, speaking Dutch, but paradoxically he would become the first president born a citizen of the United States. Now a rising forty-six-year-old political star, the short, well-mannered, elegantly dressed Van Buren was nicknamed the "Little Magician" because of his genius for political organization. Establishing the Albany Regency as a rallying point for Northern Jeffersonians, he set out to bind North and South under the rubric of limited government and states' rights. The alliance "most natural and beneficial to the country," he believed, "is that between the planters of the South and the plain Republicans of the North." And so the new Democratic Party was born.

Van Buren sent James A. Hamilton, Alexander Hamilton's son, to Nashville to act as a liaison between Jackson and Van Buren's power base in Albany. Van Buren's friend, Thomas Ritchie, the editor of the Richmond *Enquirer*, was to secure Virginia and Georgia for Jackson.

Van Buren toured the deep South, while Calhoun, Ritchie, and other Jackson men shored up support in Virginia, the Carolinas, and Georgia, and Jackson presided over a Central Committee in Nashville. With money raised from their congressional allies, they established a nationwide network of Jackson newspapers. By early 1828, Jackson's nationwide party organization was fully operational.

Van Buren met often with Jackson's allies in Congress to coordinate their siege of the Adams administration. Congressional committees inundated the administration with requests for documents and opinions, while the new Retrenchment Committee, ostensibly seeking ways to curb government spending and pay off the debt, instead sought ways to embarrass Adams. The beleaguered president denounced one Retrenchment Committee report as "full of gross misrepresentations, reckless blunders, and foul insinuations."

While perpetually dredging up the Adams-Clay "corrupt bargain," Adams's adversaries also alleged that the administration had paid off political supporters with ambassadorial junkets and was turning West Point into a "rich man's academy." Adams was accused of both being a Federalist and of having betrayed the Federalists twenty years earlier; of giving away Texas to Spain; of attempting at Ghent in 1814 to trade Mississippi River navigation rights for New England fishing rights, the charge by Jonathan Russell that Adams had demolished in 1824; and of being a lifelong politician who had grown fat at the public trough, earning an average of $12,500 a year while posted abroad—a sum that included living allowances. The distortion succeeded in outraging citizens at a time when skilled artisans were paid $1.75 per day on average.

Unwilling to build his own party machinery or to retaliate in kind, Adams was reduced to complaining to his son Charles Francis about his political enemies, who were "melted by a common disappointment into one mass envenomed by one spirit of bitter unrelenting persecuting malice against me."

Learning that his father, ex-President John Adams, was "rapidly sinking," the incumbent president set out for Quincy on July 8, 1826. He was eating breakfast at Merrill's Inn outside Baltimore when he found out that his father had died on July 4—the fiftieth anniversary of the Declaration of Independence. Then he discovered that Thomas Jefferson had died that same day. As he hurried north, Adams could not help but think, as did many Americans, that "the time, the manner, the coincidence with the decease of Jefferson are visible and palpable marks of Divine favor. . . . For myself, all that I dare to ask is, that I may live the remnant of my days in a manner worthy of him from whom I came, and, at the appropriated hour of my Maker, die as my father has died."

He reached Quincy a week after the funeral. In the bedroom where his father had died, it struck him like "an arrow to the heart" that he would never see his parents again. "I feel it is time for me to begin to set my house in order, and to prepare for the churchyard myself." While sitting in his father's pew at the Quincy Unitarian Church, Adams was suddenly moved to tears—and inspired to join the church. For all his religiosity, he had never been a church member. He resolved to keep the Quincy Big House and its acreage for his retirement, which he was certain lay in the near future.

As the dreaded 1828 election drew inexorably nearer and his sense of failure deepened, nervous tension often kept Adams awake at night. Exhausted in the mornings, he skipped his walks and Potomac swims. He lost weight, and his clothes hung loosely on him. He was lapsing into one of his depressions, which recurred throughout his life in times of stress.

> My health has been languishing, without sickness. From four to five hours of sleep, not of good repose; a continued habit of costiveness [constipation], indigestion, failure of appetite, uncontrolled dejection of spirits, insensibility to the almost unparalleled blessings with which I have been favored; a sluggish carelessness of life, an imaginary wish that it were terminated, with a clinging to it as close as it ever was in the days of most animated hopes. . . .

Yet he remained doggedly determined to endure "the protracted agony of character and reputation which it is the will of Superior Power that I should pass through." Evidently to steel himself for the ordeal, he attended three services on Sundays—Unitarian, Episcopal, and Presbyterian. Later, he took his doctor's advice and spent several weeks during August and September of 1827 in Quincy, fishing, gardening, and swimming, and he returned to the White House refreshed.

Portents of defeat pursued Adams everywhere. From the president's room in Barnum's House in Baltimore, where, in August 1828, he was spending the night while traveling to Quincy, Adams watched a speaker named McMahon loudly praise Andrew Jackson before an enthusiastic crowd in the adjacent square. Adams grumped that the man went on for three hours about "the unpardonable sins of the Administration and the transcendent virtues of Andrew Jackson." When the president retired for the night, he could still hear the man's voice, "like the beating of a mill-clapper." In Philadelphia the next day, mingled with the cheering for Adams were cries of "Huzza for Jackson!"

The previous December, as Adams and Henry Clay had gone over a speech in which Clay planned to refute the "corrupt bargain" charges, Clay had intimated that he planned to retire from public life. Adams objected to Clay's "being sacrificed as a victim to calumny" and tried to buck up his discouraged secretary of state with the prediction that his time would come. Adams conceded that Jackson would first leverage the "infamous slander" to become president. But when the public then tired of Jackson, predicted Adams, Clay would succeed him. A few months later, Clay, suffering from creeping numbness in his lower extremities, believed that he was dying and tendered his resignation. Adams, however, convinced him to instead take a vacation. The vacation revived Clay— he recovered from his illness—but nothing could resuscitate the president's re-election hopes except the political measures that he obstinately refused to take.

❖

The 1828 campaign emphasized personalities, not issues—about which Adams and Jackson were in concord for the most part, both of them being nationalistic, expansionist, and generally unsympathetic to the underprivileged. "The Combination," as Adams called the emerging Democratic Party led by Jackson, his running mate Vice President John Calhoun, Martin Van Buren, and William Crawford, succeeded in framing the election as a choice between the "old elite" and new, self-made men, contrasting Adams's "kingly pomp," "foreign wife," and inherited wealth with "Old Hickory's" self-transformation from poor orphan to entrepreneur and his wartime heroism. Of course, this was propaganda; there was nothing "kingly" about the carelessly dressed, debt-ridden Adams, or common about the wealthy businessman-planter Jackson. But such campaign rhetoric defined the 1828 election.

The rest was mudslinging. The New Hampshire *Patriot* accused Adams of having "pimped" for Czar Alexander I when he was minister to Russia, by sending a beautiful young woman to seduce him. Adams's allies tried to smear Jackson for having married Rachel Donelson Robards before she was legally divorced from her estranged first husband, Lewis Robards. Adams and Louisa were accused by Duff Green's *United States Telegraph* (Adams called Green, who was Calhoun's son-in-law, the "prince of slanderers") of having had premarital sex, while Adams's supporters outrageously asserted that Jackson's mother was a prostitute brought to America by British soldiers and that Jackson was the product of her marriage to a "mulatto man."

Adams was accused in the West of socializing with Catholic priests, and in the East of denouncing Catholics. The National Republican press published lurid accounts of Jackson's duels, his execution of militiamen and British subjects, and his slaughter of the Indians. The Jacksonians dredged up Adams's "Ebony and Topaz" toast to show that "the professor" was out of touch with the electorate.

Lost among the slanders and vilifications was the fact that under the Adams administration's stewardship, the U.S. economy had experienced one of its highest growth rates, and the national debt had been reduced from more than $16 million to just under $5 million. Despite the Democrats' opposition to federally financed internal improvements, $14 million was budgeted for canals, harbors, and roads during the Adams administration, a testament to the durability of pork-barreling.

Jackson attended a gala celebration in New Orleans on January 8, 1828, commemorating his glorious victory over the British thirteen years earlier. But Adams refused to "electioneer," thereby squandering the enormous advantages of his incumbency. Stuck in the rut of "old politics," Adams wrote, "I've never sought office, but I have no dislike of it. In a Republican Government the Country has a right to the services of every Citizen. And each Citizen is bound in duty to perform the service."

Adams made a rare exception to his policy of eschewing campaigning and ceremonies when he presided over the groundbreaking for the Chesapeake and Ohio Canal on the Fourth of July 1828. The canal marked a rare victory for Adams's Liberty with Power program, and Adams wished to celebrate it.

Thousands of people braved the heat and humidity to hear the president speak on the Potomac riverbank in Maryland. When it was Adams's moment to turn the first spadeful of earth, as luck would have it, the ground stubbornly spurned his attempts; first, he struck a stump, then hard ground. He irritably doffed his coat. "Resuming the spade, [I] raised a shovelful of earth." The large crowd responded to the slipping of what Charles Francis Adams called his father's "iron mask" by bursting into loud applause at his flash of spirit. "It struck the eye and fancy of the spectators more than all the flowers of rhetoric in my speech," he wrote in his diary with thinly disguised pleasure.

It was possibly the first time in Adams's life that a crowd had responded to him with laughter and spontaneous applause. More than a decade would pass before there would be another such occasion.

Adams refused to capitalize on the powerful backlash forming against Freemasonry as a result of the disappearance and apparent murder of William Morgan, who had attempted to publish the craft's secrets. When prominent western New York Masons tried to cover up the Masons' involvement, public indignation exploded. Yet Adams, who stood to gain support because Jackson was a Mason of high rank, stubbornly refused to state that he was not a Mason; in a cruel irony, Jackson's supporters suggested the president's silence meant that he was in fact a Mason.

To rebut charges that he was an "Old Federalist," Adams did break silence—and angered former New England Federalists, without winning new supporters. He resurrected an 1825 letter by Thomas Jefferson implying that Adams had informed him that disgruntled New England Federalists were in secret communication with the British during the War of 1812. Correcting the year to 1808, Adams wrote in a public letter that Nova Scotia's British governor had been in contact with a Massachusetts citizen about a possible New England secession conspiracy. His letter aroused indignant denials from Old Federalist leaders and prompted Duff Green to snidely observe that Adams's "betrayal" demonstrated his "true character."

By early 1828, Adams and his cabinet were certain that they and Liberty with Power were soon to be supplanted by "Jackson, Calhoun, and Liberty!" the credo of the Democrats. "It is the transition from this tempestuous gale to the calm of solitude and dereliction which I am to expect as one of the severe trials that await me," wrote Adams. Even as they campaigned on Adams's behalf—and without a cohesive party organization comparable to Jackson's—his cabinet members looked for exits from the administration. Treasury

Secretary Richard Rush and War Secretary James Barbour lobbied for the job of minister to Great Britain (Barbour got it, while Rush had the unenviable task of being Adams's running mate). Adams sympathetically wrote that they were seeking "a harbor from the storm. I cannot blame them."

The election, held during the week of October 31–November 5 (Election Day lay two decades in the future), affirmed Jackson's long-anticipated victory. Receiving 647,276 votes, Jackson easily defeated Adams, with 508,064 votes, by 56 percent to 44 percent. The outcome was far more lopsided in the Electoral College, which cast 178 ballots for Jackson and 83 for Adams. While Adams had expected to lose, the resounding defeat still stung. "I have only to submit to it with resignation," he wrote, "and to ask that I and those who are dear to me may be sustained under it."

He guiltily acknowledged that his defeat had also dragged down some loyal congressional allies. "In the ruin of our cause he has lost his election," he wrote of one of the defeated congressmen who visited him December 4 as the 20th Congress was commencing its lame duck session.

Yet, Adams was secretly relieved, too, that his ordeal was at last ended. Two years later, he would look back on his presidency with horror: "No one knows, and few conceive, the agony of mind that I have suffered from the time that I was made by circumstances, and not by my volition, a candidate for the Presidency till I was dismissed from that station by the failure of my re-election."

The Adamses moved out of the White House the night before Jackson's inauguration. Adams skipped what proved to be the first outdoor inauguration, becoming the only president besides his father to not attend his successor's swearing-in. He also placed newspaper notices requesting that friends not visit him on March 4.

Jackson had initially invited the Adamses to remain in the White House "as long as it should suit our convenience, were it even a month," but then later expressed concern that Gadsby's Tavern, his lodging place, would be too small for the crowds anticipated at the inauguration reception. So Adams sent the city marshal to inform Jackson that his family was moving out and the White House would be his on inauguration day.

Adams had pronounced, "After the third of March I shall consider my public career closed." If his failed presidency and defeat had not enunciated this fact plainly enough, he had only to recall what the ancient Seneca chief, Red Jacket, had said to him ten days before he left the White House. They both "were of the past age," Red Jacket had told Adams, "and should soon be called for by the Great Spirit." Adams had glumly agreed with Red Jacket, adding, "I hoped it would be to a better world than this."

Although he was just sixty-one years old, the age at which his father had begun his presidency, Adams was certain that his public career was over. He pessimistically believed that in the few years he was convinced remained to him, which he planned to devote to the peaceful pursuits of writing, reading, and horticulture, he would instead be "hunted down" and permitted no rest. Yet this prospect was not as unwelcome as Adams let on. If he was piously vowing to "take as little part in public concerns as possible," Adams was also sharpening his quills with the intention "to write with the boldness of truth" and "defend and vindicate my own reputation from the double persecution under which I have fallen." His first order of business was to write a scorching rebuttal to attacks on him by New England "Old Federalists" about the purported New England secessionist plot of twenty years earlier. So sarcastic and prejudiced was his 400-page response that friends and relatives persuaded Adams not to publish it.

In May 1829, George, the Adamses' brilliant, erratic, bumbling oldest son, vanished from the deck of the *Benjamin Franklin* during a night crossing of Long Island Sound while traveling to Washington. The apparent suicide shattered his family. "Blessed God! . . . Forgive the wanderings of my own mind under its excruciating torture; have compassion upon this partner of my soul [Louisa], and bear her up. . . . Deep have been her afflictions heretofore—But this! Oh, this! . . . Human suffering can go but one degree beyond what she endures." The ship's crew members said the twenty-eight-year-old lawyer, complaining to fellow passengers of headaches and claiming to hear voices, had asked to be put ashore. Then, he disappeared; his hat was found on the stern deck. "God be merciful to him and to his parents," wrote Adams in his diary. He prayed with Louisa, so prostrated by the death that her condition "is not to be described." A doctor attended to them, "but there was no medicine for this wound." Later, after his body had washed up on City Island, his family learned that he had been severely depressed and that he had fathered a child with a chambermaid, Eliza Dolph, at the Boston home where he boarded.

John Adams's depression and the alcoholism of Abigail's brother, William Smith, had been transmitted to John Quincy Adams's brothers Charles and Thomas, who both battled the bottle, and to Adams himself, who suffered from recurring depression. Now, his oldest son had succumbed to the family legacy of mental illness, while his middle son, John, had developed a drinking problem. Charles Francis, upon whom the family hopes had now settled, would be the only son to meet Adams's high expectations of scholarship and civic responsibility, yet he, too, was depression-prone, as would be his sons Brooks and Henry.

George's death served to deepen Adams's and Louisa's affection for one another. While their relationship had always been tumultuous, Adams had once been moved to declare, "My lot in marriage has been highly favored." Adams and Louisa both were intelligent, strong-willed, high-tempered, and sharp-tongued—he, irascible and harsh, and she, tending to sarcasm and using invalidism to evoke sympathy. "A more pitiable set I do not think I know than my father and mother," Charles Francis once wrote in exasperation. Yet their relationship was complex; while they sometimes angrily probed one another's vulnerabilities, at other times they helped one another compensate for them. Louisa knew her husband well enough to buffer his sensitivity to unfair criticism and outrageous innuendo, such as the report that he attended church barefooted. "Put a little wool in your ears and don't read the papers," she advised.

In Boston that summer, Adams bluntly told Charles Francis that he was the family's last hope. Lacking the qualities to succeed in public life, John II wanted to be a businessman, and it is likely that he was already drinking heavily. Adams began advising Charles Francis on how best to conduct his life, promising that if he wrote a letter once a week, "I shall give you more advice." Charles Francis wrote regularly, adopted many of his father's suggestions, and became his confidant. "I am the only one who remains to keep the name and the family in our branch at least from destruction."

In June 1829, John Quincy Adams reoccupied his parents' Quincy home, the Big House. He unpacked thirty-eight boxes and six trunks of books—he then owned nearly 6,000 books and later possessed so many that Adams's biographer Samuel Flagg Bemis pronounced Adams's collection "the best library possessed by an individual in America, not excluding that of Thomas Jefferson." Adams hired a local carpenter to build bookshelves. He also tied up loose ends from his parents' deaths: establishing a Latin academy in Quincy, as requested by his father; composing inscriptions honoring his parents for a tablet at their church; and surveying family property. He began collecting his father's papers preparatory to writing a biography, but was unable to summon much enthusiasm for the project, and never completed it. And there was Charles Francis's impending marriage to Abigail Brooks, daughter of Boston insurance broker Peter Brooks, reportedly the richest man in New England—an example of an old, established family marrying new wealth. Charles Francis would hereafter never want for money.

Adams's Quincy neighbors welcomed his return to Massachusetts, but the Boston establishment gave him a cold shoulder, resenting afresh his betrayal of the Federalists in 1808. There were no Boston dinners or receptions in his honor. The American Academy of Arts and Sciences removed him as president after having served twelve years, and the Athenaeum attempted to cancel his membership.

His sixty-second birthday on July 11 was an occasion for morbid reflections on his failure to serve others as he ought to have done and on a future that he believed only promised further disappointments. "My life for the public is closed, and it only remains for me to use my endeavors to make the remainder of it useful to my family and my neighbors, if possible." While he was tormented by rheumatism in his writing hand, he nonetheless managed to maintain his diary and a wide correspondence. He resumed his exercise regimen, taking long walks and half-mile swims between wharfs in Quincy Bay, observing with his usual exactness that he covered the distance in 16 minutes and with 531 strokes. And he immersed himself in works of history, his Bible studies, and poetry.

Poetry was a compulsion that Adams dismissingly called "the rhyming maggot in my brain." From his lifelong reading of classical poetry he rather harshly assayed his talent for poetical composition to be no better than mediocre. Yet he felt compelled to write poetry, and it frustrated him that whereas on some days the lines came to him effortlessly, other times inspiration came not at all. As a devotional exercise and an outlet for his rhyming habit, the deeply religious Adams rewrote the biblical Psalms into metric form. He often awakened before 4 A.M. and composed poetry as he lay in bed before rising at 5 to write down the words. So began *Dermot MacMorrough*. Conceived as a mock-heroic work of 50 stanzas, it evolved into a serious, sprawling epic of 266 stanzas in four cantos. It relates Henry II's twelfth-century conquest of Ireland. Once, while in the throes of composition, Adams wrote six stanzas in his mind during his morning walk.

Easily Adams's longest sustained literary effort, *Dermot Mac-Morrough* has been described as an "Irish Iliad"—beginning with the historically true story of Dermot's abduction of Prince Tiernan Ororick's wife Dovergilda (with her complicity) to abet his burning ambition to become High King of Ireland. The result was Ireland's twelfth-century conquest by the Anglo-Norman King Henry II and the end of Irish liberty. Told in "Byronic ottava rima," the narrative poem shows how the abandonment of private morality—marital fidelity, patriotism, and piety—can have tragic, far-reaching consequences, proving that private morality and public virtue both matter and are inextricably linked. Adams consciously used Byron's *Beppo* as a model, although conceding, "The unapproachable difference between *Beppo* and *Dermot* is the difference between Tokay and small beer." *Dermot*, he deprecatingly wrote, "wants vivacity, humor, poetical invention, and a large command of language." Yet, more than 2,000 copies of *Dermot* were sold in three editions.

> *Thus was the shame of servitude her [Ireland's] lot:*
> *And has been since, from that detested day,*
> *When Dermot all his country's claims forgot;*
> *And basely barter'd all her rights away . . .*

When a poem that he had written in 1789 or 1790, "The Vision," appeared in a newspaper fifty years later, Adams judged it his best poetical work, adding in a fit of self-belittlement, "My summit level, as a statesman, orator, philosopher, and proser, is about the same elevation. I leave nothing to live after me but aims beyond my means, and principles too pure for the age in which I have lived."

For his own edification, Adams translated into English the works of Juvenal, Catullus, and Rousseau, and he wrote history as well. Had he been able to suppress his manifold biases, he might have made a fine historian; he was energetic and analytical enough. He worked for three months on his article on the Russo-Turkish War (he was transparently sympathetic to Russia), sometimes devoting six hours a day to it. But as with his poetry, Adams detachedly recognized his failings as a historian and either did not finish or publish these works, among them *Parties of the United States* and a history of the Anglo-Chinese War.

Adams also completed a ten-month project of reading in the original Latin all of Marcus Tullius Cicero's known writings, lamenting the time he had wasted earlier in his life reading translations. In studying Cicero, Adams found "there is sometimes so much in it of painful reality that I close the book," he confided to Charles Francis. "I watch with his sleepless nights, I hear his solitary sighs. I feel the agitation of his pulse, not for himself, but for his son, for his Tullia, for his country." The Roman conservative's 57 orations, nearly 800 letters, and his philosophical writings, all in perfect Latin prose, revealed him in the various roles of consul and statesman, and private citizen and philosopher. Immersing himself in Cicero so soon after his own removal from public life, Adams was struck by the similarities in their thinking, and the parallels between his own situation and Cicero in retirement at his Tusculum estate: As the "military chieftain" Andrew Jackson had supplanted him, so had the triumphant Julius Caesar caused Cicero's withdrawal; as Adams mourned his lost son, so had Cicero grieved for his dead daughter.

In the meantime, Adams's family worried about his precarious financial situation. Charles Francis, who had taken control of his father's Boston affairs, was especially anxious about his parents' future, and evidently John II even expressed alarm, prompting Louisa to candidly write to him: "Your father is very well, but much depressed with a small debt of 40,000 dollars on which he is paying interest. It is a sad state of things but it is better that we should all know the truth." A particularly galling debt was Columbian Mills, the grist and flour mills on Rock Creek in Washington. Adams had taken controlling interest when Louisa's cousin, George Johnson, faced foreclosure in 1823. The mills steadily lost money, despite John II's best efforts; it didn't help that his father, wagering that demand would soar, increased production, and then watched as prices instead fell, costing him $15,000.

Adams's peaceful retirement would soon end. His decision to serve in Congress—radical for a "son of the Revolution" steeped in eighteenth-century traditions to so break with his chief executive predecessors—was no less than a minor miracle. Adams's acquiescence to becoming a candidate for the Plymouth District's congressional seat was more sensational than his anticlimactic, lopsided victory in November over a Jacksonian Democrat and an "Old Federalist." Had he been told that his subsequent congressional career, which he expected to be brief and unremarkable, would be neither, he would have suffered a recurrence of "unwilling incredulity."

On March 4, 1831, John Quincy Adams officially became a U.S. congressman, although he would not take up his duties until the 22nd Congress convened in December. His son Charles Francis understatedly observed at this point in his editing of his father's *Memoirs*, "The writer must be regarded as commencing a new term of official service. This term embraces the [17] remaining years of his life."

Chapter Four

The Freshman Congressman

---

*"I struggle against the laws of time,
and pray for cheerfulness and resignation."*

—John Quincy Adams, beginning his congressional career

DECEMBER 5, 1831, WASHINGTON

Thirty minutes before noon, John Quincy Adams, at sixty-four the oldest of the eighty-nine freshmen congressmen reporting for duty to the 22nd Congress, without fanfare took seat No. 203 in the U.S. House of Representatives. Later renamed Statuary Hall when a new House chamber was built, the old House occupied two stories of a Capitol wing. It was fitted out with a pair of fireplaces, red brocade draperies, and galleries for spectators. The representatives sat in easy chairs at mahogany desks in a semicircle around the raised Speaker's chair, which was shaded by a fringed, crimson silk canopy from the crystal chandelier overhead. In this historic room where Adams defeated Jackson in 1825 to become president, his remarkable final career began—and would end.

Speaker Andrew Stevenson of Virginia appointed him chairman of the Committee on Manufactures, ignoring Adams's petitions, "almost upon my knees to the Speaker," to be reassigned to the Committee on Foreign Affairs, for which he was better qualified than anyone alive in the United States. But the Jackson administration's massive antipathy toward Adams ruled out an appointment to such an important committee. Yet, Adams's abundant familiarity with manufactures and tariffs, and his support of a protective tariff, largely in concord with Jackson's position, made him well qualified for the assignment that he got. Moreover, looming on the horizon was a major storm over the tariff, and in the Jackson administration's view there was no better lightning rod than John Quincy Adams, unloved but respected by Democrats, fellow National Republicans, Northerners, Southerners, and Westerners. Adams resignedly accepted the assignment, grumbling, "I only know that it is not the place suited to my requirements and capacities such as they are."

The subject of Adams's first statement to the House was, almost prophetically, slavery. With the first stirring of the antebellum antislavery movement in the early 1830s, Northern congressmen had begun to present petitions to abolish slavery in the District of Columbia, which was administered by Congress and home to thousands of slaves. On December 12, Adams introduced a petition from Pennsylvania urging the abolition of slavery and the slave trade in the district. Adams then added his own opinion: "I would not support that part of the petition which prayed for abolition in the District of Columbia."

It might seem strange that Adams would present such a petition, when he believed that abolishing slavery in Washington would tear apart the nation. But Adams revered the constitutional right of petition, and whether his opinion was in concord with the petitioners' mattered less to him than that the petitions were heard.

Brief though his remarks were, Adams was embarrassed by his tentative manner of speaking. "It is so long since I was in the habit of speaking to a popular assembly . . . and I am so little qualified by nature for an extemporaneous orator, that I was at this time not a little agitated by the sound of my own voice."

But as 1831 drew to a close, he cautiously pronounced his re-entry into public life to be successful. "I have received no disrespectful treatment. Many individuals have treated me positively with respect. When I have spoken, I have been listened to with attention, and not without approbation. May I improve the lesson—remember to speak seldom, and, above all things, ask from above discernment [about] what to say!" However, he was unable to avert his eyes from his looming mortality, for "youth is the favorite of fortune, and age her victim. . . . I struggle against the laws of time, and pray for cheerfulness and resignation."

During the interregnum between his election in November 1830 and the beginning of the 22nd Congress thirteen months later, Adams had read Thomas Jefferson's sometimes dissembling memoirs and with grim satisfaction watched the current chief executive grapple with scandal. Adams read the posthumously published *Memoirs, Correspondence, and Miscellanies, from the Papers of Thomas Jefferson* with mingled indignation, contempt, and grudging admiration for the man who had been like a second father to him during his youth in Paris. "He tells nothing but that redounds to his own credit. . . . Jefferson, by his own narrative, is always in the right." Adams granted Jefferson "his ardent passion for liberty and the rights of man; his patriotism; the depth and compass of his understanding; the extent and variety of his knowledge"—all in "ceaseless operation" between 1790 and 1809. But he believed Jefferson was unfair to George Washington, Henry Knox, John Adams, Alexander Hamilton, James Bayard, "who made him President of the United States, and, lastly . . . me."

Adams observed that as Jefferson's memory "ceased to be tenacious, it became inventive." For example, Jefferson asserted that after the adoption of the Declaration of Independence on July 4, 1776, everyone present signed it. Adams, however, had seen the original Declaration in the State Department archives and knew that it bore the signatures of only the Continental Congress's president, John Hancock, and its secretary, Charles Thomson. Moreover, Jefferson's draft Declaration and Congress's alterations to it show the latter "to have been all improvements on it. The draft was declaratory, argumentative, and overloaded with crudities."

Adams also took secret pleasure in watching the Jackson administration's infighting over the "Mrs. Eaton" affair. In Adams's opinion, it was just desserts for Jackson's wholesale sacking of Adams holdovers. The president had replaced them with Democrat loyalists and fifty "writers and publishers of scurrilous newspapers, electioneering skunks" that had abetted the 1828 smear campaign against Adams.

"Mrs. Eaton" was Peggy O'Neale Timberlake Eaton, whom War Secretary John H. Eaton had married (after allegedly having an affair with her earlier) after her naval officer husband committed suicide. The indignant cabinet wives, led by Floride Calhoun, had shunned Mrs. Eaton. Remembering that his late wife Rachel had been victimized by rumor-mongering, Jackson became Mrs. Eaton's fiercest defender. To Adams's amusement, the contretemps split the Jackson cabinet. "[Vice President John] Calhoun heads the moral party, [Secretary of State Martin] Van Buren that of the frail sisterhood; and he is notoriously engaged in canvassing for the Presidency by paying his court to Mrs. Eaton." Duff Green, Calhoun's son-in-law and editor of the administration newspaper, the *United States Telegraph*, accused Van Buren of keeping the controversy alive in hopes of alienating Jackson from Calhoun, and thereby aiding Van Buren's own political prospects—which happened to be true. The scandal paralyzed the Jackson administration. Four cabinet members resigned, two of them forced out by Jackson.

And then, former Treasury Secretary William Crawford dropped a bomb: informing Jackson that Vice President Calhoun, while war secretary in 1818, had recommended punishing Jackson for his invasion of Florida. Jackson demanded that Calhoun tell him "whether it can be . . . that any attempt to effect [*sic*] me, was moved, and sustained by you in Cabinet council." The president declared that James Monroe had sanctioned the invasion, even though Monroe apparently had not. Soon, Calhoun and Crawford were both asking Adams to ransack his memory and recount what was said at the cabinet meetings thirteen years earlier.

Ironically, Adams was the only cabinet member who had actually *supported* Jackson's invasion, but that was beside the issue, caught as he was between two powerful adversaries, both of whom he bitterly resented for their "ingratitude and injustice to me." He recognized the utmost importance of his remaining scrupulously impartial. "I walk between burning ploughshares; let me be mindful where I place my foot." Adams was outraged, though, by Jackson's assertion that Monroe had dispatched Tennessee Congressman John Rhea with an authorizing letter for Jackson—a "circumstantial fabrication, [wrote Adams] beyond the comprehension of an honest mind."

Whether or not Martin Van Buren was also the secret mover behind this controversy—Calhoun said he was; Van Buren denied it—he did replace Calhoun as Jackson's second-term vice president in 1833, and four years later Van Buren became the eighth president. A collateral victim of the uproar was Duff Green, whose *United States Telegraph* was ousted as the Jackson administration's quasi-official organ in favor of Frank Blair's Washington *Globe*.

Calhoun's alienation from the Jackson administration, hardening into an advocacy of the states' purported right to nullify federal laws, had the unexpected consequence of partially conciliating Calhoun with Adams. Friends when they served together in the Monroe cabinet, they had since then become political adversaries. Although they were now friendly again, they were soon to be at swords' points over nullification. "It is on my part, as well as yours, a subject of pain, that we should differ so widely on a point, so fundamental in our political system," Calhoun wrote to Adams, when they both were "in search of truth." Adams was willing to consent to "a renewal of the intercourse of common civility," but he confessed in his diary that he had lost some of his confidence "in the qualities of his heart. . . . Mr. Calhoun's friendships and enmities are regulated exclusively by his interests."

The tumultuous, no-holds-barred politics that Adams would face in Washington was a microcosm of the nation, which was in the throes of shifting from a traditional agricultural economy to a rising industrial economy. "Go ahead! Is the order of the day," wrote sculptor Horatio Greenough upon returning to America from Europe. "The whole continent presents a scene of *scrabbling* and roars with greedy hurry." Francis Grund, an Austrian immigrant, described the "air of busy inquietude . . . which, in fact, constitutes their principal happiness." Alexis de Tocqueville, who admired the Federalist period that had ended with Jefferson's ascendancy, wrote that 1830s American politics was devoted to "material interests, not principles." In her unkind *Domestic Manners of the Americans*, Fanny Trollope, mother of the English novelist Anthony Trollope, remarked on the American obsession with making money: "Such unity of purpose, such sympathy of feeling [regarding profits] can be found nowhere else, except, perhaps in an ants' nest."

"Jacksonian democracy" would become a catchphrase, at variance with the fact that the president was a Western aristocrat who lived in a mansion, that he owned more than one hundred slaves, and that the solid support of the slaveholding states had helped elect him in 1828. That election neither extended suffrage to new constituencies, nor was it a benchmark in the rise of the "common man." It was a triumph of party organization and Democratic Party propaganda, which credited Jackson with ushering in a "government of the people." Yet in one sense, it had: More people became involved in the political process, thereby helping shape policy.

In principle, Jackson was in fact a Jeffersonian, believing that democracy flourished best in a nation of independent "yeoman farmers" living on their own land; his expansionist land policies and forced removal of Indian populations were designed to advance this purpose. Skeptical of the utility of a strong central government, he wished to dismantle the Second Bank of the United States, place the money in the state banks, and establish an independent treasury. On these questions, Jackson was distinctly at odds with Adams's "Liberty with Power" platform. Yet, on other issues of surpassing importance, Jackson and Adams were surprisingly in concordance.

They had not spoken since Adams's March 4, 1825, inauguration when, after Chief Justice John Marshall had sworn in Adams as president, Jackson had taken Adams's hand. The "corrupt bargain" uproar had dislocated their once-amicable relationship, and the surpassingly bitter 1828 election, followed by Jackson's sacking of Adams appointees, had sealed their animosity. Adams expected the very worst from the Jackson administration. It would abandon internal improvements, stop promoting domestic industries, "which from the close of the last war with Great Britain had been pursued," and relax federal control over the states while pressuring the Judiciary Department to do the administration's bidding. "The entire discharge of the national debt will dissolve one of the strongest ties which hold the Union together; and the doom of the National Bank at the expiration of its charter is already sealed." Yet Adams optimistically believed a countermovement would coalesce to rescue the Constitution from ruin; if it did not, he intended to "rely upon that overruling Providence which has so often served us before."

While Jackson might ignore Adams in retirement, he could not overlook Adams's election to Congress. The president and his allies suspected that Adams's express purpose in returning to elective office was to obstruct the administration program. Partly to blunt such a potential threat, the president's friends tried to reconcile the men. At a congressman's funeral attended by the president and ex-president, Martin Van Buren persuaded Jackson to offer his hand to Adams, but "the old gentleman, as he [Jackson] called him [both men were born in 1767]," wrote Van Buren, "had assumed so *pugnacious* a look that he was afraid he would strike him if he came nearer!"

In March 1832, Kentucky Congressman Richard M. Johnson, acting on Jackson's behalf, tried to persuade Adams to meet with the president. Jackson, and not he, had terminated their relationship, replied Adams. He said Jackson likely believed that Adams had sanctioned the "abusive charges against Mrs. Jackson" during the 1828 election—that she had cohabitated with Jackson while still married to her first husband—when he in fact had not. Assuring Adams that he had always held him blameless, Johnson said Jackson now harbored "dispositions entirely friendly" to Adams. When Adams responded that he was "disposed to receive any friendly advance from General Jackson with kindness," Johnson proposed that Adams dine with Jackson. But Adams rejected the idea of even a small dinner party, because "it would pass for mere civility to a member of Congress." When Johnson then inquired what sort of invitation Adams *would* accept, he coyly replied that he was willing to "receive in a spirit of conciliation any advance which in that spirit General Jackson might make."

Through Johnson, the president replied that he was "anxious to have a social and friendly intercourse restored." But Adams never responded. Certain that his "Old Federalist" enemies would pounce on him if he became friendly with Jackson, he thought it prudent to keep his distance. "They have drawn the sword and brandished it over my head," Adams wrote hyperbolically of the Old Federalists who, while no longer Federalists, were assuredly old—too old to be brandishing swords. "If I set my foot in the President's house, they will throw away the scabbard."

Avowals of goodwill notwithstanding, Adams remained Jackson's implacable enemy. Of Jackson's administration, he prophesied, "Its day will be the day of small things. There will be neither lofty meditations, nor comprehensive foresight, nor magnanimous purpose, nor the look for the benisons of future ages, presiding at the helm of State." While Adams might sometimes take Jackson's side on important issues, these occasions never thawed their wintry relationship.

In June 1833, Adams boycotted Harvard's ceremonial awarding of an honorary doctor of laws degree to Jackson, grumbling to his cousin, Harvard President Josiah Quincy, that he could "hold no intercourse of a friendly character with him." Moreover, as a Harvard alumnus, Adams refused to "witness her disgrace in conferring her highest literary honors upon a barbarian who could not write a sentence of grammar and hardly could spell his own name." (Adams in 1828 had seen an unedited, unsigned note believed to have been written by Jackson: "it was couched in language worthy of ancient Pistol, and set all grammar and spelling alike at defiance.") While Quincy granted that Jackson was "utterly unworthy of literary honors," he said that Harvard must extend the same courtesy to Jackson that it had to James Monroe. Adams bitterly observed, "Time-serving and sycophancy are qualities of all learned and scientific institutions."

When it was reported that Jackson had become ill while in Boston to receive his honor—so ill that some people feared he might not reach Washington alive—Adams unfeelingly wrote, "I believe much of his debility is politic. . . . He is one of our tribe of great men who turn disease to commodity, like John Randolph, who for forty years was always dying. Jackson . . . is so ravenous of notoriety that he craves the sympathy for sickness as a portion of his glory." But Jackson's illness was real enough; he had dysentery and was coughing up blood from an old dueling wound. Later, he collapsed in Concord and had to hurry back to Washington.

On his sickbed, gaunt and white-haired, Jackson is said to have declared, "The Bank is trying to kill me, *but I will kill it!*" Jackson made good on his vow. His passionate opposition to the Second Bank of the United States was popular in the South and West, where the bank had become a lightning rod for resentment against corporations and the moneyed class, and with local and state banking officials, who bridled against the bank's tight-fisted control over bank notes. While Southerners questioned the bank's constitutionality, Martin Van Buren and the Albany Regency hoped its death would cause Philadelphia to lose its cachet as the nation's financial center. In 1832, the president of the Second Bank, Nicholas Biddle, sought to recharter the bank four years early, counting on election-year politics to aid its passage, and reasoning that if the recharter attempt failed, he would have time to try again.

Adams supported the Second Bank—he in fact had recently sold fifteen shares of bank stock that he owned—and he was a close friend of Biddle, a cultivated, urbane man who shared Adams's literary tastes and often played host to the Adamses when they were in Philadelphia. After one such visit, Adams wrote to Biddle, "There is except for my own son, not a man living with whom I could open in such unlimited confidence all my impressions of public duty and of unpromising anticipation as I then did with you." So when Adams was named to a seven-member special House Bank Investigating Committee that would travel to Philadelphia on a fact-finding trip, it was unsurprising that he defended Biddle.

Adams's minority report, cowritten with South Carolina Congressman George McDuffie, assailed the majority report—which was hypercritical of the bank's operations—for its bias. The Adams-McDuffie report also alleged that the committee had violated the rights of bank officers by snooping in their private accounts, which it had as much authority to examine, Adams wrote with indignation, as it did to enter "the dwelling-house, the fireside, or the bed chamber of any one of them."

Despite the majority report, Congress voted to recharter the bank, and Jackson vetoed the bill, claiming that renewing the charter would increase stock prices by more than 20 percent, enriching wealthy foreign and U.S. investors at the public's expense. "If we must have a bank with private stockholders . . . it should be *purely American.*" Even though the Supreme Court had upheld the national bank's constitutionality, Jackson expressed the startling opinion that each branch of government "must each for itself be guided by its own opinion of the Constitution," and thus, "the President is independent" of the opinions of both Congress and the judiciary. A veto override attempt failed. After his re-election in 1832, Jackson withdrew the government's deposits from the Second Bank and placed them in state banks—for which the Senate censured him, and laid the foundation for the Whig Party's formation in 1834. But the Bank of the United States was dead.

The controversy over the national bank was only one of many issues that found Adams and the Jackson administration on opposing sides. Adams condemned the administration's passive acquiescence to Georgia's illegal assumption of jurisdiction over the Cherokee Indians. He favored higher tariffs than the administration supported. He opposed its plans to sell public lands cheaply to benefit settlers, advocating instead a "true value" land price that would generate revenue for internal improvements—another Adams "Liberty with Power" tenet that was out of favor in Jacksonian Washington. In fact, Jackson vetoed Congress's proposed extension of the National Road through Kentucky. As for Texas, which Jackson had tried to buy from Mexico, Adams granted that its acquisition was still possible but noted that Mexico's abolition of slavery several years earlier made its annexation problematic.

On the centennial of George Washington's birth, Adams, feeling discouraged over the Washington family's refusal to allow his remains to be reinterred in the U.S. Capitol, pessimistically concluded that the Union would not last twenty more years, possibly not even five.

So absorbed was Adams in his new duties as a congressman that, except for scattered fragments, he neglected his diary between March and December 1832, when he then resumed it without explanation. When Congress was in session, his diary sometimes resembled the *Congressional Globe*, the forerunner of the *Congressional Record*, in its devotion to keeping a factual record of the House's actions. But his pungent comments about the debates and his inventive descriptions of the leading characters saved it from dryness. Congressman Jesse Bynum of North Carolina was "a small thin man, with a perpetual agony in his face, a dark brow, a livid complexion, a haggard look, a ghastly smile." Joseph Underwood of Kentucky was "troubled with the conceit that he is the wisest of mankind," and Robert Barnwell Rhett of South Carolina sometimes spoke so rapidly and inarticulately that, with his head thrown back, he resembled "a howling dog." He could hear little of Louisiana Congressman Eleazor Ripley's speech, but "enough to understand that its mainspring was sycophancy." Charles Atherton of New Hampshire was "a cross-grained numbskull" who "emitted half an hour of rotten breath," while Senator Daniel Webster of Massachusetts possessed "a gigantic intellect, envious temper, ravenous ambition and rotten heart."

Adams never intended that his diary be published, containing as it did "trash inexpressible, which I pray to God may never be exposed." Yet he continued to fill his diary pages, while grumbling, "This has been an idle waste of time, and a multiplication of books to no end and without end." Charles Francis, Adams believed, might one day mine it for material for a biography before passing it on to his children and grandchildren as a family heirloom.

In August 1832, at the end of the 22nd Congress's first session, Adams observed that if he were sensible at all, the Congress's short session beginning in December and ending the following March should mark the "euthanasia" of his political career. Yet, "one short campaign more seems however to be in prospect before me, and then, if so long I live, I shall have attained the age [65] at which all our principal men have withdrawn from the stage," he wrote George Sullivan, a former Harvard classmate. Louisa Adams saw through her husband's show of preparing for retirement. "Your father," she wrote to her son John, "is in high spirits dabbling as usual in public affairs while *fancying he has nothing* to do with them. His mind must be occupied with something, and why not this?" In November, Adams learned from the Boston newspapers that he had received three-fourths of the votes cast in the 12th Congressional District race.

The 22nd Congress adjourned at 5 A.M. on March 3, 1833, with Adams persevering to the bitter end. He rode part of the way home with Edward Everett and walked the remaining distance in the freezing cold. As the new day began to dawn, the exhausted Adams crawled into bed and offered up a prayer of thanks "in bringing the affairs of the country to a condition more favorable to peace and union than it has been of late." As for himself, "My career is yet to be closed. It is in its last and lingering stage."

Indeed, in these early years of Adams's remarkably long career as a congressman, it appeared that he might best be remembered for his stubborn promotion of internal improvements and the expertise that he lent to debates of foreign affairs and the tariff. As did many congressmen, on the days each month set aside for such matters, Adams introduced citizen petitions to stop the spread of slavery to new territories and to abolish slavery in the District of Columbia. But the petitions had not so far become a flood, and after their perfunctory reading, they were referred to standing committees and never heard from again. They had not yet become nettlesome to the slaveholding South, nor were they the cause célèbre that they were destined to be for a handful of congressmen, including John Quincy Adams.

However, even before his astonishing transformation into an antislavery crusader, Adams was much more than a wise, tart-tongued sage. His devotion to principle over politics startled, infuriated, delighted, and was admired by colleagues of every political persuasion.

In 1835, Adams forfeited an opportunity to go to the Senate by patriotically standing with the Jackson administration as it pressured France to abide by its treaty with America settling U.S. claims that dated from the Napoleonic wars. The treaty of July 4, 1831, had bound France to pay American claims of $5 million, and the United States to pay $300,000 to settle French claims. France's first check bounced—the Legislative Chamber failed to appropriate the money—and then France pointblank refused to make the payment and recalled its minister from Washington. In his annual message in December 1834, Jackson urged Congress to authorize reprisals on French property. The Senate, however, adopted Henry Clay's report from the Committee on Foreign Affairs rejecting such action. When the House foreign relations committee delayed taking any action, Adams exhorted the House not to "dodge the question," which "might possibly eventuate in war."

That same week in Massachusetts, the legislature, controlled by the year-old Whig Party, was choosing a senator to serve with Daniel Webster when news arrived of Adams's support for Jackson's "war policy." Until then, Adams had been the favored candidate. But the Whigs now abandoned him, and instead selected John Davis.

The U.S. House passed a resolution asserting that the treaty "should be maintained, and its execution insisted on," without threatening reprisals. The House and Senate disagreed over whether to establish a special defense fund of $3 million for the president's use in the event of hostilities. The two houses blamed one another, and Adams made a brilliant, three-hour extemporaneous speech—inspiring the first known references to him as "Old Man Eloquent"—in which he called Webster to task for imprudently asserting that he would not vote for the appropriation if "the guns of the enemy were battering against the walls of the Capitol." Adams biographer Samuel Flagg Bemis concluded that Webster's declaration "ruined his chances for the Presidency."

Martin Van Buren later praised Adams's courage on the French spoliation issue: "No liberal mind can fail to admire the spirit and indomitable firmness with which he maintained opinions which he, doubtless, conscientiously believed to be right . . . [but] not always in harmony with those of the House."

Adams was aware that he now stood alone, without strong party ties, and he wondered how he would fare during the next congressional session. In a footnote to his father's *Memoirs*, Charles Francis Adams remarked, "This may be noted as the first of the great triumphs of Mr. Adams in the House. It is much to be regretted that he failed to record it more at large."

Nullification's origins dated to the infamous Alien and Sedition Acts of the late 1790s, whose purpose was to squelch the Republicans' criticism of John Adams's Federalist administration during the Quasi-War with France. In response, Thomas Jefferson and James Madison had secretly written, respectively, the Kentucky and Virginia Resolves, declaring that states could repudiate these and any laws that overstepped federal constitutional powers. Interest in the resolves waned with the end of the Quasi-War, Jefferson's election, and the acts' expiration in 1801.

The issue unexpectedly burst into life again in 1829, with the publication of *The South Carolina Exposition and Protest,* an early draft of which was written anonymously by Vice President John C. Calhoun. It concluded that protective tariffs were unconstitutional and could be rightfully "nullified" by any state, until such time that three-fourths of the states overrode the nullification with a constitutional amendment. With all hope gone of succeeding Jackson or even serving another term as vice president, Calhoun composed his landmark "The Relation which the States and General Government Bear to Each Other." It openly expounded upon the nullification doctrine and its corollary that "secession would apply" in some instances.

Imbibing the spirit of defiance in the Southern air, Georgia ignored a U.S. Supreme Court ruling in March 1832 that Georgia had wrongly convicted a missionary for not obtaining a required state license to live on Cherokee tribal land. Georgia had no authority over the Cherokees, the Supreme Court had concluded. Georgia refused to acknowledge the court's ruling, and the Jackson administration refused to enforce it, thus lending its tacit approval to Georgia's disobedience. To permit Georgia to extend its laws over the Cherokees, Adams fumed, was to cast aside the Constitution, laws, and treaties of the United States. "This example . . . will be imitated by other states, and with regard to other national interests—perhaps the tariff," he portentously observed.

Indeed, South Carolina punctiliously fulfilled Adams's prediction, triggering the "nullification" crisis. The flashpoint was a law bearing Adams's name, the so-called "Adams Tariff." In its Nullification Ordinance of November 1832, South Carolina nullified all previous tariffs, including the Adams law, a compromise drafted that same year by Adams, as chairman of the House Committee on Manufacture, with Treasury Secretary Louis McLane. It didn't matter to South Carolina that the Adams Tariff reduced duties to 1824 levels. South Carolina nullifiers and their Unionist adversaries began drilling their respective militia companies.

Adams had stated his implacable opposition to nullification in a Fourth of July address to his Quincy neighbors in 1831. States had no constitutional authority to annul laws passed by Congress, Adams asserted. Nullification was "neither more nor less than treason, skulking under the shelter of despotism." If he were dying, Adams said, "my expiring words to you and your children should be, 'independence and Union forever!'"

Thus, Adams was dismayed when Jackson, in his December 5, 1832, Message to Congress, did not reprimand South Carolina for nullifying all tariffs but appeared to let it pass without comment, while recommending reduced tariffs, Indian removals, and no internal improvements. These were all anathema to Adams, who bitterly observed of Jackson, "He has cast away all neutrality . . . and surrenders the whole Union to the nullifiers of the South and the land-robbers of the West." After having watched the president acquiesce in Georgia's defiance of the Supreme Court over the Cherokees, it was understandable that Adams assumed that Jackson would react similarly to South Carolina's refusal to enforce the tariff.

But anyone who had attended a Philadelphia Jefferson Day dinner in April 1830 would have known that Jackson's views on nullification were more in harmony with Adams's than with South Carolina's. Southern leaders had organized the dinner and invited Jackson, Calhoun, and Martin Van Buren, as well as Pennsylvania's congressional delegation, which the Southerners hoped to persuade to oppose protective tariffs. The Pennsylvanians, however, left the hall before the dinner began when they discerned the purpose of their invitation. The Southerners began toasting states' rights. When Jackson's turn came to offer a toast, he stood ramrod straight, raised his glass, and declared, "Our Union! It must be preserved!"

On December 10, five days after the Jackson Message to Congress that had convinced Adams that Jackson intended to truckle to the South Carolina nullifiers, the president issued a proclamation that warned citizens of his native state (he was born near Waxhaw, South Carolina) not to "lend themselves thereby to an act of disunion, under penalty of *treason*." He uncompromisingly asserted that nullification was unconstitutional, destructive, and incompatible with the very existence of the Union. The hero of New Orleans began to raise troops, intending to personally lead them into South Carolina if necessary.

South Carolina indignantly protested Jackson's threat of a military intervention. No president could order a state to repeal a law, it said. Each state has the right "to secede peaceably from the Union" if its liberties are jeopardized, or to repel "force by force, and relying upon the blessings of God, [to] maintain its liberty at all hazards." Submission would lay the foundations for despotism and monarchy. Jackson replied that no state could be permitted to flout federal law or to secede. "The Constitution and the laws are supreme and *the Union is indissoluble*." South Carolina's further recalcitrance would only assure action by his administration.

Adams wholeheartedly supported Jackson's stated intention of using troops, if necessary, to force South Carolina's compliance with the tariff. The people of South Carolina, Adams believed, possessed a uniquely disputatious character among the states. Yet he didn't quite trust Jackson's motives. Adams introduced a House resolution calling on the White House to turn over copies of the president's proclamation and South Carolina's nullification ordinance. The House refused to consider the resolution.

A House bill proposing to nearly halve tariffs over two years was referred to the Ways and Means Committee rather than the Committee on Manufacture chaired by Adams, who would surely have tried to kill it. As the 1832 Adams Tariff had already reduced federal revenues by millions, "it was not desirable to reduce it five or six millions more," he wrote. When the bill reached the House floor, Augustus Smith Clayton of Georgia argued that Southern cotton and rice producers, who would benefit from the lower tariffs, were as entitled to make a profit as Northern manufacturers. "Our slaves are our machinery, and we have as good a right to profit by them as do the Northern men to profit by the machinery they employ."

This was too much for Adams who, addressing the House in one of his first heartfelt extemporaneous speeches, accused Congress of submitting to South Carolina's bullying and enumerated for his colleagues some of the special protections already enjoyed by the South. The South had gained twenty additional U.S. House seats through the constitutional provision that allowed each slave to count as three-fifths of a white person in the census, he said. Another protection was the law requiring the North to hand over fugitive slaves. And, he said, federal troops protected the South and Southwest against domestic threats; soldiers and sailors had prevented Nat Turner's slave uprising in 1831 from spreading beyond Virginia. "My constituents possess as much right to say to the people of the South, 'We will not submit to the protection of your interests,' as the people of the South have the right to address such language to them." Retorted William Drayton of South Carolina, "The member from Massachusetts has thrown a firebrand into the Hall." Replied Adams, "The Nullification Ordinance is the firebrand."

Unhappy over the proposed tariff reductions, Adams penned a "minority report"—supported by just one fellow member of the Committee on Manufacture and opposed by the other five members—complaining that such measures would threaten manufacturing and lead to a nationwide depression.

Congress approved the tariff reduction bill and a companion "Force Bill," which authorized the use of force to collect import duties. South Carolina convened a constitutional convention, nullified the Force Bill, but then quietly repealed its offending 1832 Nullification Ordinance. The crisis had ended. Alexis de Tocqueville concisely summed up Congress's capitulation to South Carolina on the tariff: "At the same time as it altered the tariff law, it passed another law investing the President with extraordinary power to use force to overcome a resistance no longer to be feared."

Adams would later pronounce nullification "a theory of constitutional law worthy of its origin"—the South, where slaves were deemed "destitute not only of the sensibilities of our own race of men, but of the sensations of all animated nature." Slavery, he said, "flies to nullification for defence against the energies of freedom, and the inalienable rights of man."

Freemasonry was at its apotheosis in the United States in 1826. More than 200,000 men belonged to the secret fraternal organization, constituting a greater proportion of the populace than before or since; Masons held many public offices in Washington, New York, and Boston. But Freemasonry's image was dealt a terrific blow when dozens of prominent western New York State Masons evidently kidnapped a disgruntled Mason poised to publish a book revealing the order's secrets. Stonemason William Morgan's disappearance and presumed murder, and the blatant obstruction of subsequent investigations by Mason public officials provoked a backlash. Although there were indictments, Freemason-dominated juries convicted just ten of the fifty-nine men indicted, and sympathetic judges handed down light sentences. The Freemasons neither expelled the defendants nor condemned their actions, but they purged their ranks of anyone who criticized them. Public wrath in western New York and New England gave rise to a powerful anti-Masonic political movement.

Adams did not engage in the controversy at first. But as animosity toward Freemasonry coalesced into the Anti-Masonic Party, Adams finally conceded in May 1831 that he could no longer ignore the call of duty. Disliking, as Adams did, the secret Mason blood oaths that sometimes led to lawlessness, it was a small step for him to telegraph his support for the new political party by attending a convention at Boston's Faneuil Hall.

Adams cannily recognized that the Freemasonry controversy might also open a door to the White House for him. Was Adams really interested? The 1832 frontrunners, Henry Clay and Jackson, were both unrepentant Masons and therefore potentially vulnerable to a challenge by the Anti-Masonic Party, which as yet had no candidate of its own. Adams had told William Seward, "I had not the slightest desire for a nomination, nor for the office of President of the United States." But at the same time, he suggested that he would accept the nomination if it were offered. Delegates to the national Anti-Masonic convention in Baltimore, remembering Adams's defeat just four years earlier, instead nominated William Wirt of Maryland, who had served as attorney general under James Monroe and Adams. Jackson decisively defeated Wirt and Clay.

During the next two years, Adams threw himself into the anti-Masonic movement, which had strong support in his semirural congressional district, where secret oaths were viewed with suspicion. He wrote letters denouncing Morgan's murder and called on every Masonic lodge in the United States either to dissolve itself or to renounce forever "all oaths, all penalties, all secrets, and all fantastic titles, exhibitions and ceremonies hitherto used in the Institution." He objected to the Masons' use of the Holy Scriptures to justify their existence and deplored a Knight Templar installation rite in which initiates drank wine from a human skull.

Nominated by the Anti-Masonic Party for governor of Massachusetts in 1833, Adams accepted the "unwelcome" draft, believing that he might unite Anti-Masons with National Republicans and defeat the Democrats. He did not. When no candidate won a majority and the election was to be decided in the state House of Representatives, Adams, who was a distant second in the popular vote, withdrew and threw his support to the National Republican candidate, John Davis, who was then elected.

The Anti-Masonic Party's energy was spent by the mid-1830s, but it had caused a sharp drop in the number of Freemasons and lodges—in New York State, a decline from 480 lodges to 82—and the passage of laws in Vermont and Rhode Island against "extra-judicial oaths." From the ruins of the Anti-Masons and National Republicans, and the residual ill will from the national bank's demise,

William Seward and political mastermind Thurlow Weed forged the new Whig Party.

On March 12, 1832, Adams's last surviving sibling, fifty-nine-year-old Thomas Boylston Adams, died of the effects of prolonged alcohol abuse. Unable to leave Washington because Congress was in session, Adams entrusted the funeral arrangements in Quincy to Charles Francis, who efficiently managed the funeral and Thomas's burial in the family vault, while unsympathetically describing his uncle as "a man who paid a bitter penance for his follies." Adams and Louisa, scarred by their son George's suicide three years earlier, now worried about the effects of John II's growing alcohol dependence on his already deteriorating health. Even thinking about it, Adams privately admitted, was "more than I can endure, and reduces me to the weakness of a child." On his sixty-fifth birthday, he confessed to beginning the year "in great distress of mind," with his only antidote being "*occupation*. To keep the mind as constantly as possible employed. All before me is dreary."

The fifty-fourth anniversary of Adams's return to Massachusetts on August 2, 1779, from his first trip abroad to Paris, occasioned a wave of nostalgia and harsh self-examination: "Through how many scenes of good and of evil fortune have I since passed! . . . how many of overruling passion! And how few of virtuous self-denial and of disinterested exertion for the good of my fellow-creatures! I cannot say, like Rousseau of Geneva, that I am prepared to present myself before the throne of Omnipotence with my confessions in my hand, and affirm that no better man than myself ever lived."

Sometimes when Adams did try to serve others, such as when he attempted to teach his granddaughter Louisa, John's child, to read, he found his patience sorely tried. With Congress adjourned, he was able to spend up to two hours daily with the little girl. It was a frustrating exercise for Adams. "She seems to make no progress, though not deficient in intelligence," he reported as he began the project. "I find here, too, that the qualities perhaps most indispensable to a schoolmaster are patience and perseverance." Two months later, he confessed, "The lessons to my granddaughter try my philosophy." Louisa did finally learn to read.

While in Quincy in October 1834, Adams was informed that John II was dying in Washington. He set out immediately for his son's bedside. Reaching Washington on October 22, Adams found his thirty-one-year-old son alive but unconscious. Adams remained with him until two o'clock the next morning, when he lay down for a nap. Returning to his son's room two hours later, he saw that John "had just ceased to breathe." In his diary Adams recalled "the precious services that my darling child had rendered me"—especially his valiant attempts to make the family albatross, the Columbian Mills, turn a profit—and "the uncomplaining patience with which he has endured misfortune, sickness and disappointment, the hardships of his fate, and the meekness with which he has submitted to it. . . . Oh! Let me not murmur at the will of God." Charles Francis blamed his brother's death on "the scourge of intemperance," so manifest in the Adams family "that every member of it is constantly on trial." In a poem titled "John's Grave," Louisa, who chose to ascribe her son's health problems to the Columbian Mills' damp air, later wrote, "Softly tread! For herein lies/The Young, the beautiful, the wise. . . . "

Adams pledged to John's wife, Mary, "that I would be a father to her and her children." Mary and her two daughters moved in with Adams and Louisa, and began their new life there just as Adams was poised to launch the most momentous phase of his extraordinary post-presidential career.

Chapter Five

A Worthy Cause

---

*"If the Union must be dissolved, slavery is precisely
the question upon which it ought to break."*

—Congressman John Quincy Adams

---

*I*n 1835, America stood on the brink of its first great industrial era, which would upset the delicate equipoise between slave states and free established by the 1820 Missouri Compromise. Of the twenty-four states, half were slave, half were free. Thus, there was parity in the U.S. Senate, where two senators represented each state, regardless of population. But in the House, where population dictated representation, the South, whose population growth was nearly stalled while waves of immigrants poured into the North, maintained parity by leaning ever more on Article I, Section 2 of the Constitution, which deemed a slave to be worth three-fifths of a white citizen for census purposes. The fabric binding the whole complicated mechanism began to unravel.

Emancipation was in the air, but not in the United States. Since Haiti's black revolutionaries abolished slavery in 1804, five South American nations, newly liberated from Spain, had followed suit. Most significantly, England had abolished slavery in 1833 in its

West Indies colonies. America had prohibited importing slaves since 1808, but a clandestine trade thrived, despite ever-harsher penalties, alongside the legal domestic slave trade—the result of resurgent European demand for U.S. cotton and the advent of Eli Whitney's revolutionary invention, the cotton gin. English barrister Henry Tudor was repelled by the spectacle of a slave auction in New Orleans, where he observed buyers examining the slaves' joints and teeth to determine their soundness, "as if they had been so many horses in a fair." It was "an anomaly of the most startling character" in the self-proclaimed freest nation on earth.

In the aftermath of Nat Turner's bloody slave insurrection, there was a brief period of soul-searching in Virginia. Thomas Jefferson Randolph, a grandson of the third president, proposed a plan of gradual emancipation in the state legislature. After contentious debate, the Virginia assembly instead approved a bill to curb the movements of slaves and to push free blacks out of the state.

The American Colonization Society's project, sending willing American blacks to West Africa, initially had widespread support and was endorsed by presidents James Madison and James Monroe, and Chief Justice John Marshall. However, support waned in the 1830s, when the rising abolition movement denounced colonization as a scheme by Southerners to rid the nation of free blacks, thereby tightening their grip in slavery. "They [Society members] do not wish to admit [blacks] to an equality. They can tolerate them only as servants and slaves, but never as brethren and friends," wrote abolitionist leader William Lloyd Garrison in 1832. By 1860, the society would transport 12,000 American blacks to settlements near Monrovia in present-day Liberia and elsewhere in West Africa.

The American anti-slavery movement stirred to life in the 1830s as a consequence of the Second Great Awakening and the landmark emancipation debate in England's Parliament. The British abolitionists' invocation of a higher moral authority made a great impression in the United States, where newspapers closely followed the 1830 debate. Recognizing an opportunity to recruit Americans to the abolitionist cause, British antislavery leaders sent pamphlets and letters across the Atlantic, rekindling the religious benevolent societies' traditional hatred of slavery. Soon, the *New York Evangelist* was exhorting, "Let us imitate our British brethren and open the flood gates of light on this dark subject." In 1831, the American Anti-Slavery Society was established, and Garrison was launching his acrid attacks on slavery in the *Liberator* in Boston. Within a decade, membership in U.S. abolition societies soared to 200,000.

The year 1830 was also the "great revival year." The Second Great Awakening, which had begun in western New York's "Burned-Over District" in 1824 with a series of revivals led by Charles Finney, hit its stride in 1830. It was in many ways the birth of modern evangelism and its characteristic hellfire sermons and emotional conversion experiences. The Awakening burned like a prairie fire through the Northeast and the Midwest above the Ohio River. Finney preached that newly reborn Christians should "aim at being useful in the highest degree possible." Supporting the antislavery movement became one way of being useful, as was championing temperance and women's rights.

Finney's prize convert was Theodore Dwight Weld, evangelist, temperance speaker, and arguably the greatest of all abolitionists. Weld's name today elicits blank stares, which would have pleased him. He was credited with having won over to the emancipation cause the extremely influential Tappans of New York City—Arthur, founder of the New York *Journal of Commerce*, and his wealthy merchant brother Lewis—as well as Edwin Stanton, Joshua Giddings, James G. Birney, and Harriet and Henry Ward Beecher. A strict vegetarian who dressed in coarse, plain clothes—much like a penitent—Weld was an American original. He cultivated anonymity, while mocking his "morbid modesty" as evidence of excessive pride: "I am . . . proud as Lucifer that I can and do scorn applause and spurn flattery," he wrote to his wife, Angelina Grimké.

Weld accepted no title or salary, attended no conventions, published nothing under his own name—even though his searing pamphlet, *Slavery As It Is*, a catalogue of atrocity stories, was a national sensation and inspired Harriet Beecher Stowe to write the most famous abolitionist book of all, *Uncle Tom's Cabin*. Until his voice failed him after two weeks of nonstop revival speaking in 1836, Weld was easily the movement's most inspiring speaker, and thus he was targeted by the movement's enemies, who mobbed and pelted him with eggs and stones during and after his speeches.

The names Weld, Finney, Garrison, Giddings, Stanton, and Birney, and those of the Tappans, Beechers, and Grimkés dominated the antislavery movement during its 1830s heyday. It was an "age of great movements," wrote New England clergyman and writer William Ellery Channing, "of sympathy with . . . suffering, and of devotion to the progress of the whole human race." The abolitionist leaders and their followers made mass petitions and mass mailings their strategic hallmarks, just as *Slavery As It Is* became their signature literary work.

Angelina Grimké, her sister Sarah, and Weld found the material for *Slavery As It Is* in stacks of Northern and Southern newspapers. It is surprising that the book's gruesome collection of anecdotes came from Americans' everyday reading material. A Missouri woman gripped the throat of a young female runaway with red-hot tongs when the girl wouldn't answer her. "This had the desired effect. The poor girl faintly whispered, 'Oh, misse [*sic*], don't—I am almost gone,' and expired." A "Mr. Brubecker" tied large cats to a slave's naked body and whipped them "to make them tear his back." A wealthy Richmond tobacconist flogged a fifteen-year-old slave girl to death, pausing to permit his wife to sear the girl with a glowing iron; a jury acquitted them of murder. The murder of another Virginia slave was too horrific even for a Southern jury; it ordered the imprisonment of a slave owner who had tied a slave to a tree, flogged him, then piled brush around the tree, and burned him to death.

Angelina Grimké described her own experiences growing up on a plantation in South Carolina, where in Charleston slaves were sent to the workhouse to be whipped; neighbors "often heard the screams of the slaves under their torture." She knew Charlestonians who borrowed slaves for social events because their own slaves "had been so cruelly flogged in the workhouse, that they could not walk without limping at every step, and their putrefied flesh emitted such an intolerable smell that they were not fit to be in the presence of company."

The Grimké sisters "deserted the home of [our] fathers to escape the sound of the lash and the shrieks of tortured victims." "One who is a slaveholder at heart never recognizes a human being in a slave," wrote Angelina Grimké. The sisters moved to Philadelphia and left the Anglican Church, in which they had been raised, to become Quakers. They were called "Carolina's high-souled sisters"—with Angelina, tutored by Weld in public speaking, described as "an angel of life," aided by her humble, self-sacrificing sister Sarah, who in digging out the ghastly accounts for Weld's book derived "the same holy peace . . . which we found in the public advocacy of the cause."

On the streets of Washington, congressmen occasionally witnessed firsthand the abuses routinely inflicted on slaves. A congressman reported watching as a slave was knocked down by a "brick-bat" from his pursuing master and then was kicked by the master and his son as he lay bleeding on the ground. A crowd gathered, and someone exclaimed, "You will kill him!" to which the man responded, "He is mine, and I have a right to do what I please with him." The tormenters dragged the slave into a stable, so that they could continue the beating in private. But the slave's cries could be heard at the Capitol, a quarter-mile away. The paradox of slavery being condoned in a place ostensibly symbolizing human freedom did not escape observers such as the English writer Fanny Trollope, who scornfully observed of Washington: "You will see them with one hand hoisting the cap of liberty, and with the other flogging their slaves." Nor could it be said that the English barrister Henry Tudor, after touring the South, was unfair in writing, "As long as so foul a stain shall tarnish the brightness of American freedom," the United States must "forego its proud claims to superior advantages over the rest of mankind."

After organizing itself in the North, the abolition movement—the American Anti-Slavery Society in the forefront, with its affiliates in New England, New York, Pennsylvania, and Ohio—launched an unprecedented political action campaign, assisted by its two powerful newspapers, Garrison's *Liberator* in Boston and the *Emancipator* in New York. Abolitionists began to swamp Congress with petitions, while simultaneously inundating the South with antislavery literature. The aggressive campaigns spawned backlashes. Southerners placed a $200,000 bounty on Arthur Tappan, whose wealth helped underwrite the abolitionists; in Charleston, South Carolina, abolitionist pamphlets were burned in the city square. Anti-abolitionists in the North mobbed lecturers, wrecked abolitionist presses, and broke up meetings.

Jackson, who owned one hundred slaves, denounced the abolitionist mass mailings in his seventh Annual Message to Congress in December 1835. He urged Congress to pass a censorship law permitting post offices to stop delivery of the literature. The mailing campaign, he said, was clearly calculated to provoke insurrection among slaves.

South Carolina Senator John Calhoun condemned the abolitionists' "blind and criminal zeal." States have the right, he said, to stop publications that could destroy the relationship between masters and slaves, and the federal government must honor such state prohibitions. The Senate defeated Calhoun's attempt to make it a crime for a postal official to send antislavery literature to states where it was outlawed. But with Postmaster General Amos Kendall's tacit approval, postal officials did block abolitionist mailings, without any legal authority. One postmaster announced he would no longer forward the pamphlets, "out of regard for Southern feeling." The covert federal policy unofficially sanctioned Southern censorship.

Stymied by the postmasters, abolitionists shifted their enormous energies to mass-producing petitions as efficiently as they had the mass-mailed material that had so infuriated Southerners. Typically, the petitions urged the abolition of slavery in the District of Columbia, the only slave principality over which Congress had jurisdiction, or they pronounced opposition to the admission of new slave states. To assist in the petition drive, Theodore Weld wrote *The Power of Congress over the District of Columbia*, which appeared in installments in William Cullen Bryant's New York *Evening Post* and in a pamphlet. It argued persuasively that because "slavery . . . is the creature of legislation," it was "an appropriate sphere of legislation." This, together with his pamphlet, *Emancipation in the West Indies*, armed petition circulators both with arguments for emancipation and with examples of how a transition from slave to free labor might occur.

Volunteers, often women, obtained the signatures for the petitions, which were then forwarded to congressmen, usually Northern Whigs, who could be relied upon to introduce them. For many of the women petition-circulators, the campaign served as a course in how to conduct a mass movement—lessons they later put to use in seeking women's rights. Indeed, future leaders Susan B. Anthony, Lucretia Mott, Lydia Maria Child, and Elizabeth Cady were all veteran abolitionists.

American citizens had submitted antislavery petitions since the First Congress, but what was now occurring was unprecedented. During Congress's 1834–1835 session, petitions with 34,000 names were submitted; during its next meeting, Congress received petitions containing more than 150,000 signatures. By 1838, the accumulated petitions would fill a room to the ceiling in the Capitol.

During the first thirty days of each congressional session, an hour a day was devoted to petitions; thereafter, petition submissions were limited to one hour every other Monday. On petition days, the roll of states was read, starting with Maine and proceeding southward. Congressmen usually read only the petition titles, and the petitions were then referred to an appropriate committee. By early 1836, there was no congressman more dependable than John Quincy Adams for introducing antislavery petitions.

Adams's lifelong abhorrence of slavery was shaped by his first shocking encounter with the institution—not in the South, but in Eastern Europe—when he was traveling to St. Petersburg in 1781 with Francis Dana. From Poland, fourteen-year-old Adams wrote to his father, "All the Farmers are in the most abject slavery; they are bought and sold like so many beasts, and are sometimes even chang'd for dogs or horses. Their masters have even the right of life and death over them, and if they kill one of them they are only obliged to pay a trifling fine."

But nearly forty years passed before his youthful revulsion ripened to mature conviction. Until the debate that resulted in the 1820 Missouri Compromise, Adams evidently accepted Southern slavery as an immutable fact. As secretary of state, he had been slow to sign onto international treaties suppressing the African slave trade; he had helped slaveholders extradite fugitive slaves from Canada; and he had presented Southerners' indemnification claims to Great Britain for slaves taken during the War of 1812.

Although the bitter debate over Missouri statehood did not involve Adams directly, it impelled him, watching with keen interest from the sidelines, to clarify his convictions about slavery and for the first time to recognize the threat that it posed to the Union. In his diary, he unequivocally declared that slavery was "the great and foul stain upon the North American Union" and that it should be abolished. From 1820 forward, Adams never once departed from his belief that slavery was a great evil that degraded both slaves and owners. For the rest of his life, his sole questions about slavery concerned whether emancipation was possible, whether it was "practicable," and if carried out, whether it would destroy the United States. How could it be accomplished with the least loss of life?

Adams was astonishingly prescient—in effect foreseeing the Civil War forty years in the future—in assaying the appalling cost to the United States that would be required to resolve the slavery question. "A dissolution, at least temporary, of the Union . . . would be certainly necessary." He foresaw a war between the "two severed portions of the Union." But the result of this awful conflict would be emancipation, "so glorious . . . that, as God shall judge me, I dare not say that it is not to be desired. . . . If the Union must be dissolved, slavery is precisely the question upon which it ought to break."

But in 1820, the abolition movement had not yet awakened, and the Missouri Compromise at least temporarily put the slavery issue to sleep by permitting Missouri's entry as a slave state while excluding slavery in the Louisiana Territory north of 36° 30'. While Adams described the first exhaustive debate of American slavery as "the title page to a great tragic volume," that volume was not ready to be written. Until the rise of the abolition movement in the 1830s, Adams and other public men who opposed slavery would have little occasion to express their views. The time had not yet come for the opponents of slavery to begin trying to tear down the master–slave hierarchy.

The Missouri Compromise debate did have the effect of causing leaders to begin to take sides. Adams was disappointed to learn that his then friend, War Secretary John Calhoun, whose intelligence he had admired, was devoted to preserving slavery. He concluded that if Calhoun was so deaf to persuasion, there was little hope of changing other Southerners' minds about slavery. But their discussion of slavery in March 1820 caused Adams to recognize the importance of the Constitution's "morally and politically vicious" Article I, Section 2, in sustaining slavery, by allowing the South to count its slaves for purposes of representation. It would have been better, Adams concluded, for Congress to forego compromising on Missouri, and instead to amend the Constitution.

Adams also began to perceive that in penning the Declaration of Independence's assertion that "all Men are created equal, that they are endowed by their Creator with certain unalienable Rights, that among these are Life, Liberty, and the Pursuit of Happiness," Thomas Jefferson had unknowingly constructed the precipice from which slavery could be destroyed. It would be a hard death, though. Viewed as a necessary evil at the founding of the republic, slavery, wrote Adams, had developed its own "execrable sophistry" of self-justification in the South that "would make of slavery the cornerstone to the temple of liberty."

In the spring of 1836, the national capital bore all the hallmarks of a slave center. The *National Intelligencer* published numerous notices of slaves that had run away and advertisements announcing the sale of hundreds of slaves. While three traders were selling 1,200 slaves at a site near the Potomac River, Franklin & Armfield of Alexandria was offering to buy 500 of "both sexes, from twelve to twenty-five years of age. Persons having likely servants to dispose of will find it to their interest to give us a call," as the buyer was offering to pay cash and higher prices than his competitors.

The inescapable reminders of slavery in the District of Columbia grated on some public officials. Even Congressman John Randolph, representing part of slaveholding Virginia, thought it grimly ironic that "in no part of the earth, not even excepting the rivers on the Coast of Africa, is there so great, so infamous a slave market, as in the metropolis, the seat of this nation, which prides itself on freedom."

The slave insurrection led by Nat Turner, who claimed to have been acting at the behest of the Holy Spirit, was a short-term stimulus for the black colonization movement in the 1830s. Adams, however, never believed that its purpose was humanitarian. In a letter to Benjamin D. Silliman of Brooklyn, Adams described the Colonization Society as "a vast undertaking originated entirely with the Slave-holders, and by which the benevolence and humanity of the Northern and Eastern states continues to be egregiously duped." To another acquaintance, Adams said colonization would not "diminish the number of slaves in the United States by a single individual . . . [and] was rather a public injury than a public benefit."

At the beginning of his congressional career, John Quincy Adams's own warring principles placed him in the strange position of introducing petitions demanding the abolition of slavery in Washington, while simultaneously believing that they accomplished nothing, except to foster "mutual hatred" between Northern and Southern congressmen. Weeks after taking his seat in the House for the first time, he discussed his views with a Mr. Lewis, who was a Quaker, suggesting a second reason for his refusal to advocate abolition in the District of Columbia. How would Lewis like it, asked Adams, if the District of Columbia petitioned the Pennsylvania legislature to compel all Pennsylvania citizens to bear arms in national defense? Wouldn't that be "meddling"? To another Quaker, Moses Brown of Providence, Rhode Island, Adams added a third reason: His constituents did not want him to advocate abolition. While he believed emancipation would one day occur, "I am not at Liberty to take a part in promoting it. The Remedy must arise in the seat of the evil." He also believed that the Constitution bound free states not only to "abstain from all measures, the tendency of which would be to provoke insurrection among the Slaves, but to give all our aid and exertions to suppress insurrection if it should break out." Thus, he could not in good conscience support the abolitionist agenda.

But Adams also bridled at the resolutions by Southern congressmen condemning the least interference with slavery and seeking to censor the abolitionist mass-mailings. He believed Congress had neither the constitutional authority to interfere with slavery nor the power to sustain it. And he was well aware that while the Missouri Compromise had temporarily laid the issue to rest, the problem was by no means solved. He would not be long content to passively watch the South adopt more aggressive measures to preserve its "peculiar institution."

As in 1808 when he supported the Embargo Act that his Federalist Party so despised, and also during much of his presidency, Adams again found himself detached from all political parties—a "man of the whole country." The emerging Whig Party was wary of his support of the Jackson administration's tough positions on nullification and French spoliations. Democrats, however, knew that he was not one of them. Adams's friends counseled him to conform to "the main object of party pursuits," because otherwise he was just "sallying forth in search of Giants, and coming in conflict with every Windmill."

While grateful for his friends' concern, Adams wrote, "I have made moral principle, and not party or selfish purpose the standard of my conduct throughout my political life, and there is too little of the stake left that I can lose for me now to turn round and become a mere partizan [sic]." Indeed, in this respect Adams was and would always be his father's son: John Adams had defended British soldiers involved in the "Boston Massacre," because he believed in every man's right to counsel, and he had shattered his own Federalist Party, thereby forfeiting his chance of winning re-election, when he made peace with France in 1800.

Like his father, John Quincy Adams, too, accepted his isolated, principled position. On the threshold of the year 1836, the pivotal year of Adams's congressional career, Adams wrote: "I stand in the House of Representatives, as I did in the last Congress—alone."

To all appearances, Adams had reached the summit of his modest post-presidential career, and a long decline lay ahead. A host of afflictions assailed him. His old nemesis depression sapped his energy, kept him awake nights, and troubled him with "a dejection of mind which almost makes life a burthen. . . . To lie down and die is a privilege denied." Besides having recently lost two sons and a brother, Adams noticed that Louisa was now ill more frequently. He battled eye inflammations and rheumatism in his writing hand—particularly galling because reading and writing were his main occupations. His physical problems "gave me a new admonition to prepare for the close of life." At times scarcely able to write at all, Adams improvised a wrist rest that permitted him to painfully scrawl his diary entries. A cold, cloudy day could cause him to despair. "My whole life has been a succession of disappointments. I can scarcely recollect a single instance of success to anything that I ever undertook," he wrote on one such gloomy day, while yet grudgingly acknowledging that he had also achieved "signal successes which I neither aimed at nor anticipated."

Just when Adams seemed to be ready to enter permanent retirement and quietly await death, his attitude began to undergo a profound change. A pivotal event was the birth of his first grandson, named John Quincy Adams, to Charles Francis and Abby Adams.

This revived Adams's hopes and fighting spirit. He proudly handed the family seal, used by John Adams when he signed the Treaty of Paris in 1783, to Charles Francis on his son's christening day. He resumed his diary critiques of the sermons delivered at the two Sunday services that he routinely attended; he took his two granddaughters to church and to the circus; he went fishing off the

Massachusetts coast; and he extended his morning walks beyond six miles.

Adams now sought a cause worthy of his recharged energies, and prayed that "a ray of light might flash upon my eyes" so that it would be revealed to him.

Until December 1835, Adams had been content to introduce antislavery petitions without overtly criticizing the institution of slavery. But the South's suppression of the abolitionist mass mailings had spurred the American Anti-Slavery Society and its allies to redirect their efforts into flooding Congress with antislavery petitions. The deluge of petitions outraged Southern congressmen, and they railed against the petitions and the abolitionists. Adams grew increasingly irritated with this new wave of Southern abuse, following as it did their aggrieved denunciations of the abolitionist mailings and their prickly defense of their prerogatives as slave owners.

After days of listening to the Southerners vent their indignation and outline a sinister new plan to crush the petition movement altogether, Adams wrote to Charles Francis, "The voice of Freedom has not yet been heard, and I am earnestly urged to speak in her name. She will be trampled under foot if I do not, and I shall be trampled under foot if I do. . . . What can I do?"

But Adams already knew the answer; he began to reply in kind to the Southerners. "I have taken up the glove in the House," he informed his son. A few months later, he was triumphantly reporting: "They hunt me like a Partridge upon the mountains. Well—be it so. I am aware that my severest trials are yet to come."

The "glove" taken up by Adams was to stop a Southern proposal that would ban the antislavery petitions from even being referred to committees, as they now were. If they "gagged" the petitions, Adams warned his Southern colleagues, the very debate that the South wished to avoid—the debate over slavery—would certainly occur on the floor of the House. It would be reported in the newspapers, sowing indignation and dread among voters. Would Southerners then enact a prohibition on all speech "in derogation of the sublime merits of slavery?" Adams accused them of suppressing not only the right of petition but freedom of speech, freedom of the press, and freedom of religion, "for, in the minds of many worthy, honest, and honorable men . . . this is a religious question."

Leonard Jarvis, a Maine Democrat, proposed that all petitions to abolish slavery in the District of Columbia be automatically tabled without debate. Adams promptly introduced a petition by 107 women urging abolition in Washington. He requested the petition's assignment to a committee, as it was "the true course to let error be tolerated, to grant freedom of speech, and freedom of the press, *and apply reason* to put it down."

As the petitions poured into the Capitol in record numbers in early 1836, angry Southerners were ready to take radical steps. In February 1836, a nine-member select committee chaired by Henry Laurens Pinckney of South Carolina was instructed to develop a new procedure for receiving the antislavery petitions. There was a grain of truth in the professed need for a new system; with so many petitions, and so much time consumed by their very reading, congressmen were not devoting enough time to other matters. As a majority of Pinckney's committeemen were Jacksonian Democrats, there was little doubt that the committee's recommendations would favor the slaveholding South.

Just as he believed that he must defend the constitutional right to petition, so did Adams conclude that Texas's annexation, which was avidly sought by Democrats, must be stopped. A Mexican province, Texas had revolted in 1835. After Sam Houston's army crushed General Antonio Lopez de Santa Anna's punitive expedition at San Jacinto in 1836, Texas declared its independence. Even before the revolution, American settlers had defied Mexico's express prohibition against slavery in its states and provinces and had brought their slaves to Texas with them. Adams opposed the annexation of Texas because it would sanction slavery where it had formerly been outlawed. Moreover, he was convinced that Mexico would fight to keep Texas, placing the United States in the odious position of going to war to defend the extension of slavery.

Amid catcalls from the House gallery, Adams condemned all attempts to annex Texas in a memorable speech on May 25, 1836. He bluntly accused proponents of plotting to steal Texas from Mexico in order to bring new slave states into the Union. "You are now rushing into war—into a war of conquest, commenced by aggression on your part, and for the re-establishment of slavery, where it has been abolished, throughout the Mexican Republic. . . . In that war, sir, the banners of *freedom* will be the banners of Mexico, and your banners, I blush to speak the word, will be the banners of slavery."

Adams snidely inquired why more land was needed. "Do not two millions of square miles cover surface enough for the insatiate rapacity of your land jobbers? . . . Have you not Indians enough to expel from the land of your fathers' sepulchers, and to exterminate?" Besides bringing war with Mexico, said Adams, annexing Texas could provoke intervention by Britain or France on Mexico's behalf, prompt an Indian uprising, and even ignite a civil war within the United States.

Almost clairvoyantly, Adams described the consequences of such a civil war, anticipating Abraham Lincoln's invocation of war powers in the Emancipation Proclamation in 1863. "From the instant that your slaveholding States become the theater of war, civil, servile, or foreign, from that instant the war powers of Congress extend to interfere with the institution of slavery in every way by which it can be interfered with. . . ."

The hour-long speech was the most consequential of his life until that time; the barbed, sarcastic manner of delivery would very soon become Adams's recognized trademark. Afterward, he noted with evident satisfaction that it was met by "echoes of thundering vituperation from the South and West, and with one universal shout of applause from the North and East."

Adams's speech also dissuaded Jackson from pressing for annexation; he left office in 1837 without proposing Texas's admission to the Union. Yet the possibility that Texas would become a slave state remained a storm cloud on the flat horizon. The lingering threat inspired abolitionists to devote hundreds of thousands of petitions resisting it. And down through the years, the issue would be a staging ground for Adams's assaults on slavery.

The very day of Adams's triumphant Texas speech, his embryonic campaign to uphold the right to petition was dealt a severe blow by Pinckney's select committee. It announced concordance on a three-part resolution declaring that Congress had no constitutional authority to interfere with slavery in states; that asserted that Congress "ought not" interfere with slavery in the District of Columbia; and, most compellingly, that recommended that all petitions, resolutions, and memorials regarding slavery or abolition should be tabled without being read, referred, or even printed. House Speaker and future President James K. Polk of Tennessee called Adams to order when he attempted to protest the pronouncement that Congress had no right to even broach the subject of slavery. When Polk repeatedly denied Adams access to the floor, Adams finally asked in exasperation, "Am I gagged?" He was not, but his motion was out of order, said Polk.

By large margins, all three parts of the resolution won approval. When Adams's name was called to vote on the third pronouncement, later known as the "Gag Resolution," Adams said, "I hold the resolution to be a direct violation of the Constitution of the United States, the rules of this House, and the rights of my constituents," and sat down amid thunderous cries of "Order!" In his diary, Adams described what then happened: "A scene of great disorder ensued." Unsure of how to denote Adams's defiant declaration in the official report of the voting, the clerk chose to make no record. (It was approved 117–68.) Adams later demanded that the official journal reflect his refusal to vote, but he was denied the privilege. "The freedom of debate has been stifled in this House to a degree far beyond anything that ever has happened since the existence of the Constitution," he declared amid his colleagues' loud protestations.

Although the Gag Rule's declared purpose was to dispense with the time-consuming ritual of reading and debating the mushrooming petitions that endlessly repeated the same demands, its actual aim, of course, was to suppress any debate of slavery. The House renewed the Gag Rule during each congressional session until January 1840, when it was promoted to a standing rule that prohibited even the reception of petitions.

During the English Parliament's great debate on ending slavery in its West Indies colonies, parliamentarians, too, had struggled against a tide of antislavery petitions that threatened to clog the machinery of government. But after testing and discarding various expedients, British leaders hit upon one that would last a century. Petitions were divided into two classes: private petitions, which sought a benefit for the petitioners themselves; and public petitions, essentially "propaganda" that urged government action on matters in which the petitioners had no personal stake. Private petitions were presented and received as before, but public petitions—advocating abolition and other causes—were sent to a select committee, which then periodically wrote a report cataloguing the petitions' subjects and their number and toting up the sum of signatures. The United States Congress, which regarded all petitions as private, might have learned from Britain's experience, but strangely, Britain's efficient model was never discussed.

The Gag Rule set two constitutional rights at odds: the First Amendment, stating, "Congress shall make no law . . . abridging . . . the right of the people . . . to petition the government," and Article I, Section 5, asserting, "Each House may determine the rules of its proceedings." Where did one right end and the other begin? Over the next eight years, the Gag Rule's adversaries would persistently challenge its constitutionality and fairness.

Never did John Quincy Adams doubt the First Amendment's primacy. "The right of petition . . . is essential to the very existence of government; it is the right of the people over the Government; it is their right, and they may not be deprived of it." The South's adoption of the desperate measure of gagging antislavery petitions convinced Adams that the final issue between slavery and liberty would soon be decided in America.

As he took up cudgels against the Gag Rule, Adams, whose profile had always been high in Congress, now began to attract the attention of the wider public. But his family was of a divided mind over its patriarch's sudden blossoming as a national celebrity, while on the threshold of his seventieth year. Charles Francis worried about his father's "whole system of life . . . that he sleeps by far too little, that he eats and drinks too irregularly, and that he had habituated his mind to a state of morbid activity which makes life in its common forms very tedious." But he believed it impossible to calm his father down. Louisa, too, wished he could "bring his mind to the calm of retirement," while knowing that it would finish him. She generously hoped that her husband would now realize his dream to "leave a fame to posterity and awaken the justice of this nation to record his name as one of the fairest midst the race of man." But she secretly feared that he was squandering his time and energy on people who did not understand or appreciate him or his talents.

Adams's supreme dedication to safeguarding the right to petition and stopping the spread of slavery was indeed the "ray of light" that he had prayed might "flash upon my eyes." It would prove to be arguably of greater importance than even his election as president, for as Bennett Champ Clark, an early-twentieth-century Adams biographer, observed of the brewing showdown: "No contest in American public life ever exceeded in ferocity the long fight for the right of petition which John Quincy Adams waged from 1836 to 1844."

No one was more aware than Adams himself of the outcome's importance, both to the nation and to his own legacy. "This is a cause upon which I am entering at the last stage of life," Adams wrote in June 1836, "and with the certainty that I cannot advance in it far; my career must close, leaving the cause at the threshold. To open the way for others is all I can do. The cause is good and great."

Chapter Six

Adams, Science, and the Smithsonian Institution

"The pleasure I take in witnessing these
magnificent phenomena of physical nature never tires;
it is part of my own nature, unintelligible to others . . . "

—John Quincy Adams

---

*I*n January 1836, President Andrew Jackson announced that James Smithson, an obscure English amateur scientist who had never been to America, had bequeathed a half-million dollars to the United States. After Smithson died in Genoa, Italy, in 1829, his estate had initially gone to a nephew, a Continental dandy named Henry Hungerford. Smithson's will stipulated that upon Hungerford's death, the remaining property would be bequeathed to the United States, for establishment of a "Smithsonian Institution" to further the "increase & diffusion of Knowledge among men." Hungerford had died in 1835 in a Paris hotel, and Smithson's remaining money had reverted to his estate's executors, who had notified President Jackson. A half-million dollars (the equivalent of $11 million today) was an enormous amount of money in 1836; at that time, Harvard's entire endowment came to just $600,000. Never again would a U.S. institution receive a bequest of remotely comparable value. Richard Rush, the distinguished former attorney general, ex-treasury secretary, and one-time minister to Great Britain, was sent to England to secure the bequest in chancery court. The mission would try Rush's patience over the next two years.

Adams was delighted that a stranger had chosen to bestow such a large sum on American science, a cause that, nearly alone, he had championed for twenty years. An amateur astronomer, horticulturalist, arboriculturist, and silviculturist, Adams for years had passionately argued for the establishment of a uniform system of weights and measures, a national observatory, and a national university.

Although Adams described the bequest as "a high and honorable sentiment of philanthropy," he had a dark presentiment that Congress, to which Jackson had quickly delegated all responsibility for Smithson's bequest—and which Adams with good reason distrusted—would ignore Smithson's wishes and squander the money on "hungry and worthless political jackals" or "electioneering bribery." Indeed, some congressmen were already calculating how they could turn Smithson's generosity to their political benefit, while others were suspicious of Smithson's true motives and questioned his sanity. "So little are the feelings of others in unison with mine on this occasion," sighed Adams.

Why James Smithson decided to leave his money to the United States remains a great mystery. Purportedly the illegitimate son of Sir Hugh Smithson Percy, the 1st Duke of Northumberland, he changed his name from Macie to Smithson in obedience to his dying mother's request. Educated at Oxford, he became a serious, accomplished amateur chemist whose specialty was mineralogy. His groundbreaking work with calamines led to his posthumously becoming the namesake for a base ingredient found in sunscreen and lotions for treating poison ivy—"smithsonite." His friends and acquaintances included James Hutton, the "father of geology"; the French chemist Antoine Lavoisier; and paleontology pioneer Georges Cuvier. A lifelong bachelor, Smithson was a familiar figure at the Paris gaming tables. For years, he traveled in Europe, but he never crossed the Atlantic. When he died at the age of sixty-four, he had 29 published papers, 200 unpublished manuscripts, and various scientific writings—all later destroyed in the Smithsonian Institution fire of 1865.

The reason for Smithson's mysterious bequest is likely a combination of heartfelt philanthropy and a craving for posthumous fame. Besides having once been, at twenty-two, the British Royal Society's youngest member, Smithson was a charter member of the Royal Institution, founded in 1800 as an "Institution for Diffusing the Knowledge" to the people—also Smithson's description of the anticipated purpose of his American bequest. And among his unpublished notes can be found the bitter wish of a man who never forgot that he was a nobleman's bastard son: "My name shall live in the memory of man when the titles of the Northumberlands and Percys are extinct and forgotten." Finally, he undoubtedly was aware that his gesture would make a larger impression in the United States, where such wealth was rare, than in Britain, where larger fortunes were more common.

Congressional leaders recognized they could find no one better than Adams to chair the special committee that would secure the bequest and fulfill Smithson's wishes. As an amateur scientist, former minister to Great Britain, ex-president, and experienced congressman, Adams possessed the wisdom and skills to see the project through to completion. He would need perseverance, too; before the Smithsonian Institution was at last commenced, ten years would pass—years when the bequest was imperiled by apathy, graft, and extinction.

The committee's first report of January 1836, which resulted in Rush being sent to Great Britain, brims with Adams's enthusiasm. "Of all the foundations of establishments for pious or charitable uses, which ever signalized the spirit of the age, or the comprehensive beneficence of the founder, none can be named more deserving of the approbation of mankind than this."

While Adams wholeheartedly embraced his role as watchdog, he also had his own ideas about how to spend the money. He dusted off his plan for building a national astronomical observatory, one of the "lighthouses of the skies" that he had promoted without success as president. He believed "that the national character of our country demanded of us the establishment of such an institution [an observatory] as a debt of honor to the cause of science and to the world of civilized man." Any remaining money, he said, should help advance scientific inquiry and knowledge. Adams emphatically pronounced how the money should *not* be spent: "No jobbing—no sinecures—no monkish stalls for lazy idlers. . . . I feel deep responsibility as testator to the world for this."

Brooks Adams in later years described his grandfather as "a scientist of the first force," to whom in fact science was his "tenderest part, and the part where he received the least sympathy and intelligent support from his family or friends." Science was a lonely passion that Adams shared with no one else in his immediate family, yet more than being just an absorbing intellectual pastime, it was paradoxically one of the pillars of his religious faith. Science was a God-given tool, Adams believed, for improving man's quality of life. His faith in science was also the cornerstone of his failed Liberty with Power program, characterized by Samuel Flagg Bemis as "scientific planning enacted into law"—the use of central government planning to transform transportation, domestic commerce, foreign trade, internal migration, and education. In all of this, Adams was decades premature, just as he was in proposing to convert America to a metric system, an ideal that, while yet unrealized, remains alive in the twenty-first century.

John Quincy Adams's *Report of the Secretary of State Upon Weights and Measures* is a ponderous and complex historical, scientific, and philosophical treatise, as well as an incomparably authoritative and thorough government report. It is one of Adams's outstanding literary achievements and a triumph of personal will. All but ignored when Adams submitted it in 1821, it is a forgotten artifact today. This is a pity, because even at a remove of nearly two centuries, the report's historical narrative of how European weights and measures evolved through the emergence of the French metric system remains relevant.

Adams's report on weights and measures fulfilled an unusual House resolution from December 1819. Invoking Congress's explicit constitutional authority to establish a uniform system, the resolution instructed the secretary of state to examine the uniform systems of other nations and to recommend how the United States could implement its own system.

Most men would have either ignored the House resolution, as it required an enormous amount of work for a lofty, but seemingly unattainable, end—or they might have expressed a willingness to implement it at a future, unspecified time. But Adams adopted the project as his very own. Although burdened with his duties at the State Department, Adams personally researched and wrote the treatise without assistance, even conducting experiments to find the right proportion between, for example, pennyweight and troy weight.

During the summer of 1820, Adams remained in Washington to write his report, rising at 3 A.M. to labor on it, while his family vacationed. Adams enjoyed the work, and during this rare summer, he indulged his latent idealism by imagining that a uniform system of weights and measures could even unite the peoples of the world.

"The metre will surround the globe in use . . . and one language of weights and measures will be spoken from the equator to the poles." Whoever managed to accomplish this, he wrote, perhaps secretly hoping it would be he, "would be among the greatest benefactors of the human race" for having opened a golden era of commerce and communication between nations. Universal weights and measures might even result in "that universal peace which was the object of a Savior's mission . . . the trembling hope of a Christian."

Adams's treatise analyzed the British and French systems of weights and measures and displayed staggering erudition in tracing Europe's civil, political, and religious institutions back in time to the Greeks and Hebrews, and thence to Egypt. He discoursed at length on each stage, drawing from his mental storehouse of biblical and historical knowledge. Beginning with the English statute of 1266, Adams described the patchwork of measurements and weights that became the British system, "the decays of which have been often repaired with materials adapted neither to the proportions nor to the principles of the original construction."

He clearly admired the new French metric system, scarcely twenty years old, in which decimals underpinned uniform lengths, weights, and volume. Whether successful or not, he wrote, it "will shed unfading glory upon the age in which it was conceived," but he conceded that it was a "new and complicated machine . . . the adoption of which to the use for which it was devised is yet problematical."

In the United States, each state had adopted its own system of weights and measures, although all were derivatives of the British system. At the very least, wrote Adams, Congress should fix a standard for the existing U.S. system and consult other nations about establishing a "permanent universality."

Adams rated the preservation of the U.S. system as the least preferable of the four options listed in the report's conclusions. He clearly liked best the French metric system, which he believed held the greatest potential of one day becoming a universal system. The second-best alternative was restoring and perfecting the old English system, while his third option was to combine the best features of the English and French systems to form a new system.

When Adams submitted the report that he had sacrificed sleep and a summer vacation to complete, Congress, which had requested it, laid it on the table without taking any action. The report was then filed away and forgotten in the dustbins of the Capitol.

Adams had begun dabbling in science when he returned to Boston from Berlin in 1801 and was reunited with his friends from the Crackbrain Club of his early lawyer days. While he was overseas, they had launched the Natural Philosophy Club, oriented to their new interest in science. Adams bought scientific books and attended their meetings where, among other things, they experimented with electric shocks, which Adams credited with relieving his muscle pains.

But his love of nature predated even his ancient habit of early rising and brisk morning walks; it suffused his diary from youth to old age. In a representative entry, Adams described an "excursion to see the rising sun, and to visit and study my seedling plants and listen to the matinal minstrelsy of the bobolink, the spring bird, and the robin, with the chirp of the sparrow, and the new whistle of the quail . . ." At the end of a day when he had watched the sun rise and set from a hill at Charles Francis's home, he confessed, "The pleasure I take in witnessing these magnificent phenomena of physical nature never tires; it is part of my own nature, unintelligible to others . . ."—confirming Brooks Adams's later observation about this aspect of his grandfather being neither understood nor appreciated.

The spark that blazed into Adams's abiding enthusiasm for horticulture and the cultivation of trees, silviculture, had its origin in an 1826 House resolution to establish a domestic silk industry by planting groves of mulberry trees to sustain silkworms. Adams hurried to consult his "books and the forests" and discovered a new passion. Soon, he was jotting in his diary, "I propose to commence a nursery the next autumn, and to plant acorns, hickory-nuts, and chestnuts." He wished that he had begun cultivating trees thirty years earlier—he would have had a mature forest to roam—but that had been impossible with his transient lifestyle. "Now I shall plant, if at all, more for the public than for myself."

So President John Quincy Adams planted trees in the White House garden. Aided by his valet Antoine Giusta and the gardener, a man named Owsley, he put in four rows of large Pennsylvania walnuts, nine "Quincy walnuts," eight hazelnuts, and three "Peters chestnuts," while also planting apple seeds. He took equal pleasure in the garden's other dwellers: its shrubs, hedges, vegetables, kitchen and medicinal herbs, flowers, and weeds. "I ask the name of every plant I see," he wrote, after prowling the garden following one of his 5 A.M. swims in the Potomac.

His new enthusiasm carried over to public policy: He established a tree plantation near Pensacola, Florida, to cultivate 100,000 live oaks for building Navy ships. When the Jackson administration later abandoned the plantation, Adams bitterly arraigned "the stolid ignorance and stupid malignity of [Navy Secretary] John Branch and of his filthy subaltern, Amos Kendall."

At the Big House in Quincy, Adams had no gardener to attend to his trees and shrubs, and so they were neglected during his long absences. After he and Charles Francis examined some bedraggled peach trees—a species more at home in the mild South than amid New England's harsh winters—in Adams's half-acre nursery, the younger Adams pronounced their appearance "really disheartening." Charles Francis unkindly added that while his father was a "fine theorist," he "has not the least practical and useful knowledge in the world." Henry Adams, John Quincy Adams's historian grandson, at least partly agreed, observing that his grandfather, who possessed "a restless mind" and took his hobbies seriously, "probably cared more for the processes than the results, so that his grandson was saddened by the sight and smell of peaches and pears, the best of their kind, which he brought up from the garden to rot on his shelves for seed."

But Adams also planted dozens of seedlings that thrived, and several years later, he placed walnut trees at the corners of a lot where Charles Francis was building a summer home. The plantings spoiled his son's landscaping plan, but Charles Francis, resigned by then to his father's compulsive pastimes, good-naturedly sighed, "Who can resist so innocent a hobby in a father?" As happened so often with Adams, the new hobby became an occasion for self-reproach, for having "betaken myself to a pursuit which already absorbs too much of my time, and would, if indulged, soon engross it all."

But even more than silviculture, Adams loved astronomy. His passion for it was conceived in St. Petersburg, where he adopted the habit of going up on the roof at night to look at the stars. His stargazing blossomed into "a pleasure of gratified curiosity, of ever-returning wonder, and of reverence for the Creator and mover of these unnumbered worlds." As a Harvard College regent, he proposed a Harvard observatory as early as 1823; sixteen years later, the Harvard College Observatory was established.

Adams's unprecedented, albeit ultimately futile, advocacy of a national observatory as a codicil of his Liberty with Power program was an unexampled instance of governmental support for science and would be unmatched for eighty years. While his "lighthouses of the skies" initiative made him the laughingstock of Jacksonian Democrats, others welcomed Adams's interest in astronomy. Lieutenant Matthew Maury, who in future years would become a world-renowned oceanographer as well as a spokesman for the Confederacy in England, invited Adams to visit the Naval Observatory in Foggy Bottom, where the Navy

maintained its chronometers, charts, and other navigational instruments, and from where, too, it issued them to ships going to
sea. At the observatory, the Navy also operated a fourteen-foot
telescope with a nine-inch-diameter refracting lens. Maury promised to bring Adams there on the next clear night to look at the
constellation Orion, and he was as good as his word, arriving at
Adams's home in a hack on an April night to take him to the observatory, where the men gazed "at the nebula Orionis, at the
cluster of spangles in Auriga, at the blazing light of Sirius, and at
the double stars, orange and blue, in Andromeda."

The observatory's steady evolution from a supplier of ships' navigational equipment into a de facto national observatory finally un-
dermined Adams's efforts to secure approval for his proposed
observatory with Smithson's money. Forty-eight years after Lieutenant Maury conducted Adams around the facility in 1845, the
Naval Observatory moved to its present site above Georgetown.

When the Cincinnati Astronomical Society began preparing the
site for what would become one of the first professional observatories in the United States, on four acres atop Mt. Ida 400 feet above
Cincinnati, the society's founder, Professor Ormsby McKnight
Mitchel of Cincinnati College, knew that he wanted Adams to lay
the cornerstone. But would Adams, seventy-six years old in 1843,
consent to travel from Boston to Cincinnati in November, when
cold rain and snow could make the monthlong journey a grueling
test of endurance? Mitchel personally extended the invitation
while Adams was vacationing at Niagara Falls during the summer
of 1843, and Adams accepted on the spot. The cornerstone laying,
he believed, was an opportunity "to turn this transient gust of enthusiasm for the science of astronomy at Cincinnati into a permanent and persevering national pursuit, which may extend the
bounds of human knowledge and make my country instrumental
in elevating the character and improving the condition of man

upon earth." He traveled by stagecoach to the Erie Canal, thence by boat to Buffalo, across Lake Erie to Cleveland, and down the Ohio Canal to Columbus.

It was a triumphal passage through the North. Crowds and dignitaries met Adams at each stopover, to shower "empty honors . . . upon me." He was unwell, with a sore throat and fever, but he received the stream of encomiums with pleasure, be they pronouncements or the kisses of pretty women. At one stop, when he was kissed on the cheek, "I returned the salute on the lip, and kissed every woman that followed, at which some made faces, but none refused."

Although ill on the eve of the cornerstone laying, which had been postponed a day because of heavy rains, Adams stayed up until 1 A.M. composing his speech, then rose at 4 A.M. to finish it. With rain continuing to fall, on November 10 he laid the cornerstone and delivered his two-hour address—it would be his last speech to the general public.

His address was a fusion of poetry, erudition, and his own awe of the heavens. "So peculiarly adapted to the nature of man is the study of the heavens, that of all animated nature, his bodily frame is constructed, as if the observation of the stars was the special purpose of his creation," said Adams, who regarded astronomy as the preeminent scientific discipline. With his usual thoroughness, he traced astronomy's development from prehistory through the discoveries of the Egyptians, Greeks, and Romans, to Copernicus, Kepler, Galileo, and Newton. America's arts, sciences, and culture were necessarily European-derived, he said, but in astronomy, especially with the recent strides in optics, the United States might lead. The appreciative Cincinnatians renamed the observatory hill Mt. Adams.

The journey's rigors were already wearing Adams down as he traveled east through Pennsylvania—"the stamina of my constitution are sinking under the hardships and exposures of traveling at this season and at my time of life"—and when he reached

Washington on November 24 he needed several days to recover. When his strength returned, he gloomily concluded that his laborious effort on science's behalf was probably wasted. "The people of this country do not sufficiently estimate the importance of patronizing and promoting science as a principle of political action. . . . Astronomy has been specially neglected and scornfully treated." But in years to come, scientists and science historians would remember Adams's crusade on astronomy's behalf.

In May 1838, the British chancery court cleared the Smithson bequest to be placed in the hands of the U.S. emissary, Richard Rush. Gold bullion totaling 109,960 British pounds—in U.S. dollars, $508,318.46—was placed in 105 sacks and carted to the ship *Mediator* with fourteen boxes of Smithson's personal effects. It had taken two years, but Rush was finally sailing home with his prize. Reaching Philadelphia on September 4, he deposited the money in the U.S. Mint, where it would not long remain.

As Adams had feared, the Jackson administration acted quickly to reap political benefits from the bequest for the Democratic Party. Administration allies slipped an amendment, permitting Treasury Secretary Levi Woodbury to invest the Smithson funds in state bonds, into a bill that continued funding for the U.S. Military Academy. The amendment sped through Congress without attracting notice.

So authorized, Woodbury, without consulting Congress, used Smithson's bequest to buy nearly $500,000 worth of State of Arkansas bonds and $8,000 in Illinois bonds. None of the bonds was redeemable until 1860, meaning only the interest earned on them would be available until then. Adams exasperatedly demanded that Woodbury issue periodic financial statements on the status of the funds and the accrued interest, and he began a campaign to repeal Woodbury's actions and restore the money to the U.S. Treasury.

While congressmen from the West and North did not necessarily agree on what the Smithsonian Institution's mission should be, they did believe that Smithson's wishes should be honored. Southern congressmen, however, did not see any point in accepting the bequest at all. Andrew Johnson, the future president from Tennessee, said Washington already was a cesspool of "extravagance, folly, aristocracy, and corruption" and did not need another venue for its vanity and waste. William C. Preston of South Carolina sneered that Smithson's gift was "a cheap way of conferring immortality" on an obscure English scientist and "pandering to the paltry vanity of an individual." John Calhoun said accepting Smithson's bequest would not only violate the Constitution, it would "involve a species of meanness which I cannot describe, a want of dignity wholly unworthy of this government." South Carolina Congressman Joel Poinsett, an amateur scientist whose horticultural legacy would be the poinsettia, was an exception to the Southern carping about the bequest. "A flourishing state of the arts at the seat of government would be felt in the remotest parts of our country," he said. But Poinsett also hoped the money would find its way to his newly founded National Institute for the Promotion of Science and the Useful Arts in Washington.

Adams's special House committee made no progress on the bequest in joint meetings with a seven-man Senate committee. Whenever Adams proposed an astronomical observatory, his Senate counterparts suggested a national university. Whenever the subject came up in Congress—and between 1838 and 1846, it did arise 401 times in the Senate and on 57 occasions in the House—Southerners urged rejection of the bequest in its entirety. While an observatory was the centerpiece of the Adams committee plan, the committee also proposed a museum of mineralogy, "conchology," and geology; a natural history "cabinet"; a botanical garden; and an "accumulating" library. Each of these proposals had its champions in Congress, as did proposals for giving the money to education or to Poinsett's National Institute.

But there was no sense of urgency—understandable with the money locked into bonds that were unredeemable for a decade or more. Moreover, the states were not even paying the interest on the bonds that they owed the federal government. Arkansas was the worst offender—owing $75,687 by the end of 1843.

Adams treasured his denomination as custodian of Smithson's bequest, pledging to zealously guard it from "the canker of almost all charitable foundations—jobbing for parasites, and sops for hungry incapacity." In two lectures in Massachusetts in November 1839, he said there were two imperatives upon which his House committee was in agreement: that appropriations be made only from the income, estimated at $30,000 a year, and that the funds should not be appropriated to any educational institution. Adams's surpassing desire was that the United States conscientiously carry out Smithson's wishes. He urged Congress to reflect on how its actions would be perceived by the rest of the world—and future generations. The bequest must not be "wasted upon the rapacity of favourite partisans, squandered upon frivolous and visionary mountebanks, or embezzled in political electioneering. . . . How under such a result would your children dare to show their faces among the learned and polished Nationals of Europe? . . . It must not, shall not be!" Even as he was delivering these carefully written lectures, Adams, dissatisfied as always with his efforts, privately despaired that they were tedious, dull, and unfit for presentation.

Virtually alone, Adams continued to campaign for the astronomical observatory. In an 1842 committee report, he recommended that $60,000 from the Smithson bequest be appropriated to equip and build the observatory in Washington and create an astronomical library. Interest on the state bonds, he wrote, could pay the salaries of an astronomer and four assistants.

Treasury Secretary John C. Spencer, a prime specimen of Jacksonian-era anti-intellectualism, was dismissive of Adams's observatory plan when he and Adams discussed it. During their meeting,

Adams irritably noted, Spencer resurrected from the dark days of Adams's presidency the Democrats' derisive term for Adams's dream, causing Adams to pronounce "the prejudice against my plan . . . insurmountable, because I had once called observatories light-houses *in* the skies. My words were lighthouses *of* the skies. But Mr. Spencer sees no difference between the two phrases."

During the ten years that Adams, as chairman of the Select Committee on the Smithsonian Fund, stood guard over the Smithson bequest, as he had predicted and feared, there was a profusion of proposals and schemes. They included plans for a national university, a national agricultural institution, a national library, a professorship of the German language, and for using the money for literary and scientific prizes. A perennial con-tender was Poinsett's National Institute; its supporters had once even included Adams, who had nearly joined forces with Poinsett when he agreed to support Adams's astronomical observatory and the goal of spending only accrued interest. But fearing that the Institute might absorb the Smithsonian Institute envisioned by Smithson, Adams eventually chose to distance himself from the proposal.

As an antidote to these potentially distracting plans, Adams's committee reports continually reminded Congress of the Smith-son bequest's stated purpose. "*The increase and diffusion of knowl-edge* among MEN," Adams wrote in a March 1840 report, "present neither the idea of knowledge already acquired to be *taught*, nor of childhood or youth to be instructed, but of new discovery, of *progress* in the march of the human mind—of *acces-sion* to the moral, intellectual, and physical powers of the human race—of dissemination through the inhabitable globe." All branches of human knowledge should be encompassed, but espe-cially astronomy, the means of discovering "a standard for the measurement of the dimensions and distances of the fixed stars from ourselves."

Adams also used his chairmanship as a bully pulpit for pressuring the Treasury Department to collect the overdue state interest payments on the Smithson bonds and to file status reports. In a report on June 7, 1844, Adams's committee asserted that it was "indispensably necessary" to honor Smithson's bequest and not permit it to be tied up for decades in state bonds.

The entreaties and pressure failed to retrieve the bequest from the states. Therefore, Adams and his colleagues adopted an entirely new tack—drafting a bill proposing that an amount equal to the projected principal and interest through 1846 of Smithson's bequest, $700,000, be withdrawn from the U.S. Treasury and invested in 6 percent interest bonds, redeemable when Congress saw fit. It was essentially an advance by the federal government, to be repaid by the states of Arkansas, Michigan, Illinois, and Ohio when the bonds that they held reached maturity and their principle and interest were deposited in the U.S. Treasury.

While there was no apparent immediate action on the bill, in the committee back rooms things were happening. Compromises produced a salable bill that, unfortunately for Adams, omitted the astronomical observatory; the steady growth of the Naval Observatory had obviated the need for Adams's beloved project.

In April 1846, the committee bill suddenly surfaced in the House. It stipulated only that Smithson's mandate for the "increase and diffusion of knowledge" would be honored, leaving the details to the future Smithsonian Institution's secretary and regents. The House passed the bill, 85–76. Three months later, the Senate, by 26–13, forwarded it to President James K. Polk, who signed it into law on August 10. At that time, the bequest, with interest, totaled $757,298.

A month after the bill-signing ceremony, President Polk roamed the Washington Mall with the new Smithsonian Institution regents and Washington's mayor, examining prospective building sites for what would become "America's Attic." With the assistance of Secretary of State James Buchanan, the regents chose sixteen acres between 9th and 12th streets on the south side of the Mall.

In December 1846, the Smithsonian's trustees sifted through nearly one hundred applications to choose the institution's first secretary, Joseph Henry, regarded as the greatest living U.S. scientist because of his pioneering work in electromagnetism. Henry initially balked at turning the Smithsonian into a repository for collections; he wanted to focus on the institution's roles of supporting research and operating a weather data collection program. But national collections temporarily housed at the Patent Office— mainly the artifacts collected during the Lieutenant James Wilkes Expedition to Antarctica in 1837–1841—soon found their way to the Smithsonian.

The cornerstone for the "Castle on the Mall" was laid in May 1847 (slowed by a major stroke suffered the previous fall, Adams did not attend). The medieval revival–style building, designed by James Renwick Jr. (who later drew the plans for St. Patrick's Cathedral in New York City), was completed in 1855 and housed an art gallery, library, chemistry laboratory, lecture halls, and museum galleries. Its opening was an American cultural milestone. Today, the Smithsonian Institution is an archipelago of nineteen museums, nine research centers, and the National Zoo.

In January 1904, inventor and Smithsonian regent Alexander Graham Bell and his wife traveled to Genoa, Italy, and removed Smithson's remains from their resting place on a promontory that was going to be dynamited into the sea. Smithson's bones were re-interred inside the castle's main entrance on March 6, 1905—in the incarnation of his beneficence, in the country that in life he never saw.

Of Adams's determined efforts to carry out James Smithson's wishes, and of his faithful promotion of science, historian Robert

V. Remini wrote, "No one since Benjamin Franklin accomplished as much in advancing the cause of science in America." Richard Hofstadter observed in *Anti-intellectualism in American Life*: "Adams was the last nineteenth-century occupant of the White House who had a knowledgeable sympathy with the aims and aspirations of science, or who believed that fostering the arts might properly be a function of the federal government." Adams would have no governmental counterpart as a promoter of science until Theodore Roosevelt became president in 1901.

Chapter Seven

Lightning Rod of Congress

"Freedom of speech is the only safety valve,
which under the high pressure of slavery, can preserve
your political boiler from a fearful and fatal explosion."

—John Quincy Adams on why the slavery question
should be debated in Congress

JANUARY 1837, WASHINGTON

*J*ohn Quincy Adams was again defying the Gag Rule, by presenting petitions from more than 400 Massachusetts women to abolish slavery in the District of Columbia. In the view of many Southern congressmen, this was becoming a too-common occurrence; they would have been all too happy to see Adams himself gagged. Indeed, Adams's initial volcanic outrage over the House's adoption of the Gag Rule in May 1836 had settled into a flinty determination to attack, flout, and circumvent the rule whenever an opportunity presented itself. Just such an opportunity had now arisen.

When Adams presented the first petition, signed by 150 women, someone proposed that the Gag Rule, which already required petitions on slavery to be tabled without being read, be made more restrictive, so that such petitions could not even be received. Adams shot back that freedom of speech and petition had been "violently assailed" during the past year, but this was "a proposition directly in the face of the Constitution itself." Adams then tried to shame his colleagues for attempting to suppress the women's petition. "Suppose that the own mother of any member of the House was one of the petitioners. [Would] he . . . reject and turn the petition out of doors, and say that he would not even hear it read?" When his motion to receive the petition was tabled, Adams vowed to call it up every day "so long as freedom of speech was allowed." He voiced the hope that the public would not tamely submit to the injustices inflicted by the Gag Rule.

He then launched into the reading of the second petition—over shouts of "Order! Order!" Signed by 228 women, it alluded to "the sinfulness of slavery." The Speaker ordered Adams to not read the petition but to briefly state its contents. Adams replied that reading the petition was the briefest statement that he could make of its contents—and he resumed reading the petition, amid loud protestations from other congressmen.

When Adams began reading a third petition to abolish slavery in Washington, Representative Joseph Underwood of Alabama interjected: "I desire to know what right the people of Massachusetts have to petition us to repeal or modify the local regulations and laws which do not operate upon them, or within their territory." Adams's response to all such objections was that the people's constitutional rights "cannot be abridged by any act of both Houses, with the approbation of the President of the United States."

A month after the battle over the women's petitions, Adams escalated his one-man insurgency—and was nearly censured. He first introduced a petition by nine free black women from Fredericksburg, Virginia. When Congressman John Patton of Virginia venomously characterized them as being of "notoriously infamous character and reputation," Adams wryly wondered how Patton came by that information.

The petition was tabled, and just as the Southerners' crackling indignation was subsiding, Adams ignited a conflagration with a petition from twenty-two people purporting to be slaves. He was drowned out by loud cries of "He ought to be expelled!"

Alabama Congressman Dixon Lewis demanded that Adams be punished, and a resolution was instantly drafted to censure Adams for the slave petition, which demonstrated "a flagrant contempt of the dignity of this House" and "an outrage on the rights and feelings" of many Americans. Moreover, the censure resolution declared that extending the privilege of petition to slaves would incite insurrection and rebellion.

But Adams had in fact baited a trap for the Southern slave owners. He had not attempted to present the slaves' petition, he said, but had only asked the Speaker whether he deemed it proper to present the petition. And the petition itself, presumed by Lewis and other Southerners to seek the abolition of slavery, was, in fact, the very reverse: It sought the *continuation* of slavery. "My crime has been for attempting to introduce the petition of slaves that slavery not be abolished," Adams said. "The gentleman from Alabama may perchance find that the object of the petition is precisely that which he desires to accomplish." He asked to be permitted to contest the censure motion—namely to be granted the floor in order to defend the right to petition, his intent from the beginning and the eventuality against which the Southerners had labored for months.

Congressmen hastily amended the censure resolution so that it condemned Adams for having "trifled with the House." Then, it was watered down further. Democrats had largely watched in bemusement as Southern members of Adams's own Whig Party—who were upset with Adams for disrupting their agenda with his petitions—pressed for his censure. But now the alarmed Democrats intervened and attempted to table the resolution. It was too late; Adams was given the floor.

Like a wolf cornered by a pack of dogs, Adams lashed out, drawing blood. "Since the existence of the Constitution of the

United States, there has never before been an example of an attempt in the House of the United States to punish one of its members for words spoken by him in the performance of his duty. . . . Your representative was . . . threatened with a prosecution, by a slaveholding grand jury, and a sentence in the penitentiary as an incendiary, for asking a question of the Speaker of the House." If he were to be indicted, Adams said, the Speaker ought to be, too, for aiding and abetting, because the Speaker had put the question to the House.

Chastising his tormentors for attempting to suppress the Fredericksburg petition on the basis of the signatories' character, he demanded,

> Where is your law which says that the mean, and the low, and the degraded, shall be deprived of the right of petition, if their moral character is not good? . . . Petition is supplication—it is entreaty—it is prayer! There is no absolute monarch on earth who is not compelled by the constitution of his country to receive the petitions of his people, whosoever they may be. . . . And what does your law say? Does it say that, before presenting a petition, you shall look into it, and see whether it comes from the virtuous, the great, and the mighty? No, sir, it says no such thing; the right of petition belongs to all.

He mocked a critic's assertion that he would be as willing to accept a petition from a dog or a horse as he would a slave's petition. "Sir, if a horse or a dog had the power of speech and of writing, and [sent Adams] a petition, I would present it to the House." When slaves were first enjoined from petitioning, then free blacks, and then those of questionable character, Adams said, "there is but one step more, and that is to inquire into the political faith of the petitioners." Slavery, he said, is "a slow poison to the morals of any community infected with it. Ours is infected with it to the vitals."

Virginia Congressman John Robertson tried to stop Adams's "ruinous and insulting" onslaught with a brief display of melodrama. "Is the gentleman to be protected in a continued assault upon the South, and in a course of things here, which must, if persevered in, result in the overthrow of this Government, and I fear in the destruction of the liberty of the American people?" When South Carolina Congressman Waddy Thompson Jr. observed that if Adams were to attempt to introduce slaves' petitions in South Carolina, he would face a grand jury, Adams retorted, "If that, sir, is the law of South Carolina, God Almighty receive my thanks that I am not a citizen of South Carolina!"—infuriating Southern congressmen. Adams could not resist further provoking them by saying he understood that in the South "there existed great resemblances between the progeny of the colored people and the white men who claim possession of them." In fact, he mischievously added, if a slave woman was described as "infamous," might not the slave's owner be infamous, too? The House dissolved into bedlam.

To stop Adams's one-man assault on slavery, the resolution censuring Adams was withdrawn altogether. In its place were substituted a resolution declaring that slaves did not have the right to petition, approved 162–18, and a motion rejecting Adams's slave petition, which passed 160–35. Adams voted against both. So preoccupied was he with his defense that he neglected his diary during this period. His editor and son, Charles Francis, observed that the diary "passes over in silence the memorable attempt to censure Mr. Adams. . . . This was the first of his great struggles in that cause [against slavery]."

The donnybrook hardened the Southerners' antagonism toward Adams, while fortifying Adams's resolve to fight for the right to petition and against the extension of slavery to new territories. He became adroit in introducing petitions that did not appear to fall under the Gag Rule's restrictions, but then managing to conclude their reading by calling for justice, or humanity. Once, when the suspicious House Speaker, future President James K. Polk, would not allow Adams to read a petition, Adams appealed to the House, protesting that the petition made no direct mention of slavery. Another congressman said that because he did not know what the petition said, he could not judge whether it fell under the Gag Rule. Thus, Polk was compelled to read the petition, which indeed violated the rule. Adams was described as "half rabid and half laughing" during Polk's reading of the petition.

After yet another contentious floor session, the reporter for the *Congressional Globe* wrote that Adams had "wantonly tortured the feelings of [the Southern members] by the minuteness with which he . . . dwelt upon the contents of offensive petitions and the names and character of those who signed them." The *United States Magazine and Democratic Review*, which profiled Adams in its first issue, described him as "today growling and sneering at the House . . . and anon . . . lashing the members into the wildest state of enthusiasm by his indignant and emphatic eloquence." His adversaries began calling him "the Massachusetts madman," but to his allies he was "Old Man Eloquent."

Like most Southern congressmen, South Carolina Senator John C. Calhoun detested the antislavery petitions and was satisfied with the Gag Rule. "The peculiar institution of the South," he said, "that on the maintenance of which the very existence of the slaveholding States depends, is pronounced to be sinful and odious, in the eyes of God and man; and this with a systematic design of rendering us hateful in the eyes of the world—with a view to a general crusade against us and our institutions." The subject of slavery, he believed, was beyond the jurisdiction of Congress, which had no right to alter or even discuss it.

Adams agreed that slavery was a matter of state jurisdiction so long as it did not encroach on constitutional liberties, yet he also believed that the subject of slavery should be openly debated. In his 1837 Fourth of July oration in Newburyport, Massachusetts, he castigated "the learned doctors of the nullification school" who wished to suppress all discussion of slavery and who believed "that color operates as a forfeiture of the rights of human nature: that a dark skin turns a man into a chattel; that crispy hair transforms a human being into a four-footed beast." Rather than imperil the Union, open debate of slavery would help perpetuate it, he said. "Freedom of speech is the only safety valve, which under the high pressure of slavery, can preserve your political boiler from a fearful and fatal explosion."

When the 25th Congress convened in December 1837, Adams attempted to introduce petitions to abolish slavery and the slave trade in Washington and to abolish slavery in the territories. They were all tabled. Then, acting on behalf of the Massachusetts delegation, he presented resolutions protesting any attempt to annex Texas. American settlers had brought their slaves to Texas during the 1820s and 1830s, contrary to Mexican law, and had then rebelled, founding the Republic of Texas. If the United States annexed Texas as a slave state, Adams warned, it would be "damned to everlasting fame by the reinstitution of that detested system of slavery, after it had once been abolished within its borders."

Admonished by Speaker Polk and interrupted by Southern congressmen, Adams asked that the subject not "forever be smothered by . . . all the other means and arguments by which the institution of slavery is wont to be sustained from this floor . . . the same means and arguments, in spirit which in another place have produced murder and arson. Yes, sir, this same spirit which led to the inhuman murder of Lovejoy at Alton. . . ." Polk ordered Adams to sit down after this reference to abolitionist Elijah Lovejoy's martyrdom months earlier in Illinois while defending his newspaper press. But Adams was then permitted to conclude his remarks, which he did with these words: "The annexation of Texas and the proposed war with Mexico are all one and the same thing."

Adams's pronouncements on the annexation of Texas provoked a nationwide outcry, prompting the *National Intelligencer* to inquire, "Will we go to war for this [Texas]?" The Van Buren administration, which had been sitting on the fence on the Texas question, backed away from annexation. It then consented to arbitration with Mexico to settle claims by U.S. citizens for their losses during the numerous revolutions that had occurred since Mexico had won its independence from Spain in 1821.

When it was Adams's turn to vote on a resolution reimposing the Gag Rule on slavery petitions, he spoke nearly the same words as he had in 1836: "I hold the resolution to be a violation of the Constitution, of the right of petition of my constituents, and of the people of the United States, and of my right to freedom of speech as a member of the House." Adams noted that his pronouncement came "amidst a perfect war-whoop of order."

American politics had changed; Adams had not. He found himself in a political landscape dominated by disciplined, powerful coalition parties run by professionals such as Martin Van Buren, Thurlow Weed, and Amos Kendall. They demanded loyalty, often at the price of personal principle, in exchange for patronage. The parties' paramount object was power, not ideology. Although Adams's presidential administration had witnessed the birth of this second party system, by the late 1830s it surpassed anything he had ever seen. Candidates now campaigned, rather than retreating to their homes while supporters campaigned for them, and they labored to project a winning personal image. All of this was anathema to Adams, whose insistence upon principle above party, and substance over style, increasingly set him apart from his colleagues. The *Democratic Review* portrayed him at work in the House: "Alone, unspoken to, unconsulted, never consulting with others, he sits apart, wrapped in his reveries; and with his finger resting on his nose."

Besides being arguably Congress's most learned member—and undoubtedly the oldest—Adams was also one of the most resilient and hard-working of representatives, often the first to take his seat and among the last to leave. When the House sometimes recessed for dinner and then resumed work that continued into the night, Adams found it agreeable to spend the hour, while his colleagues dined at their lodgings, in a House conference room, writing letters while consuming five or six small crackers and a glass of water. "I am calm and composed for the evening session, and far better prepared for taking part in any debate than after the most temperate dinner at home or abroad."

During a marathon congressional session finale, Adams stayed at his post for seventeen unbroken hours. Edward Everett, whose seat adjoined Adams's and who left the Capitol with him after midnight, remarked that he hoped Adams had managed to eat something. "He said he had not left his seat; but holding up a bit of hard bread in his fingers, gave me to understand in what way he had sustained nature." Another time, Adams fasted twenty-eight hours during a continuous session that spanned two days. "But I felt during the whole process neither hunger, thirst, nor drowsiness. Fasting and quietude are the only way for me to pass through these ordeals." Afterward, he slept for nine hours, arising refreshed—and convinced of the utility of fasting in these circumstances.

When the House dissolved into chaos during the commencement of the 26th Congress in December 1839, congressmen looked to the highly intelligent, dependably impartial, maddeningly articulate congressman from Massachusetts to extricate them from their predicament. New Jersey had sent ten men to occupy five disputed congressional seats. Five were Whigs certified by the Whig governor, and five were Democrats certified by the secretary of state. The House clerk, Hugh Garland, called only the name of a New Jersey representative whose claim to a sixth seat was undisputed; the matter of the five contested seats, declared Garland, would be settled after the roll call. The House erupted, and the roll call stalled. Garland refused to put any question to the House until it organized itself. But the House could not organize until Garland called the roll, which he was unable to complete because of the New Jersey imbroglio. "Now we are a mob!" shouted Virginia Congressman Henry Wise. For three days, congressmen made no progress toward seating a New Jersey delegation or completing the roll call—the necessary preamble to electing officers.

Adams did not once join in the confused debate but serenely jotted notes and wrote in his diary. On the evening of the third day, a delegation of congressmen appeared at his home and asked him to assume temporary leadership and lead the chamber out of its morass.

The next day, Adams rose from his seat. "I rise to interrupt the clerk," he said. Throughout the House, representatives cried, "Hear him! Hear him! Hear what he has to say! Hear John Quincy Adams!" In the silence that fell, Adams addressed his colleagues. "What a spectacle we here present! We degrade and disgrace our constituents and our country. We do not and cannot organize, and why? Because the clerk of this house . . . usurps the throne, and sets us, the representatives, the vice regents of the whole American people, at defiance." The representatives loudly applauded when he suggested that the clerk sit down and permit them to conduct their own affairs.

By acclamation, congressmen chose Adams to preside until officers could be elected, and then they conducted him to the empty Speaker's chair, a place that in the ensuing days he found to be decidedly unpleasant. When he declared that the New Jersey governor's congressmen should be seated, "much vituperation, and much equally unacceptable compliment, [were] lavished personally upon me," he later wrote. His proposal was rejected. Over the days that followed, congressmen alternately abused, defended, and blamed Adams as he issued a stream of decisions and counter-decisions

In this house, John Quincy Adams was born on July 11, 1767, in Braintree, Massachusetts, now part of Quincy. In the background is the birthplace of his father, John Adams. *(Library of Congress, Detroit Publishing Company Collection)*

In eschewing partisan politics, John Adams and his son, the second and sixth chief executives, were unique among the early presidents, as they were in serving just one term. *(Library of Congress)*

Abigail Adams warned her son John Quincy against vice, and encouraged him to seek challenges: "It is not in the still calm of life, or the repose of a pacific station, that great characters are formed." *(Library of Congress)*

John Quincy Adams was launched into public life after writing essays assailing Thomas Paine's *The Rights of Man* and defending President George Washington's dismissal of Citizen Genêt. *(Library of Congress, Detroit Publishing Company Collection)*

The English-born daughter of a U.S. diplomat, Louisa Catherine Johnson was well-read, a poetess, and a talented musician. She married John Quincy Adams in London in July 1797, and in a dozen pregnancies produced three sons who lived to adulthood. *(Library of Congress)*

President James Monroe chose John Quincy Adams to be his secretary of state in 1817, and the men were an effective foreign policy team. They remained close friends until Monroe's death. *(Library of Congress)*

Andrew Jackson, here shown in a daguerreotype made two months before his death in 1845, was the great military hero of his age, and John Quincy Adams's bête noire. Jackson expanded the powers of the president during his two terms in office. *(Library of Congress)*

Editor-publisher John Binns is caricatured carrying Henry Clay (left) and President John Quincy Adams and their "coffins" — an allusion to the "coffin handbills" of the 1828 presidential campaign that condemned Andrew Jackson for allegedly executing military deserters. (*Library of Congress*)

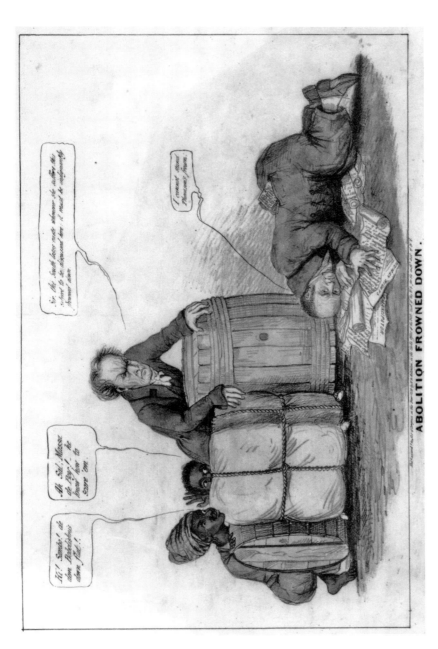

This 1839 political cartoon shows John Quincy Adams prostrated by a more restrictive Gag Rule in the act of introducing antislavery petitions. (*Library of Congress*)

John Quincy Adams, in a characteristic pose with a book in his hand, as he appeared about the time of his presidency. *(Library of Congress)*

Martin Van Buren, pictured here late in life, was the architect of Andrew Jackson's victory over John Quincy Adams in the 1828 presidential election, and Jackson's successor. *(Library of Congress)*

John Quincy Adams regarded President John Tyler as a mediocrity and ridiculed his controversial marriage, at the age of fifty-four, to a twenty-four-year-old New York socialite. *(Library of Congress, Brady-Handy Collection)*

This wood engraving shows a crowd in New Haven, Connecticut, watching a wrestling match between African captives from the slave ship *Amistad. (Library of Congress)*

Marble bust of John Quincy Adams as displayed in the office of the clerk of the U.S. House of Representatives in the U.S. Capitol. *(Library of Congress)*

Congressman John Quincy Adams died at age eighty in the U.S. Capitol in February 1848, after collapsing at his desk in the House of Representatives. *(Library of Congress)*

The "Big House," as it appears today in Quincy, Massachusetts, was the last home of John and Abigail Adams, and later, John Quincy Adams's summer home. *(Pat Wheelan)*

that inched the House toward a resolution. The seventy-two-year-old congressman presided from early morning until late at night, one day sustaining himself with just a cup of coffee and two slices of buttered toast.

Two weeks after the House first met, representatives were finally able to elect Robert M. T. Hunter of Virginia as their Speaker. Adams surrendered the Speaker's chair "with an ejaculation of gratitude to God for my deliverance," and walked home with "a lightened heart."

As Adams's anachronistic "man of the whole country" political philosophy had resolved the House's crisis, so did his equally archaic moral philosophy lead to a ban on dueling in Washington. Then, as now, violence was a common feature of American life. There were even fistfights in Congress: North Carolina Congressman Jesse Bynum once crossed the chamber to "grossly insult" Louisiana Representative Rice Garland, who punched Bynum, igniting a "fisticuff bout" until they were separated. Naturally, a select committee was appointed to investigate and issue a report. Ten days later, North Carolina Congressmen Kenneth Rayner and William Montgomery broke canes over one another's heads.

But in eighteenth- and nineteenth-century America, dueling, a byproduct of Europe's Romantic Age, was the preferred method of settling disputes among "gentlemen." Aaron Burr had killed Alexander Hamilton in a duel; Andrew Jackson had barely survived a duel in which he had slain a man; John Randolph and Henry Clay had dueled without injury.

Duels among congressmen, while not everyday occurrences, were common enough, but the duel with rifles at 100 yards between Congressmen William J. Graves of Kentucky and Jonathan Cilley of Maine—with Cilley killed during the *third* exchange of fire—proved to be the final straw. Adams, who thought dueling barbaric, sponsored a bill that prohibited dueling in the District of Columbia, and that fixed a ten-year prison sentence when a death occurred, and five years if there were no death. Adams said Southerners who lived by the *code duello* habitually insulted their Northern colleagues who deplored dueling "because it is supposed that the insult will not be resented, and that there will be no fight." He would no longer sit by idly, he said, while fellow Northerners were subjected to the law of the duelist, which obstructed free speech and debate in Congress. Despite Virginian Henry Wise's complaint that such a law would only encourage congressmen to call one another liars and cowards without consequences, the House passed Adams's bill. Samuel Prentiss of Vermont shepherded the Prentiss-Adams Act through the Senate, and it became law.

By July 1840, Adams's meager hopes for the Van Buren administration had curdled into disgust. "The most important and the worst measures of the Administration have been carried through the House by the most contemptible men in it." The politics and partisanship were bad enough, "but the worst symptom now is the change in the manners of the people." William Henry Harrison's election briefly gave him reason to hope for better things—Harrison treated Adams like an old friend—but his death only a month after his inauguration placed "a nullifier" and one of the worst of the Southern "slave breeders," John Tyler of Virginia, in the White House. Adams deplored Tyler's veto months later of a national bank bill, which he characterized as a surrender to "profligate political swindlers." Privately, Adams admitted that he did not understand how banking, currency, and exchange operated. "I am groping like a blind man to find my way, feeling for a table or chair, or bed post as I go . . . and what I want most of all, is counsel, from those who do know something about it."

With advancing age, a multitude of aggravating, chronic physical ailments bedeviled Adams. He suffered from lumbago and sciatica. His voice failed him at times, his eyes streamed tears, and he shrank an inch in stature to five feet six. His writing hand was palsied, now nearly always requiring him to use his hand rest when writing letters or diary entries. In May 1840, Adams tripped on new matting on the floor of the Capitol, fell, and dislocated his right shoulder. Although in pain, he returned to work the next day with his arm in a sling. To an inquiry by his doctor about whether he had dislocated the shoulder previously, Adams recalled that his mother had told him that when he was two or three, he had wandered into the road, and a nursery maid ran after him. "Seizing me by the right hand, [she] gave it an involuntary, sudden jerk, and dislocated the shoulder," with the result that his right hand was weaker than his left, and he was "always unable to write fast"—making his enormous production of letters and diaries all the more remarkable. "I have struggled to the utmost of my ability, considering it as the business and duty of my life to write, and receiving as admonition and chastisements of Providence these occasional disabilities."

Two months later, on his seventy-third birthday, he acknowledged that while he had reached an age at which he should "wean myself from the interests and affections of this world . . . the truth is, I adhere to the world, and to all its vanities, from an impulse altogether involuntary." He could not make himself "pack up and make ready for my voyage." He resolved to leave public life only when "the last of my political friends shall cast me off."

Adams's detached, unsmiling, yet oddly candid manner had always produced a mixture of puzzlement, respect, and occasional dislike among acquaintances, and exasperation among family members. The journalist Ann Royall's *Sketches of History, Life, and Manners in the United States* describes Adams receiving her "with that ease of manner, which bespeaks him what he really is, the profound scholar, and the consummate gentleman." He was serene, dignified, and of "middling stature, robust make, and every indication of a vigorous constitution." She remarked on his piercing black eyes. "He never smiled whilst I was in his company. It is a question with me whether he ever laughed in his life, and of all men I ever saw, he has the least of what is called pride, both in his manners and his dress."

New York Governor William H. Seward described his first meeting with Adams, who would become a close friend: "He was bald, his countenance was staid, sober, almost to gloom or sorrow, and hardly gave indication of his superiority over other men." The men talked for three hours. "He was all the time plain, honest, and free, in his discourse; but with hardly a ray of animation or feeling in the whole of it . . . hardly possessing traits of character to inspire a stranger with affection."

But where Royall and Seward perceived serenity and dignity, others saw cold civility. An Englishman who met Adams in St. Petersburg wrote that he had "a vinegar aspect, cotton in his leathern ears, and hatred to England in his heart. . . . Many were the times that I drew monosyllables and grim smiles from him and tried in vain to mitigate the venom."

Even Adams's own son, Charles Francis, sometimes despaired at his father's lack of bonhomie, as when he observed his father's reaction to an affectionate greeting by supporters. "My father has unfortunately such a cold manner of meeting this sort of feeling that I am surprised at the appearance of it any time among his supporters. . . . He is the only man, I ever saw, whose feelings I could not penetrate almost always."

So busy was Adams with public business and keeping abreast of the newspapers that he sometimes updated his diary while the House was in session. This proved to be a happy circumstance for future readers of Adams's diary, because he laced his entries with pungent observations about his colleagues as they went about their duties. A speech by George Keim of Pennsylvania, "a thick-set, squat-figured, half-Dutchman, unquestionably dull, but rich, affecting neatness of person, classical learning, and patronage of the fine arts," was an hour long, "gotten by heart, inexpressibly flat, a compound of champagne and dishwater."

Adams skewered Congressman Alexander Duncan as "a thorough-going hack demagogue," with "no perception of any moral distinction between truth and falsehood . . . coarse, vulgar, and impudent, with a vein of low humor exactly suited to the rabble of a populous city, and equally so to the taste of the majority of the present House of Representatives."

He described Robert Barnwell Rhett of South Carolina as "passing from the chrysalis state of a late voracious nullifier to a painted Administration butterfly," and Isaac Bronson of New York as "a tall, tame, tiresome conservative, who poured forth a basin of milk-and-honey democracy tinged with a scruple of arsenic." After a ranting, abusive speech by South Carolina Representative Francis Pickens, he wrote, "All this was delivered with an air of authority and a toss of dogmatism as if he was speaking to his slaves."

Adams regarded Congress as a composite of "universal mediocrity," yet he reveled in its rituals, "the echoing pillars of the hall, the tripping Mercuries who bear the calls of ayes and noes, with the different intonations of the answers from the different voices, the gobbling manner of the Clerk in reading over the names, the tone of the Speaker in announcing the vote, and the varied shades of pleasure and pain in the countenances of the members on hearing." Indeed, it "would form a fine subject for a descriptive poem."

As he approached his seventy-fourth birthday, Adams wrote: "More than sixty years of incessant active intercourse with the world has made political movement to me as much a necessary of life as atmospheric air. This is the weakness of my nature, which I have intellect enough to perceive, but not energy to control. And thus, while a remnant of physical power is left to me to write and speak, the world will retire from me before I shall retire from the world."

Chapter Eight

"True and Honest Hearts Love You"

---

*"I hope no member of the House of
Representatives will ever again be found to
treat with disrespect the sex of his mother."*

—John Quincy Adams, defending the right of women
to participate in the political process

JUNE 1838, WASHINGTON

As a public speaker, John Quincy Adams had traveled far since his early days in Congress in December 1831, when the sound of his own voice had embarrassed him. In the parlance of Ralph Waldo Emerson, Adams had become a "bruiser," capable of verbally eviscerating his adversaries for hours on end—as he was now doing in the House. Adams had fused his battle against the Gag Rule, his opposition to the annexation of Texas, and his growing antipathy toward slavery into one scorching diatribe that would continue intermittently for fifteen days between June 16 and July 7.

Adams's verbal marathon began when the Committee on Foreign Affairs tabled, without discussion, the resolutions of seven state legislatures and petitions from 100,000 people on the question of annexing the Republic of Texas as a U.S. state. Because there was no proposal before Congress to annex Texas, the committee concluded that it was not required to take up the resolutions or the petitions.

William Seward once described Adams's mind as "a perfect calendar, a store-house, a mine of knowledge," and the seventy-year-old congressman now extracted from it the 76th standing rule of the House, *requiring* committees to consider matters referred to them by the House. When Adams scornfully suggested it was unlikely that the resolutions and petitions "had ever received five minutes' consideration in the Committee on Foreign Affairs," the House burst into confused shouting. The committee members, he continued unconcernedly, not only displayed their "contempt for the right to petition" but betrayed "their duty to their constituents and to this House. . . . If I am wrong, let the country put me down."

By default and not design, Adams had become Congress's preeminent defender of the First Amendment and human rights. Before he began his fifteen-day jeremiad against the Gag Rule, slavery, and Texas annexation, Adams had been inspired by the favorable reception in the North to his guerrilla attacks to challenge the government's Indian removal policy and to defend women's political rights.

Adams's assaults on Indian policy enraged Southerners as much as had his broadsides on slavery—the reason being that the South was the prime mover behind the Indian removal program. Southern slaveholders, whose intensive cotton cultivation quickly exhausted the soil, were continually seeking new lands on which to grow cotton and rice. For a long time they had coveted the Indian lands in the Deep South's "Black Belt," whose rich soil was ideal for plantation farming. The Democratic administrations of Andrew Jackson and Martin Van Buren had obligingly adopted policies that aided the Southerners' efforts to drive away the tribes.

When a relief bill for Indian war victims came before Congress in 1836, Adams scolded the South and his colleagues for causing the suffering they wished to palliate. "The people of Alabama and Georgia are now suffering the recoil of their own unlawful weapons . . . trampling upon the faith of our national treaties with the Indian tribes." He similarly indicted his congressional colleagues: "You have sanctioned all those outrages upon justice, law, and humanity, by succumbing to the power and the policy of Georgia." He was alluding to Georgia's illegal assertion of state authority over the Cherokees, its and the Jackson administration's flouting of a Supreme Court ruling upholding Cherokee sovereignty, and Georgia's adoption of restrictive laws that targeted Cherokees and even the missionaries sent to aid them. "This, sir, is the remote and primitive cause of the present Indian war: your own injustice sanctioning and sustaining that of Georgia and Alabama," and "your never-ending rapacity and persecution."

Adams skillfully used his position as chairman of the House Committee on Indian Affairs to gain the floor and argue for more humane treatment of the tribes. He pronounced the 1830 Indian Removal Act to be a reversal of the previous U.S. Indian policy of civilizing the Indians and encouraging them to take up farming. The act banished the estimated 60,000 members of the Five Civilized Tribes of the Southeast—Choctaw, Creek, Cherokee, Chickasaw, and Seminole—to arid lands west of the Mississippi River. "We have talked of benevolence and humanity, and preached them into civilization," said Adams, "but none of this benevolence is felt where the right of the Indian comes in collision with the interest of the white man." Southern planters had turned to Andrew Jackson for help in driving the Indians from the Southeast, and he had not disappointed them. The "violent and heartless" removal policy had justifiably met resistance, said Adams, and it was a blot on America's reputation and honor.

Alexis de Tocqueville reached a similar conclusion when he witnessed a refugee band of dispirited, emaciated Choctaws being ferried across the Mississippi River on their way to the West. In a letter to his mother, Tocqueville wrote, "There was, in the whole of this spectacle, an air of ruin and destruction . . . no one could witness this without being sick at heart."

Whenever possible, Adams denounced the "merciless, treacherous, and unconstitutional course of policy toward the Indian tribes"—whose apotheosis was the Seminole War. Waged on a tribal remnant that had refused to leave Florida for the West in compliance with the Indian Removal Act, the Seminole War, said Adams, was "a war of extermination . . . to glut the avarice and revenge of bordering slave-hunters." By 1840, when Adams condemned the war in a series of speeches, the Seminole War had cost $30 million. Adams believed it was being managed with "imbecility," and he opposed a host of bills to escalate the war by sending additional regular troops and expanding the militia.

Adams scorned the army's failure to win the war after five years. "Our last resources now are bloodhounds (procured from Cuba to track Indians and runaway slaves in the Florida swamps) and no quarter. Sixteen millions of Anglo-Saxons unable to subdue, in five years, by force and by fraud, by secret treachery and by open war, sixteen hundred savage warriors!" The guerrilla war in Florida, he wrote, "is among the most heinous sins of this nation, for which I believe God will one day bring them to judgment."

Before he became president, Adams had subscribed to the predominant belief that America was entitled to the Indians' lands and could rightfully seize them by force or through faithless treaties. While negotiating the Treaty of Ghent, Adams had asserted the United States' claims to authority over the western tribes, and as secretary of state, he had supported Andrew Jackson's invasion of Florida.

But in the White House, Adams's thinking underwent a rapid change during the crisis over the Treaty of Indian Springs, in which the Creeks ceded all their lands in Georgia for $400,000 and a commensurate acreage west of the Mississippi River. The treaty was in fact fraudulent, signed by chiefs representing just eight of the Creek Nation's forty-six towns. When the other Creek leaders complained that they had been cheated, Adams intervened as their protector, opposing Georgia's determination to enforce the treaty. But the Creeks, followed by the Choctaws, lost their eastern lands.

With public opinion strongly supporting expulsion, Adams chose not to confront the Southern states clamoring for the Indians' removal, but he stopped believing that removal was a just policy. He reached the new conviction, radically out of step with the spirit of "Manifest Destiny" suffusing America, that the government should protect the Indians—a conviction that now animated his actions in Congress.

In portraying the Indians' treatment as a stark human rights issue, Adams became recognized as the tribes' friend, although in actuality he was able to do little for them. He presented a petition by two Seneca chiefs—Dartmouth-educated Chief Pierce, and the elderly Chief Two Guns—asking that Congress not appropriate funds to carry out "the fraudulent treaty by which they are to be driven like a herd of swine from their homes to a wilderness west of the Mississippi." After Cherokee Chief John Ross met with him, Adams introduced resolutions and petitions protesting the Cherokees' maltreatment.

Adams rarely retreated on a matter involving human rights, but the futility of his advocacy for the Indians—with the public and Congress overwhelmingly supporting the tribes' removal to the West—compelled him to do so now. He asked to be excused from serving as chairman of the Committee on Indian Affairs and "turned my eyes away from this sickening mass of putrefaction."

Adams had become the de facto chief spokesman for many of those denied a voice in government—abolitionists silenced by the Gag Rule, slaves, Indians, and finally, women. One may ask why Adams took on this role, but a better question is, Why did he have no company? Almost alone among his fellow congressmen, all a generation his junior or more, Adams believed in and upheld the principles of the Founding Fathers, embodied in the individual liberties of the Constitution and the Bill of Rights, in the soaring words of the Declaration of Independence, and in the antiquated ethic, which went by the board with his father's defeat in 1800, of nonpartisanship and selfless public service.

Adams's colleagues were men of a different era, who regarded these principles as quaint. Products of the second American political system, they operated within the narrow parameters of constituencies, political parties, and economic interests.

Even decades earlier, Adams had been a rarity in the Senate and White House because of his conviction that he represented *all* of his constituents, not just those who voted for him. But now, in the politically charged Antebellum Age, he was truly a singularity. As the last serving "son of the Revolution" and the last "man of the whole country," John Quincy Adams fiercely and dutifully defended the rights of those needing a champion in the halls of Congress.

Women could not vote, but they petitioned. They were ardent signature-gatherers for the American Anti-Slavery Society and its affiliates, and many of the petitions routinely tabled without discussion in the House bore the signatures of hundreds of women. As it was Adams who tried to present many of their petitions, naturally it was Adams who came to their defense in June 1838, when their right of political participation was challenged.

Congressman Benjamin Howard of Maryland aroused Adams's indignation by declaring that women did not belong in "the fierce struggles of political life," but in the home. Adams had provoked Howard's assertion by presenting a petition signed by women opposed to annexing Texas. Before Adams had finished responding to Howard's pronouncement, Howard must have wished that he had not said anything at all.

Limiting the right of women to petition would be nothing less than "vicious," declared Adams. "Are women to have no opinions or action on subjects relating to the general welfare?" Women, he said, in fact exhibit great selflessness, judgment, and virtue when they leave the confines of the home to involve themselves in matters of religion, country, and their fellows. Adams said Esther of the Old Testament "by a *petition*, saved her people and her country." There was the prophetess Miriam, Deborah, and the doughty women of Athens, Sparta, and Rome. And, Adams asked, what of Elizabeth of England, Catherine of Russia, Isabella of Castile, and the women of the American Revolution, including Adams's own mother, Abigail, who resisted the British? "Shall it be said here that such conduct was a national reproach, because it was the conduct of women, who left their domestic concerns, and rushed into the vortex of politics? . . . They petitioned!" He read a petition written by South Carolina women to the British commander in Charleston during the Revolutionary War seeking his intercession on behalf of a condemned patriot. Obstructing the legal right of women to petition was "contesting the right of the mind, of the soul, and the conscience," charged Adams. Although he was unready to grant women the right to participate in public life as men's equals, he asked, "What can be more appropriate to their sex . . . [than] a petition—it is a prayer, a supplication, that which you address to the Almighty Being above you?"

Letters of gratitude from women poured into Adams's office and home. "True and honest hearts love you, bold and strong hearts venerate you, pious hearts pray for you, and breaking hearts murmur a blessing on your name," read one such letter. Another thanked him for his "just, generous and Christian defence of the character and claims" of her sex. Adams penned a reply that said he did so in his mother's memory. "I look to women of the present age with the feelings of a father." Female antislavery petitioners took time out from their work at the American Anti-Slavery Society to draft a petition of thanks, "for having defended so wisely and so well the right of women to be heard in the halls of legislation."

Two months after his defense of women on the House floor, Adams addressed five hundred women as "my constituents" at a gathering in Hingham, Massachusetts. "You have political rights," he told them. The women of Quincy honored him in September with a picnic. "I hope your right will never again be questioned," he said to them. "I hope no member of the House of Representatives will ever again be found to treat with disrespect the sex of his mother." Women sent him hand-knitted mufflers, hand-warmers, and socks. In a thank-you note to a woman who sent him a pair of stockings, he wrote, "They fit my limbs as if they had been measured to receive them."

Ordinary people began to look upon Adams as a guardian of their rights. One day, Washington workmen who had been laid off from their jobs constructing public buildings intercepted Adams on his way into the Capitol. They were owed back wages, the workmen said, and they asked Adams to use his influence to put them back to work. So informed, Adams assailed a House appropriations bill that attempted to cut about $100,000 from public building funds by "defrauding the poor workmen." He helped defeat the proposal. Later, he slipped into another bill a provision that paid the workmen what they were owed and restored them to their jobs. As Adams was leaving the Capitol, a workman in the passageway thanked him for "giving them a lift," Adams noted in his diary.

To his surprise and secret delight, Adams's fierce attacks on the Gag Rule and slavery and his defense of women and Indians made him more popular than he had ever been. He was so sought-after as a speaker that he sometimes placed notices in newspapers announcing his unavailability on certain dates. Young women accosted him, seeking his autograph; Adams sometimes jotted an extemporaneous poem next to his signature. During his first years in Congress, he had rarely mingled socially—giving as reasons his son John's death and his and Louisa's health. But more often it was because he had little camaraderie with his House colleagues. Adams now dined often with friends, relatives, and new acquaintances. Even the Boston establishment, which had rebuffed Adams because of his battles with the Old Federalists, displayed an unexpected affability, inviting him to chair a meeting of the starchy Massachusetts Historical Society and to sit for a portrait to be displayed in Faneuil Hall.

Charles Francis and Louisa found it all a bit disconcerting. "It is singular that a man should find some sort of external excitement so essential to his health," observed Charles disapprovingly. Said Louisa, "I wish you would do as other people do." Adams himself even questioned his motives for accepting so many invitations and rebuked himself for acting less from a "desire to do good" than from "egregious *vanity* and a passion for applause."

Adams's celebrity, however, was of a far more durable quality than momentary public approval of his well-known actions and moral principles; he had also become a living public symbol of the republic's founding generation. In the 1840s, as industrialization was swiftly transforming America and partisan politics were becoming more savage by the day, the public longed for the simple virtues of the Revolutionary era—an era, they believed, when Americans were unified behind the morally just crusade for freedom. Although this was maybe an oversimplification, biographies of George Washington were selling briskly, as were histories of the Revolutionary War. And John Quincy Adams was now seen as the embodiment of the Revolutionary generation.

When a giant of the independence era died, Adams was usually asked to eulogize him, as he did the Marquis de Lafayette before a joint session of Congress, as well as former presidents James Madison and James Monroe. Every patriotic occasion brought speaking invitations. For the fiftieth anniversary of George Washington's presidential inauguration, Adams made a two-hour speech on universal human rights to the New-York Historical Society. A continuation of the battle that Adams was then waging in Congress, the speech was a smashing success and was reprinted everywhere and quoted for decades. By pledging in the Declaration of Independence to uphold human dignity, he stated in that address, the United States had "achieved the most transcendent act of power that social man in his mental condition can perform."

James Madison was the last of the founders to die, at age eighty-five, at his Montpelier home in 1836. On a day so dark and rainy that he was able to read his speech only with the greatest difficulty, Adams said of the fourth president and his gifted contemporaries: "From the saddening thought that they are no more, we call for comfort upon the memory of what they *were*, and our hearts leap for joy, that they were our fathers." After her husband's death, Dolley Madison became a Washington neighbor and friend of the Adamses, as well as the capital's grande dame.

The deaths, anniversaries, and holiday levies continually reminded Adams of his own mortality, as on a New Year's Day, when after receiving visitors for hours he noted that "this ceremony becomes more and more irksome every year. The young and the prosperous may take pleasure in the recollections of the past and the anticipations of the future, but not one . . . whose overriding thought is the probability that it will be the last."

In the early summer of 1838, as Adams verbally besieged Congress for fifteen days about the right to petition, the annexation of Texas, and slavery, to the manifest annoyance of Southern congressmen, he declared slavery to be "a sin before the sight of God." Making Texas a state would only give greater latitude to this evil. Adams then uttered some of his strongest words against slavery: "I want to put my foot upon such doctrine . . . I want to drive it back to its fountain—its corrupt fountain—and pursue it till it is made to disappear from this land, and from the world."

America's toleration of slavery had tarnished her moral standing in the world, he said. "This philosophy of the South has done more to blacken the character of this country in Europe than all other causes put together. They point to us as a nation of liars and hypocrites, who publish to the world that all men are born free and equal, and then hold a large portion of our own population in bondage." And the true purpose of annexing Texas, he said, was to "strengthen the slaveholding interest, and perpetuate the *blessing* of that 'peculiar institution.'"

During his frontal assault, Adams also managed to read aloud the tabled resolutions of Vermont, Rhode Island, Ohio, Michigan, and Massachusetts, all opposing the annexation of Texas, and the resolutions from Tennessee and Alabama supporting it—scoffing at Alabama's preamble declaring that Texas's border extended to the Rio Grande River. He proposed a resolution, which went nowhere, asserting that only the American people should have the right to decide whether to annex an independent foreign state, and stating that if Congress attempted to annex Texas, its action would be void.

The U.S. government's machinations to annex Texas were veiled in double-talk, said Adams. And the government's policy toward Mexico, he charged with great prescience, was duplicitous and hostile, "a deliberate design of plunging us into a war . . . for the purpose of dismembering her territories, and annexing a large portion of them to this Union." Americans would not go to war with Mexico on the "false pretense" of unpaid U.S. citizens' claims against Mexico. (In this, too, Adams would be proven correct; the immediate cause of the future Mexican War would be the ambush of American troops occupying disputed territory along the Rio Grande.) Van Buren administration officials, Adams said, must "cast their lust for Texas to the winds."

Shifting the point of attack to the right of petition, he blamed slaveholding congressmen for suppressing freedom to petition and freedom of speech on the House floor. "If it had been their object to bring odium on the Administration, they could not have done it more effectually." But that was unsurprising, he said, for Martin Van Buren was "a Northern man with Southern principles."

Adams emphasized that the House's suppression of freedom of speech and petition, the proposed annexation of Texas, and the "war-whoop" of two successive presidents against Mexico all were symptomatic of a "deadly disease seated in the marrow of our bones, and that deadly disease is slavery. The Union will fall before it, or it will fall before the Union." He also warned that the slave-holders' strategy of suppressing free speech, which he said had already "shed its mildews" on the banking and currency issues, would next be employed to squelch petitions protesting the removal of Indian tribes.

His variegated speech appeared in a widely read pamphlet that convinced more of his Northern colleagues to resist Texas statehood. It was as pivotal as Adams's 1836 speech on annexation in persuading the president to not press the annexation issue during the next congressional session.

The administration reluctantly reopened negotiations with Mexico on spoliations after Adams forced it to acknowledge that Mexico had expressed a willingness to submit the question to arbitration. A commission and umpire reached a settlement in which Mexico agreed to pay $2 million to American claimants.

Menacing letters from south of the Mason-Dixon line began to land on Adams's desk. Surprisingly, many were signed, even threats made on his life. Richard Rinald of Augusta, Georgia, demanded "that satisfaction which nothing but your life can satisfy" for Adams's evident wish to make blacks the equal of whites. He warned Adams that if he did not cease his efforts, "you will when least expected, be shot down in the street, or your damned guts will be cut out in the dark." Peter Longate of Carter's Hill, Alabama, wrote that on "the first Day of May next I promise to cut your throat from ear to Ear." Another threatening message bore a letterhead of a raised bare arm, outlined in red, with a bowie knife in hand, and the words, "Vengeance is mine, say the South!" Shylock Shelton of Lawrenceburg, Kentucky, confidently predicted that Adams's life would end on February 10, 1839. From Philadelphia, north of the Mason-Dixon line, came the warning, "I shall be in Washington next March and shall shoot you. *Remember*!!!" In Charleston, this Fourth of July toast was drunk to "unbounded applause": "May we never want a Democrat to trip up the heels of a Federalist, or a hangman to prepare a halter for John Quincy Adams."

If anything, the malevolent letters, matched by a commensurate volume of letters of praise from the North, goaded Adams to greater exertions. In the House, amid a roar of "Order! Order!" he concluded his presentation of some antislavery petitions by repeating a threat uttered in the Senate against abolitionists: "If a Northern abolitionist should go to North Carolina and utter a principle of the Declaration of Independence, that if they could catch him they would hang him." His words were met by a "deafening shout," and the Speaker ordered him to sit down—which he did, only to immediately rise again and introduce another petition.

Even though the independent-minded Adams was the abolitionists' congressional point man, he was not altogether one of them. Grateful for his impassioned defense of their right to petition, abolitionists were nonetheless troubled by his refusal to join their campaign to abolish slavery in the District of Columbia. But

Adams believed an emotional debate over abolition in Washington could potentially bring on "a conflict for Life and Death between Freedom and Slavery."

Abolitionists William Lloyd Garrison, Sarah and Angelina Grimké, and the New York philanthropist Lewis Tappan all paid visits to Adams to persuade him to become an advocate for ending slavery in the District of Columbia. Next came Adams's friend Benjamin Lundy, the Quaker abolitionist leader who was editor of the *National Enquirer*. "He and the abolitionists generally are constantly urging me to indiscreet movements, which would ruin me and weaken and not strengthen their cause," wrote Adams, who was unmoved by their arguments. He privately believed the abolitionists would willingly destroy the Union to achieve their goal.

At the same time, Louisa and Charles Francis were pulling him in the other direction, urging Adams to break with the abolitionists; they feared the issue would consume and destroy him. But Adams continued to present the abolitionists' petitions, and deputized Lundy to act as his researcher for his attacks on the annexation of Texas—an unrealized working arrangement, it would turn out, with Lundy's papers destroyed in a fire set by a Philadelphia mob, followed by his untimely death in 1839.

The tug of competing loyalties upset Adams's peace of mind. "Between these adverse impulses my mind is agitated almost to distraction," he wrote in his diary. "I walk on the edge of a precipice in every step that I take." In addition, because his Massachusetts district was not strongly abolitionist, he had to be careful to not alienate his constituents, lest he lose his seat. This helps explain why he chose to attack slavery obliquely, by way of the Gag Rule, and it was a factor in his reluctance to press for abolition in the District of Columbia. As abolitionist newspapers laced into him for not going all the way on the latter question, abolitionist leaders were inviting him to their national convention. He declined the invitation, but in a letter to the convention he attempted to explain his views. To John Greenleaf Whittier, the poet who succeeded Lundy at the *Enquirer*, Adams wrote, "Under these circumstances, you will perceive that great prudence and caution become indispensably necessary to me."

To demonstrate that it was possible to achieve gradual emancipation without doing violence or injustice to slaveholders, Adams introduced three constitutional amendments in the House. The first declared that all children born in the United States on July 4, 1842, and thereafter would be free; the second prohibited the admission of any new state, Florida excepted, whose constitution tolerated slavery; and the third abolished slavery in the District of Columbia effective July 4, 1845. Stillborn in the House, Adams's amendments angered hard-line abolitionists, who continued to demand immediate emancipation.

Radical abolitionists' dissatisfaction with Adams reached the point where they put up a Liberty Party candidate against him in 1838. The third-party candidate splintered Adams's support so that his Democratic opponent nearly won. After the close call, Adams bitterly observed, "The moral principle of their interference to defeat elections when they cannot carry them appears to me to be vicious; and I think the first result of their movements will be to bring the two parties together against them."

While Adams's crusade had raised his profile in the House, it had also exacted a price: Many of his colleagues regarded him as political poison. "Scarcely a slave-holding member of the House dares to vote with me upon any question," he wrote. Sometimes when he was feeling particularly beleaguered, Adams longed to be shut of his self-appointed mission. If another congressman were capable of leading the cause of "universal emancipation" that Adams had now embraced, he would contentedly "withdraw from the contest . . . for which my age, infirmities, and approaching end totally disqualify me." But he conceded, "There is no such man in the House."

Concerned that his battle against the Gag Rule was losing momentum because of his habitual prescutation of abolition petitions, Adams asked abolitionists to take aim instead at thwarting the annexation of Texas. This would supply him with new angles of attack, he said, and help him avoid being marginalized as an abolitionist zealot. Antislavery leaders tried to oblige Adams. While the changeover was not absolute—abolition petitions continued to reach Adams's desk—the volume of anti-annexation petitions increased.

Although they never altogether accepted his refusal to become one of them, the movement's leaders welcomed Adams as their ally. His relentless attacks on the now-notorious Gag Rule had recruited many Northerners to the abolitionist banner. Even astute Southerners could see that Adams had turned the Gag Rule into a weapon against them. But whenever he went on the attack against their "peculiar institution," they could not stop themselves from clinging all the tighter to the rule, even while recognizing that its unintended consequence was to aid the abolitionists.

The volume of petitions arriving in Washington grew to gargantuan proportions. By April 1838, antislavery, anti-annexation, and anti–Gag Rule petitions filled a 600-square-foot room in the Capitol to its 14-foot ceiling; their disposal and cataloguing sometimes occupied several government clerks at once. Most of the petitions were addressed to the abolitionists' leading House allies: Adams, William Slade of Vermont, and Joshua Giddings of Ohio. They poured into Adams's office and home, where Louisa and Mary, John II's widow, logged each one. They "flow upon me in torrents," Adams wrote. On December 20, 1838, he presented 50 petitions to Congress; on January 7, 1839, he introduced 95; on March 30, 1840, he presented 511. All were tabled without debate under the Gag Rule.

On January 22, 1840, as was his practice in the early weeks of each congressional session since 1836, Adams proposed that all antislavery petitions be received and heard—and not laid on the table without being read or printed. He repeated his warning that the Gag Rule could not stop the subject of slavery from being debated in the House. "You will have the question of slavery and of abolition forced upon you every day; you cannot keep it out of the House; and, if you persevere, you will before you are aware of it, have a civil war raging, while you are excluding the only means that can put an end to it." It would be better to put to a vote the question of abolishing slavery in the District of Columbia; the question would probably get no more than ten "yes" votes, said Adams, and it would then be a dead issue. But Congress must not continue to violate the right of petition, "essential to the very existence of government; it is the right of the people over the Government; it is their right, and they may not be deprived of it."

He challenged Southerners to candidly debate the merits of slavery. "Why will you not discuss this question? Do you fear the argument? . . . Show us the 'blessings' of this institution. . . . Perhaps we shall come round; who knows but you may convert us?" This last comment was met with laughter.

The House ignored Adams's appeal and a week later adopted a "permanent" Gag Rule that prohibited even the *reception* of any petition, memorial, or resolution that proposed the abolition of slavery in the District of Columbia, or any state or territory, or that called for the elimination of the slave trade within the United States and its territories. It was worse than Henry Laurens Pinckney's 1836 Gag Rule, which had at least permitted the petitions to be received before they were automatically tabled. While the Pinckney rule had won approval with the support of nearly two-thirds of the House, the 21st standing rule was adopted by only 114–108. Many Northern congressmen complained that the rule explicitly violated the First Amendment right of petition.

Of the new Gag Rule, Adams noted with exasperation, "The difference between the resolution of the four preceding sessions of Congress and the new rule of the House is the difference between petty larceny and highway robbery."

Chapter Nine

The *Amistad*

---

*"Was ever such a scene of Liliputian
trickery enacted by the rules of a great,
magnanimous, and Christian nation?"*

—John Quincy Adams, on the U.S. government's
plans to return the *Amistad* Africans to Cuba

---

*W*hen the case of the mutineer slaves of the Cuban
ship *Amistad* reached the U.S. Supreme Court in late
1840, abolitionists sought a lawyer experienced in arguing before the highest court in the land to assist their two attor-
ney-advocates. But their first choice, Daniel Webster, declined the
case, as did Rufus Choate of Boston, who begged off on account of
poor health and a long hiatus from Supreme Court pleadings. In
truth, neither man was particularly fond of abolitionists.

Their third choice was Congressman John Quincy Adams, no
abolitionist, but an enemy of slavery. Lewis Tappan, the New York
philanthropist and abolitionist, believed the legal team would benefit from Adams's station, age, and character. Adams tried to turn
down the request, on the grounds of his seventy-three years, his
general "inefficiency," his pressing congressional duties, his unfamil-
iarity with appellate work, and his more than thirty-year absence

from the bar of the Supreme Court. When the abolitionists insisted, he accepted with great reluctance and trepidation, as evidenced in his diary entry that night, October 20, 1840: "I implore the mercy of almighty God so to control my temper, to enlighten my soul, and to give me utterance, that I may prove myself in every respect equal to the task."

Abolitionist leaders were far more optimistic than Adams about his anticipated contribution. Theodore Weld wrote to an English-woman abolitionist: "Thou has probably heard that John Quincy Adams is engaged as counsel in the case of the Amistad captives; it is noble in him thus to plead the cause of the oppressed."

Like his countrymen, John Quincy Adams had followed the high drama surrounding the thirty-nine Africans of the *Amistad* with great interest. After they commandeered the vessel near Cuba, the Africans had tried to return to their home but had been tricked into sailing up the U.S. East Coast to Long Island, whence they were arrested by U.S. naval officers on August 26, 1839, at Sag Harbor. Abolitionist leaders rallied to their defense, opposing the Martin Van Buren administration's efforts to pack them off to Cuba for trials on capital crimes. Adams was soon enough drawn into the sensational case, involving as it did his closely held principle of human freedom.

The central question was whether the Africans were slaves or kidnapped freemen. If they were indeed slaves, and therefore property under the Anglo-Spanish Treaty of 1795, the United States was required to return them to Spanish authorities. Spain insisted that this was the case and that the blacks' Cuban owners had the same rights as U.S. slaveholders. Spanish officials demanded custody of the Africans.

Abolitionist attorneys argued that the Africans were not slaves but abducted freemen who had justifiably regained their freedom by killing their ship's captain and seizing the ship. They should be released, said their attorneys.

In 1820, Spain had outlawed the importation of African slaves into all Spanish territories, including Cuba. And while the Africans' papers identified them as *ladinos*, slaves brought to Cuba before 1820, they were clearly recent arrivals, or illegal *bozales*; in fact, just months earlier they had been kidnapped in Sierra Leone and transported in chains to Cuba, in violation of the Spanish prohibition.

Angel Calderón de la Barca, Spain's minister to the United States, pressured Secretary of State John Forsyth to keep the case out of the U.S. courts. Return the *Amistad* and its cargo to their owners, he said, and hand over the blacks to Spanish custody for proceedings in Cuba. They would receive a fair trial, Calderón added reassuringly, and if they had been illegally imported, it would be a mitigating circumstance in judging their crimes. Calderón insisted that the United States had no authority to interfere with "Spanish officials enforcing Spanish laws." He cited "the law of nations" and the Treaty of 1795, portions of which were recognized in the Adams-Onís Treaty of 1819 transferring Florida from Spanish to U.S. ownership.

Because of the lingering economic malaise from the Panic of 1837, President Martin Van Buren faced a tough re-election campaign in 1840. Under different circumstances, his administration might not have intervened in the *Amistad* case. But the "Little Magician," the cleverest politician of his era, had forged the Democratic coalition of Southern slaveholders and Northern anti-abolitionists that had elected Andrew Jackson to two terms, and then in 1836 had himself ridden the same coalition to the White House. Van Buren and his advisers recognized that although they stood to gain nothing from the *Amistad* affair, if the Africans went free they could lose the South.

Therefore, the administration adopted a damage control strategy: intervention for the purpose of quickly removing the case from the judicial system, and then meeting Spain's demands for custody of the blacks. Van Buren would distance himself from the affair but retain the last word on the captives' fate. In the meantime, the U.S. attorney's office would surreptitiously give legal advice to the slaves' ostensible owners.

Secretary of State Forsyth, a former Georgia congressman, took operational control. He requested an opinion on the case's proper jurisdiction from Attorney General Felix Grundy of Tennessee, who predictably concluded that it was a matter between the U.S. and Spanish governments. It was of paramount importance, Grundy declared, that the blacks "may not escape punishment. . . . These negroes deny that they are slaves; if they should be delivered to the claimants [their purported owners], no opportunity may be afforded for the assertion of their right to freedom. For these reasons it seems to me that a delivery to the Spanish minister is the only safe course for this Government to pursue." But the abolitionists stood in the administration's way.

While the Van Buren administration wished for a quick, quiet resolution that would not inflame slaveholders, the *Amistad* affair perfectly suited the abolitionists' need for a high-profile case that could win public sympathy for enslaved blacks, while further tarnishing slavery's already unsavory image. Abolitionists made the most of it, splashing it in the pages of William Lloyd Garrison's fiercely abolitionist Boston newspaper, the *Liberator*, and in the *Emancipator* of New York, the organ of the American Anti-Slavery Society, where defense attorney Theodore Sedgwick argued that it was "not murder for a free man to kill his kidnapper."

Of the U.S. government's manifest lack of impartiality, John Quincy Adams wrote to the New York *Journal of Commerce*: "Is this compassion? Is it sympathy? Is it justice?" The hungry, ragged refugees had come ashore at Long Island, and their condition "claimed from the humanity of a civilized nation compassion . . . it claimed from a Republic professing reverence for the rights of man justice—and what have we done?"

Upon the urging of Ellis Gray Loring, a Boston attorney, abolitionist, and occasional Adams fishing companion, Adams began informally advising—prior to his consenting to argue before the Supreme Court—the attorneys defending the Africans in federal court in Hartford, Connecticut: Sedgwick, Roger Baldwin, and Seth Staples.

Kidnapped by other Africans and sold into slavery in early 1839, the *Amistad* captives were taken with about 150 others to Lomboko (south of Freetown, Sierra Leone), where they were imprisoned in fort-like pens, or barracoons. Slave-trader Don Pedro Blanco sold all 200 to Don Pedro Martinez and Company of Havana. The Africans were chained in the stiflingly hot hold of the schooner *Tecora* and transported across the Atlantic. In Havana, Don Jose Ruiz, a plantation owner and Cuban slave-trader, purchased 49 of the captives for $450 apiece, or $22,000 total. Ruiz reasoned that if he could smuggle them into the United States, he could make a 100 percent profit; if not, he would use them on his plantation at Port Principe, Cuba.

Ruiz bribed the Cuban governor-general, at the "head tax" rate of $15 per slave, to falsely certify them as *ladinos*. He then marched them to the *Amistad*, a "clipper-built schooner" anchored in Havana harbor. Captain Ramon Ferrer and his crew of four had agreed to take the Africans, Ruiz, and three young female slaves owned by Don Pedro Montes, also a passenger, to Port Principe, 300 miles away—a sea journey of two or three days. The *Amistad* departed Havana on June 28, 1839.

At sea, when strong headwinds promised to double the anticipated length of their journey, Captain Ferrer cut the Africans' rations, and the first seeds of discontent were sown. The unhappy blacks asked the ship's cook, a slave named Celestino, what would happen to them when they reached their destination. White men would eat them, Celestino mischievously replied. He underestimated their reaction. Instead of quaking with fear, the Africans began to plot. A kidnapped rice planter named Cinque—his African given name was Singbe—became their leader.

On the fifth night at sea, the Africans broke the padlock on the chain connecting their iron neck collars, armed themselves with machetes from the ship, and pounced on the troublemaking Celestino and Captain Ferrer as they slept on a mattress on deck, killing them both; before he died, Ferrer dispatched two of his assailants. Two sailors fled in a boat, but Ruiz, Montes, and a ship slave, Antonio, became the Africans' prisoners.

Now began a deadly serious contest between Cinque and Montes, who was a former ship captain and now, although wounded during the mutiny, was the only man aboard the vessel capable of sailing her. Cinque demanded that Montes steer for Africa, and he looked over Montes's shoulder to make sure that the *Amistad* was indeed sailing east. But at night, when Cinque wasn't watching, Montes tacked to the north and west. Proceeding in this manner, the *Amistad* during July zigzagged along the East Coast of the United States, just out of sight of land, slowly traveling north. As the weeks passed, her sails rotted, her bottom became fouled, and food ran low.

Near New York Harbor, the *Amistad* encountered the *Blossom*, whose crew gave the hungry Africans bread and water. The *Blossom's* officers immediately reported the meeting to New York's federal collector of customs, who sent an armed revenue cutter to investigate the tatterdemalion African-crewed ship plying U.S. coastal waters. The collector broadcast an alert throughout the Northeast with a description of the strange vessel and its crew, and the sightings and reported encounters multiplied. The spectral *Amistad*, barnacled and lank-sailed, and her desperate-looking, emaciated black passengers, armed with long knives, hovered off Long Island throughout August. Cinque and the Africans knew Montes had deceived them, but they did not retaliate against him because of the immutable fact that only he knew how to sail the *Amistad*. In the meantime, the two escaped crewmen had landed in Cuba, and reports of the mutiny began to reach the United States.

The Africans were so tormented by thirst that some of them unwisely drank liquid medicines found below, became violently ill, and died. These deaths, and the two killed in the mutiny, reduced the 49 men and three children that had sailed from Havana to a total of 42.

Cinque ordered Montes to steer the *Amistad* close to shore near Culloden Point on Long Island, where he hoped to obtain fresh water and provisions. Some of the Africans went ashore, and with Spanish doubloons from the ship bought casks of fresh water, two dogs, sweet potatoes, and a bottle of gin.

Before they could row the foodstuff and water to their ship and put back out to sea, a U.S. naval vessel suddenly appeared—the surveying brig *Washington*. Aware of the reports about the mysterious ship and suspicious of the activity on the beach, Lieutenant Commander Thomas R. Gedney, Lieutenant Richard W. Meade, and their crew acted quickly, seizing the *Amistad* and disarming the Africans on August 26. Cinque jumped overboard with a belt loaded with 300 doubloons that nearly dragged him to the bottom, before he removed it and Navy crewmen reeled him in. Gedney towed the reeking ship and its passengers to New London, Connecticut.

The capture of the rotting hulk crewed by mutineer slaves caused a great sensation. Newspaper reporters converged on New London to describe the scene for a public eager for details. The New London *Gazette* described Cinque, the ringleader, as being about twenty-six years of age, "well built and active . . . a match for any two men on board the schooner . . . [with] a composure characteristic of true courage, and nothing to mark him as a malicious man. . . . He expects to be executed, but nevertheless manifests a *sang froid* worthy of a stoic under similar circumstances."

Aboard the *Washington* in New London's harbor, U.S. District Judge Andrew Judson convened the first court hearing in the case. With Lieutenant Meade translating, Ruiz, Montes, and Antonio, the surviving slave of Captain Ferrer, described in Spanish everything that had occurred since they left Havana. Also introduced as evidence were the two licenses signed by Cuban Governor-General Ezpeleta that identified all the slaves as either Cuban-born, or Cuban residents since before 1820, and that authorized Ruiz and Montes to transport them to Port Principe.

The licenses and eyewitness testimony furnished ample grounds for Judson to charge Cinque and the 38 other adult Africans with murder and piracy and to hold them without bond in the New Haven jail for trial. Unsure what to do with the three girls, who wept in the courtroom from fright, Judson sent them, too, to jail under $100 bond each. In a subsequent proceeding, U.S. Circuit Judge Smith Thompson, an associate U.S. Supreme Court justice whose circuit included Connecticut, agreed with Judson that charges were warranted and denied the defendants bond. Thompson ordered them bound over for trial in Judson's federal court.

Opportunistically hoping to capitalize on the case's publicity to attract new recruits, abolitionists dispatched attorneys Baldwin, Sedgwick, and Staples to New Haven. The attorneys acted quickly to prevent the Van Buren administration from handing the Africans over to Ruiz and Montes and bypassing the judicial process altogether. In a letter to the president, Sedgwick and Staples argued that the Cubans had no legal claim on the Africans. They expressed the hope that the Africans' fate would not be decided "in the recesses of the cabinet, where these unfriended men can have no counsel and can produce no proof, but in the halls of Justice, with the safeguard that she throws around the unfriended and oppressed."

Lewis Tappan threw up a legal barrier to the Van Buren administration simply handing over the Africans to Ruiz and Montes by charging the purported owners in a civil lawsuit with assault and battery, and false imprisonment. Arrested in New York City, Montes was released on his own recognizance; Ruiz remained in jail under $250 bond.

The arrests outraged Southerners and anti-abolitionists. "The next step we shall hear of will be the arrest and imprisonment of Southern gentlemen traveling in the Northern States at the suit of their own servants," wrote the New York *Advertiser & Express*. Further complicating matters, Gedney and Meade filed a civil lawsuit seeking prize money for having seized the *Amistad*.

At a hearing before U.S. District Judge Judson in November, all the principals in the case testified, except the Africans. Defense attorneys were frantically canvassing the New York waterfront for anyone familiar with the Mende dialect that they spoke. During the hearing, arguably the most telling testimony came from Dr. Richard R. Madden, a British expert on the Cuban slave trade. During the previous three years, he stated, 20,000 to 25,000 Africans were illegally landed in Cuba each year and, after their owners paid the government a small bribe, were falsely licensed as either *ladinos* or Cuban-born *creoles*. He pronounced the *Amistad* blacks to be "bona fide *bozale* Negroes, quite newly imported from Africa," and the licenses identifying them as *ladinos* to be fraudulent. Madden's testimony planted the first substantial doubts about the *Amistad* Africans' documentation. Their attorneys were confident that when someone was found to translate for the Africans, the government's case would collapse.

While hunting for translators on the New York waterfront, Josiah Gibbs, a Yale College professor of linguistics, found two men who knew the Mende dialect: James Covey and Charles Pratt, crewmen on the British warship *Buzzard* and former slaves. The *Buzzard's* captain permitted Covey to travel to Hartford to interpret for the Africans.

Early in the proceedings, U.S. Attorney William Holabird had asked Secretary of State Forsyth, who was second-guessing every decision made by Holabird, whether there was any extant Spanish-American treaty that *required* the U.S. government to return the blacks to Cuba, "and if so, whether it could be done before our court sits." Forsyth had replied that he was investigating this avenue, but in the meantime, Holabird must "take care that no proceeding . . . places the vessel, cargo, or slaves beyond the control of the Federal Executive."

In an attempt to keep the case out of the judiciary's hands, Holabird dropped the piracy and murder charges and invoked the Anglo-Spanish Treaty of 1795. He said that in the event of piracy, shipwreck, or other accidents, the treaty obligated the United States to return all Spanish property, including slaves, to the Spanish.

But nested within Holabird's assertion lay what would become the great flaw of the government's case: The Africans were not slaves but kidnap victims; their mutiny was not piracy but an act of self-defense. Not only did Ruiz and Montes "have no title . . . to these Africans," the Africans' attorneys would argue, but the Treaty of 1795 was never intended to "warrant the delivery of these individuals as offenders."

During the Africans' first three days in the Hartford jail, more than 3,000 people paid twelve and one-half cents to see them, with jailers promising that the money would defray the Africans' expenses and buy them good food and clothing. The most popular captives were Cinque and Konoma, who was nicknamed "the Cannibal" because he had filed his teeth to points—although not for carnivorous purposes but to appear more attractive to Mende women. For weeks on end, curiosity-seekers, newspaper reporters, linguists, phrenologists, ministers, and abolitionists paraded through the jail without surcease. Before Josiah Gibbs found the Mende-language translators in New York, Thomas Gallaudet, who in Hartford had begun the first free American school for the deaf, improvised a rudimentary sign language for the Africans. Peale's Museum in

New York cast their wax effigies in scenes melodramatically depicting the mutiny. Amory Hall in Boston adorned its own wax figures with swatches of the captives' actual hair. In New Haven, a garish, 135-foot-long painting titled "The Massacre on Board the 'Amistad'" depicted twenty-six men at the putative height of the mutiny, while at New York's Bower Theater, the theatrical production "The Black Schooner" was a great success.

The Van Buren administration's actions complicated the defense's preparations as the federal trial date of January 7, 1840, neared. The administration withheld documents, including two major treaties that Forsyth claimed that he could not find in the State Department. One document that the State Department did produce appeared to have been altered, for which the administration was condemned by the New York *Express*, the *Emancipator*, and the *Liberator*.

The president secretly dispatched the USS *Grampus* to New Haven harbor to whisk the *Amistad* Africans off to Cuba the moment Judge Judson ruled, as prosecutors expected, that the blacks were Spanish property and not free men. (The Van Buren administration believed Judson was reliably anti-abolitionist, because he had a few years earlier rid his Connecticut hometown of a school for black girls.) The *Grampus* was to instantly put to sea, before defense lawyers could file an appeal. "The President has, agreeably to your suggestion," Forsyth wrote Holabird, "ordered a vessel to be in readiness to receive the negroes from the custody of the marshal as soon as their delivery shall have been ordered by the court." Van Buren also ordered Lieutenant Commander Gedney and Lieutenant Meade to be ready to sail to Cuba to testify against the Africans in legal proceedings there. In making these preparations for a hasty removal, the Van Buren administration demonstrated that it was willing to violate the judicial appeals process in order to safeguard its political standing in the South.

The Africans' removal could not happen soon enough for Forsyth, badgered by Spanish Minister Calderón de la Barca and his successor, Pedro Alcántara Argaiz, to send the Africans to Cuba to be punished. The secretary of state had patiently tried to explain to the diplomats that the U.S. government, unlike Spain's monarchy, could not simply order this done, because "the judiciary is, by the organic law of the land, a portion, though an independent one, of that Government." This explanation evidently made no impression on the ministers, who replied that the 1795 treaty superseded the courts' jurisdiction. They pressured the administration to stretch its executive prerogative to the breaking point by sending the *Grampus* to New Haven.

When abolitionist newspapers somehow obtained a copy of the *Grampus*'s orders and published them, Lewis Tappan and his brother Arthur laid a counterplan. They, too, dispatched a ship to New Haven harbor—but with the aim of spiriting the Africans away to freedom if Judson decided to send them back to Cuba. Thus, two ships with contradictory objectives lurked in the harbor, awaiting Judson's decision.

The New Haven courtroom was packed when the trial began January 7—public interest having remained at an extraordinary pitch since the *Amistad*'s capture in August. Just as they had in Hartford, visitors besieged the New Haven jail. They included a Yale Divinity School teacher who was teaching the Africans to read and write English, and Yale students who led them in prayer each morning and preached to them about Christian morality. Professor Gibbs was hard at work on a Mende dictionary.

Abolitionist lawyers Staples, Sedgwick, and Baldwin and prosecutor Holabird argued the main issue: Were the Africans mutinous slaves or kidnapped freemen seeking liberty? Then Cinque testified. The spectators who jammed the courtroom watched, spellbound. Wrapped in a blanket and standing ramrod straight, Cinque, with Professor Gibbs translating, described how he was abducted from a road crew in Mende, sold in Lomboko, and then chained with other slaves in a crowded ship's hold. Each day of their ocean voyage, the captives were fed one plantain and two potatoes and given a half-cup of water. Four were whipped; one died.

Attorneys teased out a similar story from James Covey, the British sailor, former slave, and translator. Eight years earlier, Covey testified, he, too, had been abducted in Mende, sold at Lomboko to a Cuban slave-trader, and placed on a ship bound for Havana. But an English cruiser captured the slave ship, and Covey was freed and later enlisted in the Royal Navy.

Besides sometimes translating for Cinque, Professor Gibbs acted as an expert defense witness, testifying that new slaves usually swiftly adopted their captors' tongue, but that these Africans knew no Spanish. He could only conclude that they were "native Africans and recently from Africa."

Holabird presented a Spanish consul's sworn testimony that the *Amistad*'s papers avouching that the Africans were *ladinos* and not *bozales* were in order and legitimate.

In January 1840, Judge Judson stunned prosecutors and defense attorneys by ruling that the Africans had been "born free," kidnapped, and "unlawfully sold as slaves." In attempting to win their freedom and return to their families, the Africans had committed no crime. The judge placed them in the custody of President Van Buren, who was instructed to transport them to Africa. He ordered the late Captain Ferrer's slave, the *creole* Antonio, returned to Cuba. The judge ruled that the *Amistad* and its cargo were to be handed over to the Spanish government, but that Gedney, along with his shipmates, and Ruiz and Montes would share salvage rights to the vessel and goods.

Holabird immediately appealed the verdict. In April, Circuit Judge Smith Thompson, the associate U.S. Supreme Court justice whose circuit included Connecticut, upheld Judson's ruling.

The government appealed again—this time to the U.S. Supreme Court, which agreed to hear oral arguments when it next convened in Washington, in early 1841. Believing that if the Africans were released, they would disappear, federal authorities professed concern about their safety and kept them in jail, although they no longer faced charges.

John Quincy Adams, who had avidly followed every twist and turn of the case, presented a House resolution protesting the Africans' continued imprisonment. He requested the Van Buren administration's correspondence with the Spanish ministers and Holabird and proposed a congressional inquiry into whether the State Department had deliberately mistranslated a document given to the House, Document 185. The phrase "sound negroes" had been wrongly substituted for the term *ladinos*. The New York *Express* called it "a cunningly devised fraud" that implied the *Amistad* Africans were slaves, when the District Court had declared they were not. The House organized a five-man investigative committee, chaired by Adams. The mistranslation turned out to be a proofreader's error, although Adams was unsatisfied by the explanation.

William Henry Harrison, whose supporters successfully remade the farmer-politician's staid image into that of an exciting frontiersman–Indian fighter, defeated Martin Van Buren in November 1840. The president's management of the *Amistad* case, especially the attempt to use the *Grampus* to thwart a defense appeal, may have cost Van Buren six Northern states that he had won in 1836, when he defeated Harrison.

Since consenting to argue the *Amistad* case before the Supreme Court in early 1841, Adams had pushed himself ever harder to master the case's details, while worrying that he was not equal to the task. "Oh, how shall I do justice to this case and to these men?" he fretted in his diary. In December, before the 26th Congress's Second Session began, Adams conferred with co-counsel Roger Baldwin at his New Haven home, and then, for the first time, he visited the Africans, who had been moved from the jail to a house in the city. He noted that none was taller than five and a half feet or older than thirty. "Cinque and Grabow, the two chief conspirators, have very remarkable countenances. Three of them read to us part of a chapter in the English New Testament, very indifferently. One boy writes a tolerable hand." After Adams's visit, Ka-le, one of the three African children, sent Adams an imploring letter, undoubtedly ghost-written by the abolitionists who mailed it: "We want you to ask the court what we have done wrong. What for Americans keep us in prison. . . . We want to be free very much. . . . All we want is make us free."

As Adams labored at home and in the Supreme Court library on his arguments, he vowed to find "means to defeat and expose the abominable conspiracy, Executive and Judicial, of this Government, against the lives of those wretched men. . . . Of all the dangers before me, that of losing my self-possession is the most formidable." The long days of research, added to his heavy congressional workload, overtaxed his eyes to the extent that he feared he might not be able to perform his final duty before the Supreme Court. But as the hearing date neared, Adams's eyesight improved. And then, Justice Joseph Story's absence on January 16 delayed the hearing until February 20, giving Adams more precious time to ready his presentation.

In its last days, the Van Buren administration, through its quasi-official Washington *Globe*, reflexively lashed out at the *Amistad* mutiny and Judge Andrew Judson's decision countenancing it. At the same time, perhaps wishing to osmotically influence the Supreme Court through the membrane of the Senate, Van Buren wrote a letter to the Senate recounting the Spanish minister's demands under the Anglo-American Treaty of 1795. The letter included Spanish newspaper clippings describing the Africans as pirates and murderers. No other purpose suggests why Van Buren went to such trouble in the days before the February 20 court hearing, with his successor due to take office on March 4.

The seven justices—the Supreme Court would not have nine until 1869—who would hear the *Amistad* case were Chief Justice Roger Taney, and associate justices Philip Barbour, James Moore Wayne, Henry Baldwin, John McLean (Adams's former postmaster general), Smith Thompson (the New Haven circuit judge), and Joseph Story. The justices sat at mahogany desks on a raised platform above the railed bar, which adjoined a visitors' gallery. Benjamin Latrobe in 1810 had designed the small courtroom and its vaulted ceiling, located beneath the Senate chamber in the Capitol. Heavily damaged when British soldiers set fire to the Capitol in 1814, the courtroom was repaired and returned to service in 1819. The Supreme Court would move upstairs during the 1850s when wings were added to the Capitol, and in 1935 it would take up residence in its own building.

The government's attorney, Attorney General Henry Gilpin, a Philadelphia lawyer and former federal prosecutor, led off by arguing that the Africans were slaves, and therefore property that must be returned to Cuba under the Treaty of 1795. Thus, the president acted properly when he intervened for the purpose of transferring the Africans to Cuban custody, said Gilpin. The United States must honor the "golden rule" of international relations: "Let us do to them as we wish them to do to us." At times, Gilpin veered into sophistical quicksand, observing that because slavery was legal in the United States, freeing the Africans would necessarily contravene established law. "No nation recognizing slavery admits the sufficiency of forcible emancipation," he said. Gilpin not only saw no contradiction in pronouncing the blacks both criminals and property but attempted a strange conflation of the two categories. "If they are property, they are property rescued from pirates, and are to be restored," he said, glossing over the fact that this meant the blacks had been simultaneously property and the pirates from whom they needed rescuing.

The defense team had decided that Roger Baldwin, the Africans' trial lawyer in Connecticut, would argue the case's legal points, and Adams would probe its moral underpinnings. In his opening argument, Baldwin alleged that Ruiz and Montes had used "artifice" in obtaining false documents that stated the Africans were *ladinos* when they were clearly *bozales*. And because the Africans were illegal prisoners aboard the *Amistad*, they, like impressed U.S. seamen, could rightfully utilize any means to gain their liberty, he said. How could America, the self-proclaimed beacon of liberty, permit the enslavement of people who entered her borders as free men? asked Baldwin.

When Adams's turn came to address the court, he began by modestly observing that he might well "exhibit at once the infirmities of age and the inexperience of youth." He then proceeded to demonstrate over the next four and a half hours that he was operating under neither handicap. He assailed, in turn, the behavior of the Van Buren administration and Attorney General Gilpin's belief in the applicability of the Treaty of 1795. The case, Adams said dismissively, was in fact "anomalous," and no law or statute applied—only the Declaration of Independence.

Adams arraigned the Van Buren administration for its extreme bias. It had occupied "the ground of utter injustice," compelling the Africans to unfairly face "the array of the whole Executive power of this nation," whose sympathies lay with "the slave-traders, and against these poor, unfortunate, helpless, tongueless, defenseless

Africans." The administration's loyalty to the slaveholders was the real reason for the proceedings, he charged. "By what right was [sympathy] denied to the men who had restored themselves to freedom . . . and why was it extended to the perpetrators of those acts of violence themselves?"

The Spanish ministers' assertions notwithstanding, the *Amistad* was engaged in the slave trade, Adams flatly stated. "It is universally known that the trade is actually carried on, contrary to the laws of Spain, but by the general connivance of the Governor General [of Cuba] and all the authorities and the people of the island." The passport identifying the Africans by Spanish names and as *ladinos* "is not worth a cent," yet the U.S. government honored Ruiz's and Montes's spurious claims, when the Cubans had in fact violated the laws of Great Britain, Spain, and the United States.

The *Amistad*'s voyage, said Adams, was part of the illegal journey that originated in Africa. Ruiz's and Montes's final destination was Port Principe, Cuba, "and of course the voyage was to them an unlawful one." However, "the object of the Africans was to get to port in Africa, and their voyage *was* lawful," he said. After Captain Ferrer's death, Adams asserted, the ship belonged to the Africans.

Adams mocked the demands by the Spanish ministers, Calderón de la Barca and Pedro Alcántara Argaiz, to return the Africans on the ground that "public vengeance has not been satisfied. . . . The vengeance of the African slave-traders, despoiled of their prey and thirsting for blood! . . . Surely, this is very lamentable. Surely, this is a complaint to be made to the secretary of state of this government." The Spanish wished for the president to "first turn man-robber; rescue from the custody of the Court . . . those forty odd Africans; next turn jailer, and keep them in his close custody . . . and lastly, turn catchpoll and convey them to Havana, to appease the public vengeance of the African slave-traders of the barracoons. Is it possible to speak of this demand in language of decency and moderation?"

If the president were permitted to send the Africans to Cuba to be tried for their lives, Adams warned, he could invoke the same authority to act against American citizens. "By a simple order to the marshal of the district, he could just as well seize forty citizens of the United States, on the demand of a foreign minister, and send them beyond the seas for trial before a foreign court." Pointing to one of the copies of the Declaration of Independence that hung in the courtroom, Adams said, "I will not recur to the Declaration of Independence—your Honors have it implanted in your hearts—but one of the grievous charges brought against George III was that he had made laws for sending men beyond seas for trial. That was one of the most odious of those acts of tyranny which occasioned the American Revolution." The present case should end with the Declaration of Independence, he said, because once its words are read declaring that each man has an inalienable right to life and liberty, "this case is decided."

Adams, arguably the greatest American secretary of state, scorned Forsyth's eagerness to cooperate with Spain's "inadmissible and insolent" demands. His voice dripping with sarcasm, Adams said the Spanish minister wished the president to use "absolute fiat" to pluck the Africans from the courts and send them to Cuba. "Is the Khan of Tartary possessed of a power to meet demands like these? I know not where on the globe we should look for any such authority, unless it be with the Governor General of Cuba with respect to negroes."

Forsyth should have protested that Spain was treating the president of the United States as "a constable," said Adams. By not so responding and proceeding as if the president was anxious to comply with Spain's demands, Forsyth "has degraded the country in the face of the whole civilized world." While never disabusing the Spanish of their belief that Van Buren could decree the Africans' transport to Cuba, Forsyth had at the same time splashed cold water on the British minister's expressed wish that the president free the blacks; the secretary of state had reminded the British minister that the president could not control the judiciary. "How sensitive the Secretary is now!" Adams caustically said. "How quick to perceive an impropriety! How alive to the honor of the country.

. . . How different his course, from that pursued with the Spanish minister." To the Spanish, Adams asserted, Forsyth communicated "soothing hopes . . . that the decree of the judge, dooming the Africans to servitude and death in Cuba, would be as pliant to the vengeful thirst of the barracoon slave-traders, as that of Herod was in olden times to the demand of his dancing daughter for the head of John the Baptist in a charger."

Spain had insisted that the Treaty of 1795 required the United States to return the Africans to Spanish custody, but Adams pronounced the treaty irrelevant to Spain's demand. Having negotiated a renewal of the treaty with Spain's minister in 1819 when he was secretary of state, Adams said, "I am certain that neither of us ever entertained an idea that this word merchandise [in Article 9] was to apply to human beings." Not a single article of the treaty had any application to this case, he said. If the treaty had any utility at all in the question, it would be in the sense of assisting those in need—namely, the Africans. "They were in distress," he said. The Africans' enemies had brought them into U.S. waters and even now were trying to reduce them from freedom to slavery, as a "reward" for the Africans having spared the slave-traders' lives in the fight for the ship. "If the good offices of the government are to be rendered to the proprietors of shipping in distress, they are due to the Africans only."

Adams asked the justices to imagine that the *Amistad* was an American vessel with a cargo of African slaves that had tied up at a U.S. port. "The captain would be seized, tried as a pirate and hung! And every person concerned, either as owners or on board the ship, would be severely punished."

Yet President Van Buren had acted wholly to the contrary by his "lawless and tyrannical order" that the *Grampus* remove the Africans to Cuba before their lawyers could file an appeal. "The cold-blooded cruelty with which it was issued was altogether congenial to its spirit," he sneered. "It is questionable whether such a power could have been exercised by the most despotic government

of Europe. Yet this business was coolly dispatched by a mere informal order." He sarcastically suggested that perhaps the president
was ignorant of the right of personal liberty and didn't know that
"no greater violation of his official oath to protect and defend the
Constitution of the United States could be committed than by an
order to seize and deliver up to a foreign minister's demand, thirty-
six persons, in a mass." Adams added, "Was ever such a scene of
Liliputian trickery enacted by the rules of a great, magnanimous,
and Christian nation?"

Although he had spoken for four and a half hours without inter-
mission, Adams observed "little flagging of attention by the
Judges." With an almost audible sigh of relief for having survived
the ordeal, he confessed in his diary that until the moment that he
began speaking, he was "deeply distressed and agitated"—a severe
case of butterflies—but that once he was under way, his spirits rallied. He humbly professed his "gratified heart for aid from above,
though . . . [due to] the weakness incident to the limits of my
powers. . . . I did not, I could not, answer public expectation, but I
have not yet utterly failed."

That night, Associate Justice Philip Barbour died in his sleep.
The court adjourned until March 1, delaying the conclusion of
Adams's arguments.

On March 1, after speaking four hours more to complete his arguments, John Quincy Adams indulged in a moving reminiscence
before leaving the presence of the Supreme Court for the last time.
Because Adams's own life was so entwined with the formative
years of America, as he spoke it might almost have seemed that the
titans of the early republic walked the halls of Capitol again.

Adams observed that he had first entered his name on the
Supreme Court's rolls on February 7, 1804—thirty-seven years

earlier—and that he had last appeared before the Court in March 1809, as Thomas Jefferson was leaving the White House. "Little did I imagine that I should ever again be required to claim the right of appearing in the capacity of an officer of this Court; yet such has been the dictate of my destiny—and I appear again to plead the cause of justice."

Scanning the faces of the six justices, he did not see any of the men before whom he had argued in 1809. "Marshall-Cushing-Chase-Washington-Johnson-Livingstone-Todd. Where are they?" Absent, too, were his co-counsel, Robert Goodloe Harper, and their adversary, Luther Martin, as well as the clerk and the marshal. "Where are they all? Gone! Gone! All gone!" He hoped they had reaped their eternal reward, just as he wished that the current judges may "after the close of a long and virtuous career in this world, be received at the portals of the next with the approving sentence, 'Well done, good and faithful servant; enter thou into the joy of thy Lord.'"

On March 9, Justice Joseph Story, whose service since 1812 made him the court's senior member by ten years, read the decision. After reviewing the facts and case law, he concluded, "There does not seem to us to be any ground for doubt that these Negroes ought to be deemed free; and that the Spanish treaty interposes no obstacle to the just assertion of their rights." In seizing the *Amistad*, the Africans had only exercised "the ultimate right of all human beings in extreme cases to resist oppression, and to apply force against ruinous injustice." The decision made no mention of the Van Buren administration's efforts to thwart the legal process. Justice Story later wrote to his wife that Adams's presentation was an "extraordinary argument. . . . Extraordinary for its power and its bitter sarcasm, and its dealing with topics far beyond the record and points of discussion."

"The captives are free!" Adams wrote to Roger Baldwin, who had returned to New Haven. "Yours in great haste and great joy.

J.Q. Adams." The New York *Commercial Advertiser* described the ruling as "a great and glorious triumph for humanity."

With relief, Adams expressed his private conviction—a mistaken one, as events would show—that "it was the last occasion upon which I should ever be called to stake my personal, moral, intellectual, and political character upon issues involving the lives, fortunes, and characters of others, as well as my own."

Upon Adams's request, the new secretary of state, Adams's Massachusetts colleague Daniel Webster, spoke to the secretary of the Navy about transporting the Africans home on a U.S. ship. When it became clear that Secretary Abel Upshur would do nothing, abolitionists organized a fund-raising tour for the former captives; during their many appearances, the Africans demonstrated their newly learned abilities to write, read the Bible, and pray. By November, the abolitionists had raised enough money to buy a ship and provisions for the sea voyage to Africa. On November 25, the thirty-five survivors, including the three children, sailed from New York on the *Gentleman*, reaching Sierra Leone fifty days later.

Denied legal custody of the Africans, the *Amistad,* and its cargo, Spain demanded that the United States pay reparations. In 1847, at the request of Secretary of State James Buchanan, the Senate proposed a $50,000 payment to satisfy the claim. The House killed the amendment, 113–40, after Adams argued against it in his last House speech. No reparations were ever paid, although Spain persisted in its demands until the Civil War.

The *Amistad* case reinforced Adams's determination to crusade against the slave trade and the South's efforts to plant the "peculiar institution" in new states and territories. "No one else will undertake it; no one but a spirit unconquerable by man, woman, or fiend can undertake it but with the heart of martyrdom."

Adams accepted the challenge with cheerful fatalism, aware that he was in a last race against old age and death. "My conscience presses me on; let me but die in the breach."

Chapter Ten

"Old Nestor"

"I see where the shoe pinches, Mr. Speaker.
It will pinch more yet. . . . I'll deal out to
the gentlemen a diet that they'll find it hard to digest!"

—John Quincy Adams, battling his congressional adversaries

"Well, that is the most extraordinary man on God's footstool."

—South Carolina Congressman Francis Pickens,
after John Quincy Adams's censure hearing defense

At the pinnacle of his reputation, popularity, and powers as an orator and debater, John Quincy Adams had become the congressional lightning rod on the slavery question. Abolitionists directed more petitions to him than to any other congressman. His biting, relentless attacks on the Gag Rule and the South's "peculiar institution" had placed him squarely in the South's crosshairs. In June 1841, Congressman Henry Wise of Virginia made a six-hour speech that was little more than a "continual invective" against Adams, who was more entertained than offended. In his diary, Adams described how Wise began each sentence with "a loud and vehement clatter," then bowed over his desk "till his head and chest became horizontal, his mouth pouring out all the time his words in a whisper. . . . He represented me as a fiend, the inspirer and leader of all abolition." Another annoyed Southern congressman proposed that the House "adopt some mode of getting rid of [Adams] peaceably, either by creating some office for him for life, or in such other as the wisdom of Congress might devise."

Southern animus toward abolitionism sometimes exploded in a shower of threats on the House floor. "Waste no more words," warned a Southern representative, "and if you really think you can effect your darling purpose of robbing us of our property, *come and try it*. . . . We will not meet you then with 'paper bullets of the brain,' but we will give you a reception that shall *touch your feelings*." A colleague vowed that abolitionists would first have to "march over hecatombs of bodies" before they would be permitted to emancipate Southern slaves.

The Gag Rule, which in 1840 was promoted to a House standing rule that substituted a ban on the very *reception* of slavery-related petitions for the previous automatic tabling of them, remained a barrier to the open debate of slavery. Six years after the Gag Rule was first enacted, it endured despite Adams's crusade to rescind it. Yet, public opinion was slowly turning against it, due to its obvious violation of constitutional rights and the avalanche of petitions denouncing slavery in the District of Columbia and opposing the admission of new slave states. The rule barely survived, as the support of Northern anti-abolitionist congressmen steadily ebbed. In December 1841, Adams's attempt to repeal the "permanent" Gag Rule failed by just three votes.

At an age when his contemporaries were winding up their earthly affairs, Adams improbably had become the subject of magazine profiles and the object of either reverence or hatred. "There he sits hour after hour, day after day, with untiring patience, never absent from his seat, never voting for an adjournment . . . his ear ever on alert, himself always prepared to go at once into the profoundest questions of state, or the minutest points of order," observed a *United States Magazine and Democratic Review* reporter. Unless he was ill, Adams attended every House session; he was one of the House's hardest-working members, and his name appeared in the official record more often than nearly any other congressman. "He looks enfeebled, but yet he is never tired; worn out, but ever ready for combat; melancholy, but let a witty thing fall from any member, and that old man's face is wreathed in smiles."

In the *Democratic Review* Adams was described as "a wonderful eccentric genius" with a phenomenal memory—all accounts suggest a photographic memory—who "belongs to no party, nor does any party belong to him. . . . He is original—of very peculiar ideas, and perfectly fearless and independent in expressing and maintaining them." Upon deciding to speak, "he rises abruptly, his face reddens, and, in a moment throwing himself into the attitude of a veteran gladiator, he . . . becomes full of gesticulation, his body sways to and fro—self-command seems almost lost—his head is bent forward in earnestness till it sometimes nearly touches the desk; his voice frequently breaks; but . . . nothing daunts him."

Adams's sarcastic eloquence made him a dangerous opponent, but his adversaries could not resist attacking him—thereby risking a withering riposte—because of his "wonderful power of exasperation." Ralph Waldo Emerson said Adams's advanced age and venerability were deceptive. "He is like one of those old cardinals, who, as quick as he is chosen Pope, throws away his crutches and his crookedness, and is as straight as a boy. He is an old roué, who cannot live on slops, but must have sulphuric acid in his tea." Woe to the man who challenged the accuracy of his statements, or his facts or dates. "Sure discomfiture awaited him," observed Adams's friend William Seward.

Even Adams's enemies respected his intellectual and oratorical powers. Wise of Virginia described him as "the acutest, the astutest, the archest enemy of Southern slavery that ever existed."

Benjamin French, chief clerk of the House and a staunch Democrat, was repelled by Adams's "sneering, bitter, *devilish*" manner, which made him appear to French "like a demon just from Hell, with all his passions under the influence of the red heat of the infernal regions."

It would have been surprising to those who saw only the stern and caustic Adams to learn that Martin Van Buren regarded him as "one of the most entertaining table companions of his day." When Van Buren was president, he had invited Adams to small White House dinners and had "always derived unqualified delight . . . and valuable information from his society."

Southerners were already seething over his irritating persistence in presenting petitions that were inevitably rejected because of the Gag Rule, when on January 21, 1842, Adams introduced new petitions—and touched off a firestorm in the House. Petitioners from Massachusetts were urging Congress to permit free blacks to own property and asking that action be taken against the thirteen slave states whose governments were "absolutely despotic, onerous and oppressive." Another Massachusetts petition declared that the signees would never take up arms to protect slaveholders. A petition from free black seamen sought redress for their mistreatment in Southern ports. All of the petitions were tabled without being received. Ohio Congressman Joshua Giddings observed "a deep feeling of hostility" rising against Adams.

Undeterred, Adams began reading a Pennsylvania Anti-Slavery Society petition stating that a U.S. war with England to uphold slavery would be more unjust than England's war in 1776 to keep America in bondage. The Speaker declared Adams to be out of order, but Adams continued to read until he was shouted down. The petition was tabled; Adams asked that it be printed, but his request was denied; Adams then asked that his request that it be printed be noted in the journal, and this, too, was refused.

Then he read a petition from Georgia requesting Adams's removal as chairman of the House Committee on Foreign Affairs, on the grounds that he was incompetent and biased against people of color. The petitioners suspected that Adams suffered from "a species of monomania on all subjects connected with people as dark as a Mexican." Although obviously a hoax, the petition survived a motion to table it, and Adams requested that he be permitted to defend himself. Events now began to unfold that would result in a determined attempt to censure the former president.

Still having the floor the next day, Adams delivered a scathing diatribe against slavery and the slave trade. Watching from the House gallery, Theodore Weld wrote to his wife and fellow abolitionist Angelina Grimké: "So the Old Nestor," as Weld sometimes called Adams, likening him to the aged Greek king who inspired young warriors at Troy to fight harder, "lifted up his voice like a trumpet, till slaveholding, slave trading and slave breeding absolutely quailed and howled under his dissecting knife." Angry Southerners milled around where Adams stood speaking, shouting, "That is false! I *demand* Mr. Speaker that you *put him down!*" and, "I demand that you shut the mouth of that old harlequin!" Every two or three minutes, wrote Weld, "a perfect uproar like Babel would burst forth . . . as Mr. A. with his bold surgery would smite his cleaver into the very bones."

Adams shot back at the adversaries crowded around him, "I see where the shoe pinches, Mr. Speaker. It will pinch *more* yet. . . . I'll deal out to the gentlemen a diet that they'll find it hard to digest!" Over objections and shouted protests, Adams continued speaking until the Speaker pronounced him to be out of order and declared that he "must take his seat." Adams replied, "I am in my seat," and continued to speak. Congressmen shouted, "Sit down, sit down, oh, let him go on!" Adams promised to give them "further cause for reflection before I have done" and resumed presenting petitions.

Still retaining the floor on January 24, Adams lit the match. Because he revered the right to petition, Adams occasionally introduced petitions that were abhorrent to him, such as one from Virginia asking Congress to require all free blacks to be sold as slaves or be expelled from the United States. Now, he presented a petition from Haverhill, Massachusetts, calling for the dissolution of the United States, as it "does not present prospects of reciprocal benefits . . . because a vast proportion of the resources of one section of the Union is annually drained to sustain the views and course of another section without any adequate return." Adams's colleagues were stunned. "This is a petition for the dissolution of the Union," Isaac Holmes of South Carolina said in wonder.

As Adams calmly proposed that the offending Massachusetts petition be referred to a select committee, Southern congressmen angrily interrupted with the suggestion that the petition be burned. Wise of Virginia asked if it would be in order to "censure any member presenting such a petition," and he then asked the House to proceed accordingly. "Good!" replied Adams.

That night, Southern Whigs caucused in a House committee room and began drafting a resolution to censure their maverick fellow Whig, Adams, whose hurricane-force assaults on slavery threatened to split the party along geographical lines.

Reports of Adams's impending censure spread throughout Washington, with the result that when the House reconvened on January 25, the visitors' galleries were full. Congressmen Thomas Gilmer of Virginia and Thomas Marshall of Kentucky, a nephew of the late Supreme Court chief justice, presented the censure resolutions. Marshall's resolution asserted that Adams's introduction of the offending petition was tantamount to espousing "the destruction of our country and the crime of high treason." Another of the resolutions called for Adams's "expulsion from the national councils." Adams's conduct could not be ignored this time, declared Marshall. "He, sir, from whom the proposition was made to pull down the temple of liberty, was once its high priest and ministered at its altar. It was no obscure hand and no obscure name that was connected with this procedure."

The Constitution defines treason, shot back Adams, "and it is not for [Marshall], or his puny mind, to define what high treason is, and confound it with what I have done." He asked the clerk to read the first paragraph of the Declaration of Independence. "The first paragraph of the Declaration of Independence!" Adams shouted twice. As the clerk read it, Adams repeated the words asserting the people's "right and duty to alter or abolish" government after "a long train of abuses and usurpations." "I rest that petition on the Declaration of Independence," he declared, but added that he wished to say to the Massachusetts petitioners that it was not yet time for the dissolution of the Union, and that a greater grievance was the suppression of the right to petition.

Adams promised to show during his defense that the South wished to destroy the essential rights of habeas corpus and trial by jury, as well as other constitutional liberties. If the South prevailed, worse would come, he predicted. "We shall next have a declaration that it is high treason to ask for the abolishment of slavery in the District of Columbia; that it is high treason to ask for the prohibition of the infamous slave trade." The threat of prosecution might then be used to compel congressmen to vote for legislation they opposed, Adams warned. "If a repeal of the Bankrupt law, hurried through without the ordinary forms of legislation, is objected to, why, make it high treason."

Wise of Virginia made the astounding assertion that Adams was acting in concert with a sinister English plot whose aim was to overthrow the United States, to free its slaves, and to establish a monarchy that would turn white Americans into virtual slaves. It was well known, said Wise, that Adams had been a member of "the old English party"—the Federalist Party. Now, he had fallen under the sway of English abolitionists, whose "foreign emissary [referring to abolitionist Joseph Sturge, the English Quaker who had founded the British Anti-Slavery Society] . . . openly appealed to Americans against their own Government." But Adams could never carry out the British abolitionists' "vile aims" because he was "politically dead, dead as Burr, dead as Arnold. The people would look upon him with wonder, would shudder, and retire."

While Adams appeared to stand alone against Southern and Western Whigs as well as Democrats, who were enjoying the spectacle of a family quarrel among Whigs, Adams was not utterly forsaken. The abolitionists, in the persons of the redoubtable Theodore Weld and Joshua Leavitt, came to Adams's aid. Weld and Leavitt lived with the House's abolition "insurgency," as they called themselves, in Mrs. Spriggs's boardinghouse, located across the park from the Capitol and nicknamed "Abolition House." The self-proclaimed House insurgents included congressmen Giddings of Ohio, Seth Gates of New York, and William Slade of Vermont. Leavitt was reporting for the *Emancipator* while lobbying Giddings, Slade, Gates, and Adams to introduce bills, petitions, and resolutions whose purpose was to provoke a debate on slavery.

With Adams facing possible censure, the insurgency huddled in Giddings's room and agreed that Leavitt and Weld would assist the embattled ex-president in preparing his defense. "I . . . offered him my services to relieve him from the drudgery of gathering the requisite materials for his defense," Weld wrote to his wife Angelina. The gesture delighted Adams. "I accept your offer gratefully," Adams replied, according to Weld.

The Anti-Slavery Society had begun emphasizing local organizing efforts after its big petition push in 1837, with the result that more congressmen with abolitionist leanings were being elected in the

North. Then, Weld and the society's other leaders decided to formally dissolve the organization in 1840. But William Lloyd Garrison, editor of the *Liberator* and a controversial and sometimes polarizing figure within the abolitionist movement, took it over, and its operational headquarters moved from New York to Boston. Weld, Leavitt, and their allies, meanwhile, threw themselves into lobbying Congress, with Leavitt moving to Washington in January 1841, and Weld joining Leavitt at the end of the year. Abolition House became a magnet for antislavery petitions from around the country, which were then doled out to congressional allies for presentation. Giddings described Mrs. Spriggs's boardinghouse as "the headquarters of abolitionism."

Theodore Weld attended the White House reception on New Year's Day 1842. Its "pomp and tinsel, fashion and display of magnificence" made him sad and uneasy. From the White House, Weld walked to the Adamses' levee, where the former president impressed Weld at their first meeting. "[I] found him and his wife living in a plain home, plainly furnished, and themselves plainly dressed—the old gentleman *very* plainly," he wrote to his wife. A week later, Weld, Leavitt, and the antislavery "insurgents" dined at the home of the Adamses. "The old patriarch talked with as much energy and zeal as a Methodist at a camp meeting," wrote Weld. "Remarkable man."

A vegetarian and teetotaler, Weld exercised in the Capitol park in the early mornings: "I walk, run, and jump about an hour every morning before breakfast," he informed his wife. The rest of the day, he worked in an alcove at the Library of Congress, from which he supplied abolitionist congressmen with ammunition for their forays against slavery. But with Adams now under attack, Weld channeled his enormous energy into collecting material for his defense. At the height of the censure hearing, Weld wrote, "We are not the agents God has chosen for the deliverance of the slave if fear of *anything* swerves us from duty."

While working together to thwart Adams's censure and expulsion from the House, Adams and Weld became friends. Adams's vigor astonished Weld. After watching Adams fend off his opponents' ferocious assaults for hours in the House one afternoon, Weld went to Adams's home to help him prepare the next day's defense. "He came to meet me as fresh and elastic as a boy," Weld informed Angelina. "I told him I was afraid he had tired himself out. 'No, not at all,' said he, 'I am all ready for another heat.'" Adams rehearsed the main points of his next day's speech in a loud voice, as though addressing a large audience. Although Weld tried to convince Adams to save his strength for the next day, "it was all in vain. . . . Wonderful man!"

During one of their nighttime sessions, Weld and Adams discovered that they were distant relatives and that Weld's father, Ludovicus Weld, had been a Harvard classmate of Adams's. Moreover, Weld's grandfather Ezra Weld, a Congregational minister at Braintree, had baptized Adams. The stories that Adams told Weld about Weld's family were passed down by Weld to his children.

John Quincy Adams's censure trial was the sensation of Washington—and small wonder. A former president stood accused in the House of Representatives of committing high treason, for having presented a petition espousing the dissolution of the United States because of the "peculiar institution" that the South so desperately wished not to discuss. And Adams was not only an ex-president, he was the son of a president, a living symbol of the Revolution and America's founding, and a man of the highest moral fiber who had devoted his life to serving his country. Each day, people filled the galleries and thronged the hallways long before the House convened at its usual hour, noon. Foreign ministers, attachés, and other personages crowded the House lobbies and the areas inside the chamber where spectators were permitted. They came to watch Adams battle his enemies on the House floor. The spectacle lasted nine days.

Anyone could see that Ralph Waldo Emerson was right in describing Adams as a "bruiser"; he clearly relished this rare opportunity to speak without interruption about slavery. Adams declared that he would disdain the House's mercy. "I defy them. I have constituents to go to that will have something to say if this House expels me." Even as Congressmen Thomas Marshall, Thomas Gilmer, and Henry Wise were presenting their case against Adams, he was fighting back. When Marshall sedulously remarked that Adams would withdraw the petition to dissolve the Union over slavery if he, "instead of looking into books, could travel among us," Adams interjected, "They would lynch me." Replied Marshall, "If you endeavored to kindle the flame there which you do here, I must admit that, in all probability, they would." Said Adams, "You are doing them that service now, as much as you can." Exasperated, Marshall responded, "It is the gentleman's privilege to interrupt and to insult every man on this floor; it is his privilege, and I accord it to him freely."

Wise said Adams was not "mad," but that if he were indeed suffering from "monomania," as the Georgia petitioners had alleged, "no matter what might be its cause, it was dangerous—deadly."

Gilmer said he wished "to prevent the music" of Adams, who was a "poet, fiddler, statesman, and buffoon." Days later, Adams received a letter with a sketch of himself, with a rifle ball in his forehead. Beneath the drawing were written the words, "Stop the music of John Quincy Adams," and "statesman, poet, babbler, and buffoon." Adams displayed the letter and drawing to the House, remarking that the members presumably knew its source, but he noted that Gilmer had said "fiddler," not "babbler." Adams made a joke of it: That he was "a babbler I cannot deny, but that I am a fiddler was a new discovery." His comment evoked laughter.

When it was Adams's turn to speak, he chastised Marshall as though he were a wayward boy. If he were Marshall's father, he said, he would advise him to return to Kentucky, go to law school, "and *commence* the study of that profession which he has so long disgraced." Marshall stood, with arms crossed, and faced Adams, who then launched a scorching attack on the "dark conclave of conspirators" that sought to arraign him for "half a dozen capital crimes" and censure him for having presented a petition. Show me, he said, where in the Constitution it says that it is a crime to present a petition. "Was there a Government on the face of the earth that would punish a man for a crime, when there was no law which constituted that crime?" He charged there was "a conspiracy here, concocted in this house, for the purpose of ruining me." Adams jeered at "the nullifiers" for wanting to punish him for having presented a petition "exactly agreeing with [their] views."

"A breathless silence reigned throughout the hall and in the vast galleries," wrote Giddings. "There was no loud breathing, no rustling of garments; reporters laid down their pens." Adams declared that the House had no jurisdiction to try or punish him for high treason, a capital crime for which "the life of the party accused is at stake." He repeatedly demanded a criminal court trial, government documents, and a postponement to prepare his defense. Gleefully, Adams said he might argue his case for ninety days.

Adams turned his rhetorical guns on another architect of the charges against him, Henry Wise. He recalled that four years earlier, the House had attempted to try the Virginian for murder, for having been a second at the duel in which Congressmen Graves of Kentucky had killed Congressman Cilley of Maine. But a special committee had pronounced the matter beyond Congress's jurisdiction—even though Wise had entered the chamber "with his hands and face dripping with the blood of murder, the blotches of which were yet hanging upon him." Wise, Adams said, was undoubtedly the guilty man, and Graves, the man who pulled the trigger, nothing but an instrument in his hands. Yet Wise had avoided punishment, while Adams was now being tried for his life, for having presented a petition.

Adams accused Southerners of kidnapping free blacks from the North and enslaving them and presented resolutions calling for government documents that Adams said would support the allegation. He then read from a pamphlet that compared New York State's rise to prominence with Virginia's corresponding decline—the pamphlet attributed Virginia's demise to slavery—and that questioned whether slavery should continue to be tolerated. "And now, who is the author of these glorious sentiments?" Adams asked triumphantly. The author was Thomas Marshall, who was now attempting to restore his "broken reputation" in the South by "turning like a tiger on another man with charges equally false with those under which he had himself suffered," for having written the pamphlet. Marshall responded reproachfully, "I knew that the gentleman respected nobody." Replied Adams, "Ah! The gentleman is touched, is he? He makes a personal matter where I intended none. These [the pamphlet's words] are glorious sentiments. Would to God I had powers of eloquence equal to the utterance of such language." Marshall's political career did not recover from this blow, and he did not seek re-election.

Adams deplored the time wasted on the proceeding and said he would not oppose any attempt to table the censure resolution. But when just such a motion was made—for the third time—it failed, 100–90. The spectacle continued.

Benjamin French, the House's chief clerk, was staggered by Adams's virulence. "He spares no one. . . . He has exhibited more temper, more obstinacy, & more desire to attack everybody, friend & foe indiscriminately, than I ever saw either him or any other mortal exhibit before." Indeed, the Washington newspapers stopped carrying Adams's speeches when he rebuked them on the House floor for inaccurately reporting his remarks. "So they refuse to report them at all," Weld informed his wife, adding, "Old Nestor has cast all their counsels headlong, turned all their guns against themselves, and smitten the whole host with dismay and discomfiture."

Gilmer offered to drop his charges if Adams would withdraw the offending Haverhill petition. Adams declined. The House's reaction to the petition perfectly illustrated the issue at hand, he said. Withdrawing it would be tantamount to sacrificing the right of petition and, indeed, the very right to liberty. Southern congressmen incorrectly believed they had truncated all discussion of slavery by gagging Northern congressmen and their antislavery petitions. "It would *not* be ended," said Adams. "They would have the people coming here . . . 'besieging, not beseeching.'" He advised his prosecutors to read the Northern newspapers' condemnations of the proceeding. To Lewis Tappan, Weld wrote, "Yesterday and today Mr. A. has accomplished more for our cause than at any previous stage."

Sitting in church on February 6, Adams's mind drifted to the "fiery ordeal . . . the struggle to avert my ruin" that now absorbed him day and night. As the service proceeded around him, he pondered the fact that "one hundred members of the House represent slaves; four-fifths of whom would crucify me if their vote could erect the cross; forty members, representatives of the free, in the league of slavery and mock Democracy, would break me on the wheel, if their votes or wishes could turn it round." Many of the rest were poised to desert him at the "very first scintillation of indiscretion on my part." But amazingly, despite the forces arrayed against him, Adams left the church confident that he would survive the attack on him.

The next day, Congressman John Botts, a Virginia Whig, moved a fourth time to lay the censure resolution on the table, and this time the motion carried, 106–93. The House then tabled the Haverhill petition that had started it all, 166–40.

Adams's "fiery ordeal" was ended. Abolitionists believed they had won a major victory. "I am confident that the charm of the slave-power is *now broken*," wrote Joshua Leavitt. "The triumph of Mr. A. is complete," Weld announced in a letter to Angelina. "This is the first victory over the slaveholders *in a body* ever yet achieved since the foundation of the government, and from this time their downfall takes its date." Giddings pronounced Adams's victory to be "not only complete but important," because he "had now met the advocates of slavery upon their chosen field of combat, had driven them from the conflict."

Even Adams's Southern adversaries grudgingly professed admiration for his intellectual and rhetorical gifts. "They call Adams a man of one idea," South Carolina Congressman Isaac Holmes was heard to say, "but I tell you what it is, he has got more ideas than all of us put together." South Carolina Congressman Francis Pickens remarked, "Well, that is the most extraordinary man on God's footstool." Even Marshall, badly mauled by Adams's rhetorical onslaught, granted that if somehow Adams could be removed or silenced on the subject of slavery, "none other, I believe, could be found hardy enough, or bad enough, to fill his place."

While Adams was undergoing his ordeal, Charles Dickens, who had recently dazzled British readers with his serialized *Oliver Twist* and *The Old Curiosity Shop*, was in the middle of a disheartening trip through Virginia, where he observed "an air of ruin and decay abroad," which he ascribed largely to Southern slavery. Arriving in Washington just days after the censure battle had ended, Dickens welcomed the news of Adams's triumph as an anodyne to his dismay at the coexistence in America's capital city of the actual Declaration of Independence with its antithesis, slavery. "It was but a week since this old man [Adams] had stood for days upon his trial before this very body, charged with having dared to assert the infamy of that traffic which has for its accursed merchandise men and women." Adams was "a lasting honor to the land that gave him birth . . . and . . . will be remembered scores upon scores of years after the worms bred in its corruption are but so many grains of dust."

Eight congressmen resigned from the House Committee on Foreign Affairs as a protest against Adams's refusal to step down as chairman. In the February 15 *National Intelligencer*, three of them published letters that Adams characterized as "so insulting personally to me that they are unquestionably breaches of privilege." He chose to ignore them, but he was under no illusion that his recent victory had routed his enemies. Twice in five years, they had tried to censure him "for the single offence of persisting to assert the right of the people to petition, and the freedom of speech, and of the press." They had not given up. "The leader of the associated legion banded against me has had the candor to avow his motive of hunting me like a partridge upon the mountains."

Having failed to silence Adams, the Whig leadership six weeks later took aim at Ohio Congressman Joshua Giddings, one of the self-proclaimed House "insurgents" of Abolition House. In October 1841, 135 slaves had mutinied while being transported on the *Creole* from Virginia to New Orleans. They killed a crewman and forced the mate to sail to Bermuda. There, British authorities tried the murderers and freed the rest of the slaves. In vain, the U.S. government demanded that Britain return "the mutineers and murderers." Giddings presented resolutions upholding the mutineer slaves' right to go free. Angry Southerners tabled the resolutions, proposed Giddings's censure, and voted its approval, 125–69. Giddings promptly resigned.

This lightning stroke stunned Adams. "Giddings rose from his seat, came over to mine, shook cordially my hand and took leave. I had a voice only to say, 'I hope we shall soon have you back again.'"

Adams's wish was quickly fulfilled. In April, Giddings's constituents re-elected him to the seat that he had just vacated, and by the end of May he was again at his desk in the House—and again presenting his *Creole* resolutions, this time without the threat of censure.

Discouraged Whig leaders gave up their high-handed efforts, now twice thwarted, to squelch the insurgency within their party. It was nothing less than a watershed in American politics: the commencement of the sectional realignment that foreshadowed the Civil War. By the 1850s, tensions between abolitionist and "cotton" Whigs would fracture the party, preparing the way for the rise of the Republican Party, a fusion of Northern Democrats and Northern Whigs whose greatest champion would be Abraham Lincoln.

Chapter Eleven

Triumph

"It is hard to steer and row against
wind and tide, but even in the agony of death we
must say, like Lawrence, 'Don't give up the ship.'"

—John Quincy Adams,
on his struggle against slavery and old age

---

y mind and body are rapidly falling into decay,"
John Quincy Adams wrote after leg cramps
awakened him one night and loosed a flood of
sobering middle-of-the-night thoughts. "The position that I have
taken is arduous enough to crush any man in the vigor of youth;
but . . . with failing senses and blunted instruments, surrounded by
remorseless enemies and false and scary and treacherous friends,
how can it end but in ruin? But I must meet the shock."

As Adams passed the midpoint of his seventies, these episodes
of memento mori happened more often. When he walked up a hill
in Quincy one day to watch the sun set, he spied "the shaft of the
Bunker Hill monument," and it occurred to him that eighty years
earlier to the very day, his parents had been married. "Not a soul
now lives who was then in the bloom of life. . . . My own term—
how soon it will close! . . . What a phantasmagoria is human life!"

It was becoming increasingly difficult to keep up his diary, but he somehow managed. "I rose this morning at four, and with smarting, bloodshot eye, and shivering hand, still sat down and wrote . . . but my stern-chase after Time is, to borrow a simile from Tom Paine, like the race of a man with a wooden leg after a horse." Another time, exhausted after preparing and delivering a speech to the Young Men's Whig Club, he described his struggle against old age in nautical terms: "it is hard to steer and row against wind and tide, but even in the agony of death we must say, like Lawrence, 'Don't give up the ship.'"

Even while battling the dragons of slavery, his enemies in Congress, and encroaching age, the septuagenarian Adams struggled with the quotidian. There were cash-flow problems: He was forced to sell off some property to repay a $5,000 loan from his former valet, Antoine Guista; he was dunned for coal and wood payments; and he owed pew rental at St. John's Church and back pay to his servants. To economize, Adams walked to the Capitol rather than pay 25 cents for a hack.

At times, it must have seemed to Adams that he could please no one. Even Louisa chided him—for procrastination on his father's biography. Even though she and her husband were living under the same roof, she wrote him the kind of admonishing letter that Adams had once written to his sons. Why had he not repaid his parents "for their inappreciable blessings?" she wanted to know. "Let me implore you to commune with your own heart, and do justice to yourself as well as to them and to redeem the past in exertion for the future." For once, Adams had no rejoinder other than, "Good advice." Adams still reproved himself whenever he wasted a day, even when ill. "As the hours pass over in succession, I know I might be working," he wrote while in his sickbed one day. "I brood over projected labors and never commence working. . . . Approaching midnight summons me to repose, and I have lost a day."

Whether he was aware of it or not, Adams's predawn walks and his immersion in nature were tonics for his inclination to brood. In the warmth of summertime, even when he was in his eighth decade, Adams could not resist taking an occasional dip in the Potomac. He wrote in his diary, "From the practice of personal ablution and the exercise of swimming I cannot totally abstain, for I believe they have promoted my health and prolonged my life many years."

Just as swimming toned up his body, witnessing the rising and setting of the sun renewed Adams's spirit and his sense of God's presence in the world. "The pleasure that I take in witnessing these magnificent phenomena of physical nature never tires; it is a part of my own nature, unintelligible to others, and, I suppose, a singularity which I should suppress or renounce."

"The struggle," as Adams characterized his long battle against slavery, "can terminate only with my life." In the meantime, he tried to improve his speaking skills, finally hitting upon a speech preparation method that ensured that he would consistently meet the House's one-hour limit, yet that enabled him to easily expand an address, if circumstances warranted it, to two hours or more. Highly critical of himself as always, Adams pronounced his new method "but partially successful."

Retirement was an impossibility, but not because Adams was reluctant to abandon his crusade against slavery, or believed himself indispensable as a representative of Massachusetts's 8th Congressional District (before 1842, the 12th District). "I cannot afford it," he confessed, but added that another reason—and certainly the paramount one—was "the vacuity of occupation in which I could take an interest."

Adams, who despised Andrew Jackson and distrusted Martin Van Buren, rated President John Tyler, the first "accidental president," as a "mediocrity." Tyler also proved to be an inept politician. Elected vice president in 1840, Tyler reached the White House upon the unexpected death of William Henry Harrison, a Whig whom Adams described as "amiable and benevolent," only a month after his inauguration. Tyler was "a political sectarian, of the slave-driving, Virginian, Jeffersonian school," wrote Adams, and "incapable of expansion to the dimensions of the station on which he has been cast by the hand of Providence." As a U.S. senator, Tyler had abandoned the Democratic Party when he voted to censure Jackson for withdrawing funds from the Second Bank of the United States. But when he became president, Tyler angered Whigs by vetoing two bills to re-establish the national bank; he was expelled from the Whig Party, and his cabinet resigned in protest. Muttering about impeachment when Tyler vetoed an import duties bill, Adams complained that the government was "in a state of suspended animation, strangled by the *five* times repeated stricture [veto] of the executive cord."

Thus, it was not surprising that Adams, who had boycotted Andrew Jackson's inauguration and his honorary degree ceremony at Harvard, also embargoed the commemoration of Boston's Bunker Hill monument, for the reason that Tyler would be present. It made no difference to Adams that as a boy he and his mother had in fact witnessed the actual battle from Penn's Hill in Braintree, or that Daniel Webster had invited him to attend as a guest of honor. "Upon this pageant has been engrafted another, to bedaub with glory John Tyler, the slave-breeder," he wrote in disgust, "who is coming with all his court, in gaudy trappings of mock royalty, to receive the homage of hungry sycophants, under color of doing homage to the principles of Bunker Hill martyrdom." Webster, and Tyler, too, hoped to "whistle back his Whig friends, whom he had cast off, as a huntsman his pack, and who now threaten to hunt him, like the hounds of Actaeon." While cannon thundered in the distance, Adams spent the day alone at home in Quincy fuming that the president and his entourage would retire to Faneuil Hall "to swill like swine, and grunt about the rights of man." Yet the cannons' roar, too, revived memories of smoke, fire, and cannonades witnessed by a seven-year-old boy sixty-eight years past.

As Adams dined one day in February 1844 with General of the Army Winfield Scott and others, a man burst in to report an explosion on the USS *Princeton* during a tour by President Tyler and other dignitaries. The warship's big gun, "Peacemaker," had blown up during a demonstration, killing five men, including Secretary of State Abel Upshur and Secretary of the Navy Thomas W. Gilmer. Of Gilmer, who had attempted to censure him two years earlier, Adams unsympathetically observed, "His instantaneous and violent death . . . may point a moral, but will not heal the wound inflicted upon freedom and the rights of human nature by his life." Amid the smoke and flames, Tyler had carried to safety Julia Gardner, whose father, David, died in the explosion. Months later, the fifty-four-year-old widower president married the twenty-three-year-old New York socialite. "Captain Tyler and his bride are the laughing-stock of the city," reported Adams with a tincture of satisfaction. "Under circumstances of revolting indecency, [he] is performing with a young girl from New York the old fable of January and May."

Adams was dismayed when his old adversary, former House Speaker James K. Polk of Tennessee, won the 1844 presidential election. Because Polk favored the annexation of Texas, Adams had campaigned for Henry Clay, who opposed it. Polk's election, Adams believed, surely portended events that would result in "my retirement from public life"—although he had just been re-elected to an eighth House term by 2,000 more votes than he had received in 1842. "It is the victory of the slavery element in the Constitution of the United States. Providence, I trust, intends it for wise purposes, and will direct it to good ends. . . . My removal now is but a few days in advance of the doom of nature." Adams was unmoved by Polk's pledge to be president "of the whole people," believing him to be "sold body and soul to that grim idol, half albino, half negro, the compound of Democracy and of slavery, which, by the slave-representation in Congress, rules and ruins the Union." Although invited, Adams attended neither Polk's inauguration nor the two inaugural balls.

His manifest discontent radiated outward to encompass John Calhoun, "the high priest of Moloch, the embodied spirit of slavery"; Stephen Douglas, who "had the air and aspect of a half-naked pugilist"; and even the Transcendentalists and Utopians. The Utopian leader, Robert Owen, had come to Adams to request a portion of James Smithson's bequest to carry out his plan for a new order of society, one renouncing war and poverty. Adams was unmoved; he knew all about Owen's utopian community in New Harmony, Indiana, which had failed, and had read part of his book, "a farrago of confused, indefinite ideas." Wrote Adams, "All this I had heard twenty-five years ago, and the humbug is too stale." Owens received no public money.

By challenging the status quo, Transcendentalists, who sought knowledge through nature and "spiritual intuition," offended Adams's reverence for society's institutions. "Transcendentalists not only dig up the corner-stones of human society, but pronounce them decayed, rotten, and worthless," Adams irately noted. Their putative leader, Ralph Waldo Emerson, a minister-cum-skeptic, was the son of a friend of Adams, William Emerson, and the former Harvard classmate of Adams's late son, George. This did not mitigate Adams's displeasure with Emerson or Transcendentalism, whose "deadly sophistry . . . consists in the alliance of atheism with hypocrisy," and whose "bubbling cauldron of religion and politics . . . dregs and froth . . . are boiled up into one impure and poisonous compound and administered to the body politic for healing medicine" and to incite the working class to hatred and violence. It was "every man's duty [to] take the field" against this "sect," Adams believed.

His victory in 1842 over the enemies who had tried to censure him and his constituents' emphatic vote of confidence in that fall's election freed Adams to fearlessly crusade on behalf of the right of petition. At a rally in Braintree, after marching in a procession held in his honor, Adams described the situation regarding the "permanent" Gag Rule, which prohibited even the reception of slavery petitions, and his efforts to defeat it. "Your enjoyment of the right of petition to the Congress of the United States, and that of every freeman in this Union, rests upon the arbitrary fiat of the slaveholding Speaker. Would to God that I could give you any encouragement to expect a better order of things in this respect."

But he could now take greater risks, knowing that he would not be censured and that he was supported by his constituents and, in fact, by the state of Massachusetts. Adams encouraged his friends at Abolition House to open the petition stopcocks, and he continued to present antislavery petitions in Congress over the vehement protests of his Southern colleagues. He denounced the Gag Rule whenever possible, while trying to file down its sharp edges so slavery petitions would at least be received, even if they were then tabled. His so-called "Adams Gag"—unpopular among abolitionists, who opposed gags of any kind, and never adopted—would have deposited these objectionable petitions directly with the House Speaker, who could then dispose of them as he pleased. Another proposal by Adams would have required the reception of all petitions, but those unacceptable to a House majority could be tabled without being read or discussed.

When Adams attempted to rescind the Gag Rule in December 1843, his amendment failed by just 95–91, and a committee that included Adams was appointed to review all the House rules. One of the committee's recommendations was to eliminate the Gag Rule; it and the committee's other proposals were tabled, 88–87. By doggedly keeping the right of petition alive as an issue, Adams was slowly wearing down his adversaries—and winning over Northern Democrats, one by one.

Adams's censure ordeal had inspired a determination not only to restore the right of petition in Congress but to defeat slavery. Although he was more than ever the antislavery movement's great champion, he had yet to declare himself an avowed abolitionist. But he was one, he finally acknowledged in private notes for a speech on the annexation of Texas and the right to petition. "If the most ardent desire, and a most vivid hope of the total extinction of Slavery on Earth, and especially at no distant day throughout this North American Union, constitutes an abolitionist, I am one, to the extent of readiness to lay down my life in the cause." He would one day declare himself so, he pledged in his diary. "Before my lamp is burnt out, I am desirous that my opinions concerning the great movement throughout the civilized world for the abolition of slavery should be explicitly avowed and declared. God grant that they may contribute to the final consummation of that event!"

Adams had demonstrated a rare willingness for someone of his years to challenge his own assumptions and fixed opinions about slavery and then to make a last, great ideological leap to an abolition position. It had been a long journey spanning decades—one that began in obliviousness and then progressed to a dawning awareness of the implications of the 1820 Missouri Compromise; thence to a moral revulsion tempered by fears that pushing too hard for abolition might shatter the Union; and finally, to a conviction that civil war was inevitable, with the alternative being a surrender of constitutional liberties to the South. Not only had Adams's beliefs evolved on slavery, but the evolution had occurred despite overwhelming opposition from colleagues in Congress and under the all-seeing eye of public opinion. Some credit surely was due Adams's abolitionist collaborators—Theodore Weld, Joshua Leavitt, Joshua Giddings, and Lewis Tappan—for arousing his moral objections to slavery to such a pitch that they vanquished his fear of upsetting the tense equipoise between North and South. But it was Adams who took the risks by choosing to steer by his moral principles.

Louisa Adams, who had previously exhorted her husband to break with the abolitionists, underwent a similar conversion. It happened after she began corresponding with Theodore Weld's sister-in-law, Sarah Grimké, who challenged Louisa to become an activist on abolition and women's rights. As a consequence, Louisa's opposition to slavery grew to the extent that she became a contributor to *Slavery As It Is*, the collection of slavery horror stories edited by Weld, Sarah Grimké, and her sister Angelina. Later, Louisa helped purchase the freedom of her cook, Julia, using money she inherited from her brother, Thomas Johnson.

Adams's opening salvo as an avowed abolitionist was a letter to the people of Bangor, Maine, who had invited him to speak at a tenth anniversary celebration of Britain's abolition of slavery on July 4, 1843. Adams did not attend the commemoration, but his letter, as he had intended, was no less than a manifesto for emancipation and a frontal assault on the Constitution's concession to slaveholders, the three-fifths rule. "The soul of one man cannot by human law be made the property of another," he declared. Yet, "by a fraudulent perversion of the Constitution," not only was slavery sanctioned in the United States, but slave owners could use their human chattels, counting each one as three-fifths of a white man, to increase their representation in Congress without granting them any human rights. The founders' compromise with the slave power had encouraged slaveholders to commit even greater outrages: rifling the mail and destroying abolitionist flyers mailed to the South; denying habeas corpus to escaped slaves; and jailing black sailors in the South. "Have we not seen printing-presses destroyed; halls erected for the promotion of human freedom leveled with the dust, and consumed by fire; and wanton, unprovoked murder, perpetrated with impunity, by slave-mongers? Have we not seen human beings, made in the likeness of God, and endowed with immortal souls, burnt at the stake, not for their offences but for their color?"

His letter was widely reprinted, but evidently no one noticed that Adams, already known far and wide as the great enemy of slavery, had crossed an invisible boundary of importance only to him and a few abolitionists. He had purposely made the letter "bold and startling": "I meant it as a note of defiance to all the slave-holders, slave-breeders, and slave-traders upon earth." Yet his bold pronouncement had received little attention, "the worst fate that can befall it."

But he did not stop. During a House debate, Alabama Congressman James Dellet quoted from a speech in which Adams had predicted the emancipation of blacks, "whether in peace or blood, let it come." As all eyes shifted to Adams, he forcefully enunciated, "I say *now*, let it come. . . . Though it cost the blood of millions of white men, let it come. Let justice be done though the heavens fall." Ohio Congressman Joshua Giddings, who was present, observed, "A sensation of horror ran through the ranks of the slave-holders . . . all were silent and solemn."

"My soul is oppressed," Adams wrote after making this pronouncement; the struggle between slavery and abolition could only end in calamity. "The deepest of my afflictions is the degeneracy of my country from the principles which gave her existence, and the ruin irreparable of them all, under the transcendent power of slavery and the slave-representation." Such thoughts were still preying on his mind and spirits when he visited Governor William Seward's home in Auburn, New York. At breakfast someone suggested that slavery might be peacefully abolished in twenty to fifty years, and Adams, who had been lost in thought, snapped to alertness and said, "I am satisfied that it will not go down until it goes down in blood."

In an 1836 speech in which he derogated proposals to annex Texas as disguised attempts to expand slavery, Adams had suggested that in the event of a civil war, the president had the power to emancipate the slaves. After his Southern colleagues' failure to censure him, Adams was emboldened to elaborate on this theme in a House speech that "stung the slaveocracy to madness," observed his son, Charles Francis. In wartime or amid a slave insurrection, declared Adams, "an invaded country has all its laws and municipal institutions swept by the board ... [and] the laws of war are in force." One unwritten wartime law permits "the commanders of both armies ... to emancipate all the slaves in the invaded territory. ... I lay this down as the law of nations. ... Not only the President of the United States but the commander of the army has the power to order the universal emancipation of the slaves." These very actions were taken by Union generals at the Civil War's outset, and then by President Abraham Lincoln in his 1863 Emancipation Proclamation.

Adams's popularity was at its zenith. Before his triumphal journey to Cincinnati to dedicate its observatory, Adams, his daughter-in-law Abigail, her father, and a grandson visited upstate New York, where they were welcomed with cannon salutes, bell-ringing, speeches, parades, and an unending procession of dinners. Five thousand people greeted him in Buffalo, where a future president, Millard Fillmore, delivered the welcoming address. In Auburn, several hundred free blacks paraded with lit torches. In Utica, men unharnessed the horses from the Adamses' carriage and pulled the carriage themselves. Women waved handkerchiefs from mansion and hotel balconies in Saratoga Springs. Crowds stood in the rain awaiting his arrival at Niagara Falls. And in Montreal, the Canadians lining his parade route waved small American flags.

"Old Man Eloquent," as newspapers had taken to sometimes calling Adams (from Milton's "Sonnet 10"), addressed constituents and lyceums in Boston, Salem, Lowell, Lynn, and Brookline. In Braintree, banners proclaiming, "Let there be light!" hung around the pulpit where he spoke for three and a half hours, and where he was serenaded with an ode sung in his honor, set to the music of "My Country, 'Tis of Thee." Its five stanzas included these lines: "Times shall touch the page/That tells how Quincy's sage/Has dared to live."

People accosted him on his daily walks in Quincy and crowded around him to shake his hand when he rode the steamships between Quincy and Washington. A literate black tailor from South Carolina, Joseph P. Humphries, called at Adams's Quincy home, seeking advice on whether he should settle in Boston or in the Massachusetts countryside. Adams recommended Boston; there he could ply his trade and live among other free blacks. "He cannot live in that glorious exemplification of democracy, the State of South Carolina," Adams noted with deep sarcasm.

He remained the living symbol of the nation's origins. In New York State, Governor Seward observed, "The hand we now so eagerly grasp, was pressed in confidence and friendship by the Father of our Country." Congressmen asked Adams to sponsor a resolution placing George Washington's Revolutionary War sword and a cane belonging to Benjamin Franklin in Joel Poinsett's National Institute for the Promotion of Science and the Useful Arts.

The mail brought letters from autograph-seekers, who frequently asked him to pen a few lines of poetry, causing him to repent his former freedom in dispensing extemporaneous compositions. "It has brought down upon me such a shower, or rather such a waterspout, of applications that my ship sinks under them." From the South, of course, arrived letters of a different order, filled with "insult, profane obscenity, and filth," as well as threats of assassination and lynching. Adams was not surprised; it was "the natural offspring of slave-breeders and slave-traders."

In the Capitol, a man tried to assault Adams. "You are wrong, you are wrong, and I will kick you," said the man, Thomas Sangster, and he drew back his hand to strike Adams. Adams had the presence of mind to pin the man's arms before he could deliver the blow, and bystanders subdued him. Sangster later wrote Adams a letter of apology, and Adams recommended clemency, but Sangster was indicted anyway.

While all the attention secretly pleased Adams, he grew weary of the dinners and pageants, which he attended "with feelings of a culprit to punishment, rather than of a victor to triumph."

Adams grasped the essential fact that slavery's robustness and its attendant evils were "traceable to that fatal drop of Prussic acid in the Constitution of the United States"—Article I, Section 2, the "three-fifths rule." The rule's raison d'état was apparent enough, but it puzzled him that the Constitution's wise framers had "deluded" themselves into evidently believing that by merely excluding the words "slavery" and "slave" from the Constitution, they had somehow kept it free of those evils. But even without the three-fifths rule, Adams recognized that Southerners were bound in common cause by their shared property interest—a total of "twelve hundred millions of dollars in human beings," a state of affairs neither allowed nor tolerated in the North. The three-fifths rule had the effect of buttressing this natural unity of interests with a rigged census that made the South the North's equal in Congress, he believed. But in practice it was more than parity, wrote Adams, for the South, by voting as a bloc, always prevailed when its interests were involved. Consequently, the United States was neither democracy nor republic, but "a government of two or 300,000 holders of slaves, to the utter exclusion of the remaining part, and all the population of the other States in the Union." Because the slave power's very survival depended on preserving the three-fifths rule, abolitionists attempted to rid the Constitution of it.

Following the family tradition of public service, Charles Francis Adams had sought and won election to the Massachusetts House of Representatives in 1840 and was re-elected in 1842. He proceeded to create a sensation by writing a series of resolutions, the most provocative of them recommending a constitutional amendment eliminating the three-fifths rule, a direct challenge to the slave-owning South. Another of his resolutions sought an enumeration of all congressmen who owned slaves and the value of their slave property. Charles Francis shepherded the so-called "Massachusetts Resolves" through the state legislature, and they were then forwarded to his father in Washington to be presented to the House of Representatives.

John Quincy Adams had long waited for just such an opportunity to shine a spotlight on the slave power's constitutional underpinning, and now his son and his colleagues had handed it to him. "They have allowed me the first and probably the last opportunity of leaving to my country and to the world my deliberate sentiments and opinions upon this disastrous feature in the composition of our political institutions." The Senate tabled the resolutions without printing or discussing them, but the House sent them to a special committee, whose chairman was Adams.

As he prepared his speech on the three-fifths rule, Adams challenged the slave totals of the 1840 census, suggesting that they were inflated to increase the slaveholding representation in the U.S. House. On a motion by Adams, the House asked Secretary of State John Calhoun, who was responsible for the census, whether he had corrected "gross errors" pointed out to him earlier. Calhoun responded ambiguously, while promising nothing. Calhoun's reply, Adams complained, was "at once insulting to the House, evasive of enquiry, and false by equivocation." When the House took no subsequent action on the census, Adams condemned its inaction and lack of moral fiber and blamed "the fanaticism of the slave-monger."

❋

Dominated as it was by slavery sympathizers, Adams's select committee was foreordained to recommend the rejection of the Massachusetts Resolves. The House leadership had guaranteed the outcome by carefully choosing the committee members. And to no one's surprise, the House signaled its concurrence, 156–13. But the minority report—written by Adams and Joshua Giddings of Ohio, and proposing adoption of the Massachusetts Resolves—was the real reason that Adams and his supporters had brought the matter before the House.

The report, which condemned the three-fifths rule and slavery itself, did not disappoint abolitionists or their allies. "I regard this Report as the crown of your fame," William Seward wrote Adams. The rule, wrote Adams and Giddings, was "repugnant to the first and vital principles of republican popular representation; to the self-evident truths proclaimed in the Declaration of Independence. . . . If the fundamental principles proclaimed in the Declaration of Independence, as self-evident truths, are real truths, the existence of slavery, in any form, is a wrong." The rule purported to represent persons, when in fact it represented property. Slaveholders had learned to manipulate it in order to advance their "secret, imperceptible, combined and never-ceasing struggle to engross all the offices and depositories of power to themselves."

Adams and Giddings calculated that 88 of the House's 223 members represented slaves—2.5 million slaves in all, worth $1.2 billion. And in a twisted paradox, while being simultaneously denied constitutional rights and exploited for the purpose of padding the slaveholders' congressional representation, the slaves were also ostensibly represented not by their friends or agents, but by "the most inveterate of [their] foes," their owners. It was further proof that "slavery is an evil of portentous magnitude" that corrupted all that it encountered, its sins ranging from prejudicing ordinary people against blacks to abrogating citizens' First Amendment rights.

In urging Virginians to emancipate their slaves, Adams and Giddings argued ingeniously that Virginia stood to *gain* representation in Congress by so doing; in future censuses, each former slave would count as a whole resident, instead of three-fifths of one. Moreover, Virginia emancipation would eradicate two looming dangers. "So shall you no longer live under the perpetual panic-terror of a servile insurrection. So shall you no longer have in prospect, rapidly approaching upon you, an exterminating war, in which the Almighty has no attribute that can take your side." The minority report was neither appreciated nor heeded.

Adams normally refused gifts, but he made an exception for the milky white ivory cane presented to him in March 1844 by Henry Ellsworth, commissioner of the U.S. Patent Office, acting on behalf of the firm Julius Pratt and Company of Meriden, Connecticut. A yard long, silver-tipped, with a gold-inlaid American eagle on its head, the cane bore a ring beneath its pommel with Adams's name and a well-known inscription from Horace, "Justum et tenacem propositi virum" ("The just man and firm of purpose"). The gift came with one condition—and its implicit challenge persuaded Adams to diverge from his usual policy of declining valuable gifts. The donors requested that when the Gag Rule was finally repealed, Adams inscribe the date beneath the Roman poet's epigraph. "I accepted the cane as a trust to be returned when the date of the extinction of the gag-rule shall be accomplished," he wrote in his diary. Until that day, Adams entrusted the cane to Ellsworth's safekeeping.

When the 28th Congress convened in December 1843, Adams had once again attempted to strike down the House's standing rule gagging the reading of petitions about slavery. But the Gag Rule was preserved on a 94–91 vote. The next day, Adams antagonized

Southerners by presenting a petition by 585 New Yorkers asking Congress to separate New York State from all connection with slavery. Speaker John Jones of Virginia pronounced the petition gagged. When Adams appealed Jones's decision, the House hurriedly adjourned. Adams interpreted the Southerners' anger and evasive tactics to be symptoms of their growing desperation.

To test that premise, Adams again pricked the sensibilities of slavery's defenders—thereby inciting a verbal brawl that continued intermittently for days—when he once more protested the Gag Rule's blanket ban on the debate of slavery petitions. In sustaining the rule, the House was dictating to Americans "how they shall exercise the rights secured to them by the letter of the Constitution," charged Adams. Called to order for irrelevancy, Adams witheringly riposted, "Why, according to the construction of some human skulls, nothing that bears directly on the subject before the House is relevant; and it sometimes happened that skulls of that kind have sympathy with the skull of the Speaker." Shouting erupted. Speaker Jones declared that he would not permit such remarks, as Jones's supporters roared, "That's right!" Adams shouted back, "'That's right,' say all the slave representatives on this floor!" As aroused congressmen exclaimed and gestured, Speaker Jones ordered Adams to sit down. From his chair, Adams continued to argue that the offending petition should be read, received, assigned to a committee, and reported upon. He wore down his adversaries to the point where they permitted the petition to be read before tabling it.

But Southerners were unwilling to let Adams have the last word. Isaac Holmes of South Carolina belligerently declared he would fight to uphold the Gag Rule. "[I] would say to Southern men, Gird up your loins, put on your armor and prepare for it. You must meet it; and the sooner you secure the rights which your fathers transmitted to you, the better." That evening, Adams was so upset by what he had heard that day in the House that when he went home, "I could do nothing but pace my chamber." He tried to calm down by reminding himself, "The crisis now requires of me coolness, firmness, prudence, moderation, and fortitude, beyond all former example."

In the House the following day, Adams publicly enunciated his personal views regarding slavery as he had never done before, after first expressing the hope that Congressman Holmes would "throw aside his epaulets; that he will take off his sword. . . . This is not the place for brandishing that sword." Surely to no one's surprise, Adams pronounced himself to be an abolitionist, but in the sense that Thomas Jefferson was an abolitionist when, at the age of seventy-six, he said in a statement addressed to all slaveholders that "abolition was a thing which they must grant, and the sooner the better."

In other words, Adams believed emancipation must not be imposed on the South; slaveholders should voluntarily and peacefully free their slaves. Adams disavowed any wish to interfere with "the institutions of the South." Proponents of immediate emancipation, he said, were "greatly mistaken," because bloodletting would be the certain result of forcible emancipation.

Adams's surprisingly conciliatory words did nothing to mitigate the Southerners' detestation of him. In a one-hour speech defending the Gag Rule, freshman Congressman Andrew Johnson of Tennessee made it a point to be "especially abusive" to Adams. Adams wrote resignedly, "So they all are. I am compelled not only to endure it with seeming insensibility, but to forbear, so far as I can restrain myself, from all reply."

Eight and a half years had passed since the House adopted the Gag Rule recommended by Henry Laurens Pinckney's select committee. The strictures added in 1840 and the Gag Rule's elevation to a standing rule had privately dismayed some supporters, who believed it went too far, thereby hastening its demise—which ultimately occurred. After December 1843, with the Gag Rule's survival preserved by just three votes, it was clear that it could not last much longer. Two factors coalesced to ensure its extinction: Adams's crusade on behalf of the right of petition, and the emerging realignment of the major political parties, with slavery acting as a magnet at once attracting the South and repelling the North.

On December 3, 1844, the second day of the 28th Congress's Second Session, the seventy-seven-year-old congressman from Massachusetts, as he had every year since 1836, once again asked his colleagues to restore the absolute right to petition. His resolution called for the repeal of the 25th standing rule, which forbade the House to receive petitions, memorials, or resolutions to abolish slavery in the District of Columbia, or in any state or territory, or to eliminate the slave trade between states or territories.

Scarcely daring to hope, Adams requested a vote on his resolution. Mississippi Congressman Jacob Thompson moved that it be laid on the table. But on this day the House was not of a mind to acquiesce to the slaveholders' wishes. Thompson's motion to table the resolution failed, 104–81. As the votes on his resolution were tallied, Adams spirits rose. The final count was 108–80 in favor of abolishing the Gag Rule.

That night, Adams wrote in his diary: "Blessed, forever blessed, be the name of God!" Not only was it a personal victory for Adams, it was the antislavery movement's first consequential victory over the American slave power—and a turning point in the nation's history.

Exactly a week later, Adams presented a petition to prohibit slavery in the District of Columbia. The predictable motion was made to table the petition. The House, evidently weary of gags and such evasions, unexpectedly defeated the motion 99–88, furnishing the pleased Adams with "much matter for reflection on these proceedings."

The 28th Congress officially ended its Second Session on March 3, 1845. Patent commissioner Ellsworth sent Adams the commemorative ivory cane, having added to the golden-eagle inlay a scroll inscribed with the words, "Right of Petition Triumphant." Adams paid a jeweler to engrave the date "3 December, 1844" above the scroll, on the eagle's breast, and returned the cane to the Patent Office. In his will, Adams bequeathed the cane to the United States. Fittingly, the cane today resides at the Smithsonian Institution.

Chapter Twelve

A New War and Decline

---

*"The chain which linked our hearts
with the gifted spirits of former times,
has been rudely snapped."*

—South Carolina Congressman Isaac Holmes,
in his eulogy for John Quincy Adams

---

*A*dams's triumph over the Gag Rule assured his place as the Southern slaveholders' great nemesis. Thus, it puzzled him when "several of the bitterest political opponents that I have in the world" attended his annual New Year's Day levee in 1845. By nature pessimistic and suspicious, Adams did not see that while his adversaries might denounce him, they respected his independent principles and, more so with every passing year, his association with the nation's hallowed past. Instead, Adams pictured himself "bound hand and foot and chained to a rock . . . by the slave-monger brood linked together with the mongrel Democracy of the North and West."

Adams once more angered Southerners—ironically, this time by supporting their leader, President James K. Polk of Tennessee, in his decision to end the Anglo-American joint occupancy of the Oregon Territory and to seek Oregon's annexation. Because the new northwestern states would not tolerate slavery, the South opposed their annexation, which would cancel out any benefit from Texas's admission as a slave state. Adams, they charged, was being maddeningly inconsistent on Oregon; he had consented to joint occupancy in 1818 and 1827. Publicly, he said the situation had changed: Few American settlers had lived in Oregon previously; many lived there now. "I want the country for our western pioneers . . . to go out and make a great nation . . . instead of it being hunting grounds for the buffaloes, braves, and savages of the desert." In reality, Adams regarded Oregon as a needed counterweight to a slavery-tolerant Texas, whose annexation he believed was inevitable.

Adams supported Polk's bold assertion of U.S. rights to all of the Oregon Territory, clear to 54° 40' (present-day Alaska's southern border), while recognizing that Polk was trying to bluff England into accepting a 49° boundary (today's Canadian-U.S. border). Adams and James Monroe had both proposed dividing the territory at 49°.

During a House speech endorsing Polk's proposal to give one year's notice to England of the termination of Oregon joint occupancy, Adams asked the clerk to read aloud the verses in the Book of Genesis in which God created man and gave him dominion over the earth. Dominion, the foundation of property rights, he said, required "actual possession," not merely discovery or exploration. England, which wished to preserve the status quo in Oregon for the Hudson Bay Company's benefit, certainly knew the territory would lose its value to her once it was settled by "tillers of the ground." Americans must possess Oregon, declared Adams, "to make the wilderness bloom as a rose, to establish laws, to increase, multiply, and subdue the earth." By 163–54, the House approved the termination of U.S.-British joint occupancy of Oregon.

In 1844, President John Tyler, disowned by both Whigs and Democrats, launched his own party, the Democratic-Republicans, in the hope of being elected president in his own right. Then, he wagered his presidency and candidacy on the single issue of Texas annexation, by cleverly sowing the idea that the annexation of Texas, which he advocated, would also extend slavery. He believed that this so-called "Texas bombshell" would compel the major party candidates to declare their opposition to annexation in order to appease Northern voters—thereby costing them the support of the South and West. While his opponents fought over Northern votes, Tyler would sweep the South and West and win the election—or so he thought. His strategy was initially successful: Former President Martin Van Buren, the leading Democratic candidate, and Henry Clay, the Whigs' nominee-apparent, both announced their opposition to annexing Texas.

At the Hermitage near Nashville, seventy-seven-year-old Andrew Jackson, his health steadily declining, watched with rising concern as his former vice president, Van Buren, was mousetrapped by Tyler. Long a frustrated proponent of Texas annexation, Jackson recognized that if Democrats now nominated Van Buren, they would be beaten. The Democrats' patriarch cast about for a candidate who supported annexation. He didn't have to look any further than his protégé and fellow Tennessean, former House Speaker James K. Polk. With little fanfare, Polk, whose great ambition was to become Van Buren's running mate, had recently stated in a letter that he favored "the *immediate re-annexation* of Texas." Polk asserted that Texas had once belonged to the United States as part of the Louisiana Purchase—a spurious claim never recognized by Spain, which obtained clear title to Texas in the 1819 Adams-Onís Treaty.

Polk's "dark horse" Democratic nomination in May 1844 spurred Tyler and his allies to try to push annexation legislation through Congress, in order to lock up the South and the West for the election. But the Senate rejected the proposal, 35–16.

Adams's brief elation at this setback was tempered by his conviction that the determined advocates of annexation, by honest or dishonest means, would eventually prevail. "Treachery of the deepest infamy marks every step of this Jackson project . . . portentous beyond conception." Indeed, Adams gloomily apprehended that annexation would be the ruinous "first step to the conquest of all Mexico, of the West India [*sic*] Islands, of a maritime, colonizing, slave-tainted monarchy, and of extinguished freedom."

Tyler stubbornly remained in the race until Jackson, concerned that he would siphon off support for Polk, persuaded him to withdraw.

With the ailing Jackson leading them, Democrats campaigned largely on the issue of annexing Texas and unexpectedly vilified Adams for his actions thirty-five years earlier. Texas, said the Democrats, had belonged to the United States by virtue of the Louisiana Purchase—until Secretary of State Adams traded it to Spain for Florida in 1819 in the Adams-Onís Treaty.

As did any threatened blot on his reputation, the allegation acted on Adams like a fire bell. He flung himself furiously into a defense of his actions. The Florida treaty, he wrote in a fiery overstatement, was "the most successful negotiation ever consummated by the Government of this Union." He denounced the "utterly baseless lies of Andrew Jackson" and the attacks by the "bloodhounds" loosed upon him by the Democrats. Muttering that the allegation was "an engine for the total destruction of my good name, and to charge me with treachery to my country and to my trust," he marched to the State Department archives in search of supporting documents.

Adams's enemies had learned to not casually provoke him on questions that placed his reputation in jeopardy, knowing that he would harness his daunting memory and relentless work habits in an obsessive crusade to defeat them, while even seeking divine support, as he now did. "I have put myself upon trial by God and my country. May God be my judge!" In the archives, he discovered instructions dated May 1816, written by then Secretary of

State James Monroe, which stated that if Spain ceded its lands east of the Mississippi to the United States, the Sabine River (the present-day Louisiana-Texas border) should become the boundary between the United States and Spain's southwestern provinces, "rather than our shadow of a claim to the Rio Del Norte." Monroe "had no confidence" in the latter claim, and Monroe, Adams, and Jackson had all agreed the "the extension of the boundary [to the Rio Grande] would weaken us for defence," by exposing a long, vulnerable coastline to attack. In New York, Adams obtained an 1819 letter from then General Andrew Jackson to President Monroe in which Jackson had avouched his unqualified approval of the Florida treaty. These discoveries led Adams to exult in a diary entry, "I . . . can wind the whole body of conspirators round my fingers."

In large measure to avenge himself on Jackson, Adams campaigned for the Whig nominee, Henry Clay. It was a watershed for Adams, who had eschewed presidential campaigns since his own failed re-election attempt. In speech after speech throughout the Northeast, Adams lashed out at the "conspiracy" by Jackson and other expansionist Democrats "to ruin my good name and fabricate a fable to justify the robbery of Texas from Mexico." Speaking invitations poured in to "Old Man Eloquent," whom Southerners preferred to call the "Madman of Massachusetts." Jackson declared that Adams was either "demented" or "the most reckless and depraved man living." Adams's address on the subject of Texas to the Young Men's Whig Club of Boston was so well received that it was made into a popular pamphlet.

Righteous and proud, Mexico even now regarded Texas as a rebellious province, although the Republic of Texas had existed as a sovereign nation since 1836. Texas was irretrievably lost to Mexico, and Mexican leaders privately realized this. But they also were very aware that, as coup followed coup, it would be political folly for them to permit Texas to join the United States without Mexico being compensated for its loss. American leaders were equally aware that it was too politically risky for them to show Mexico any consideration as they pursued the annexation of Texas. As Adams concisely summarized the stalemate, "The root of the danger is in the convulsive impotence of Mexico to maintain her own integrity, geographical, political, or moral, and the inflexible perseverance of rapacity of our South and West, under the spur of slavery, to plunder and dismember her." Consequently, Mexico and the United States were drifting toward a collision from which neither was willing to turn. "My heart sinks within me for the cause of human freedom and for our own," confessed Adams.

As tensions increased between the nations, Mexican leaders recognized a true friend in Adams and sent Minister Don Juan N. Almonte to express Mexico's gratitude for his "candor and generosity" toward their country. The gesture pleased Adams. He had attempted to "observe the law of justice on the part of my country towards Mexico and all other nations," he told Almonte.

After Polk defeated Clay in November 1844, Tyler mounted one last effort to bring Texas into the Union. In early January 1845, with less than two months remaining in his presidency, Tyler redoubled his efforts to secure Texas, justifiably believing James Polk's victory to be a mandate for annexation. Almost daily now, Democrats presented Congress with an annexation resolution of one order or another; they were invariably tabled or assigned to a committee. Behind this curtain of preliminary resolutions, however, the forces of annexation were preparing their principal effort, Joint Resolution 46, to admit Texas straightaway as a state, bypassing the usual intermediate period as a territory. A provision of Joint Resolution 46 that especially alarmed antislavery forces permitted Texas to be divided into as many as five states—with probably all of them sanctioning slavery, as only a narrow strip of Texas lay north of the 36° 30' Missouri Compromise line.

The evident futility of trying to stop annexation when the stars were seemingly aligned for the Republic of Texas to become the

twenty-eighth state momentarily paralyzed Adams, who uncharacteristically vacillated over whether to even make the effort to
speak against it. In the fullness of his bitterness he wrote, "The
Constitution is a menstruous rag, and the Union is sinking into a
military monarchy, to be rent asunder like the empire of Alexander
or the kingdoms of Ephraim and Judah."

But Adams was constitutionally unable to bear silent witness to a
monumental wrong. On January 24, 1845, he addressed the House
for an hour, speaking in opposition to the myriad pending resolutions. Texas had never belonged to the United States as part of the
Louisiana Purchase, he asserted. As president, he twice attempted
to buy Texas from Mexico, and he would have annexed it if Mexico
had consented and if slavery were prohibited. His position remained unchanged, said Adams. "If slavery were totally abolished
forever in Texas, and the voluntary consent of Mexico could be obtained, I would vote for the annexation of Texas to-morrow."

The next day, the House threw out every annexation resolution
except Joint Resolution 46 and then approved it, 107–102. In his diary, Adams wrote, "Let the will of God be done!"—an emphatic
self-admonition to accept the unacceptable. Next came weeks of
lobbying in the Senate, culminating in the resolution's narrow,
27–25 approval on February 28. "The heaviest calamity that ever
befell myself and my country was this day consummated," Adams
somberly wrote. Tyler signed the resolution into law on March 2,
two days before leaving office. All that remained was Texas's acceptance and its formal admission as a state.

"I have opposed it for ten long years," Adams wrote in his diary,
"firmly believing it tainted with two deadly crimes: 1, the leprous
contamination of slavery; and, 2, robbery of Mexico. . . . The sequel
is in the hands of Providence. . . . Fraud and rapine are at its foundation. They have sown the wind" and would reap the "whirlwind."

John Greenleaf Whittier portentously wrote in "To a Southern
Statesman": "Crimson as blood, the beams of that Lone Star!/The
Fates are just; they gave us but our own;/Nemesis ripens what our
hands have sown."

Britain secretly persuaded Mexico in 1845 to extend official recognition to the Republic of Texas, hoping this would convince Texas's Congress to remain independent rather than join the United States. It might have worked five years earlier, but it was too late now. And when Britain's involvement became known—the British envoy, supposedly traveling incognito, wore a hat so blindingly white that it turned heads—the Polk administration press pounced on it as evidence of British meddling, to advance her own selfish interests. Britain's attempted intervention, which might have averted the result that Adams so dreaded, only revived his reflexive suspicions about England: "I perceive nothing, as yet, to relieve the deep distrust, which I would fain discard if I could, of the British ministerial policy."

The revelation destroyed the slender chance that Texas might have remained independent; on July 4, Texas officially accepted the U.S. invitation of annexation and rejected Mexico's recognition of Texas's sovereignty. Mexico declared it would never recognize the U.S. annexation of Texas, hinting of war, a pronouncement mocked by the Polk administration's quasi-official Washington *Union* "as gasconading about her pretended rights and wrongs. . . . [Mexico's] absurd threats of war . . . will exhaust what remains of disposition on our part to deal generously with her." But President Polk was disinclined to be generous; he had already ordered U.S. troops to advance toward the disputed U.S.-Mexican border.

On December 9, 1845, Adams presented up to twenty petitions that he described as "remonstrances" against admitting Texas into the Union as a slave state. The petitions were referred to the Committee on the Territories. Three weeks later, Congress voted to admit Texas as the twenty-eighth state.

With the annexation of Texas, Adams had reached his seventy-ninth year and yet remained an iconic, highly visible national figure. The New York *American* described him as "ancient, venerable, time honored . . . the coeval of the Constitution, its illustrator and guardian . . . the glory of three ages." At times, he displayed signs of mellowing, as when he confided to a fellow congressman that he, like his hero Cicero, would "wish my enmities to be transient, and my friendships to be eternal." He accepted an invitation to address the Norfolk City Temperance Society, and his speech was "faintly applauded" by its five hundred listeners because he forthrightly told them he neither approved of nor practiced teetotalism. After addressing the Mercantile Library Association in Baltimore, the last in a series of speeches, he pessimistically prepared himself for a severe correction after weeks of applause. "It augurs some deep humiliation awaiting me, to teach me in the last stage of my existence upon earth what I am, and the real estimation in which I am held by the very small portion of my fellow-creatures who know or care anything about me."

Andrew Jackson died on June 8, 1845. The death of his old enemy, who shared Adams's 1767 birth year, did not move Adams to forgiveness. "Jackson was a hero, a murderer, an adulterer . . . who in his last days of his life belied [*sic*] and slandered me before the world and died," he wrote. Later, he elaborated upon his flinty thoughts about the man who helped wreck his presidency, denied him a second term, and abused him even as Adams supported Jackson's controversial policies on French spoliations and nullification. Unquestionably, Adams was burdened by a long, punishing memory: "Jackson's vengeful hatred of Monroe was stimulated by his disavowal of his conquest of Florida; his hatred of me was stimulated by my services in saving him from the public indignation; and he glutted his revenge upon us both in the same way—by spinning out of his own brain fictitious and slanderous charges against us." Neither was Adams moved to sympathize with South Carolina Congressman John Campbell, "dying by inches of pulmonary consumption," when he cast what would be his last House vote two months before his death. "He is one of those who, in the commission of crimes, think they are doing God service," Adams dryly observed. "He represents about eighty thousand slaves." But he mourned the passing of his friend Nicholas Biddle, who had retired in his midfifties after the demise of his Second Bank of the United States. He remembered Biddle's "smiling face and stifled groans over the wreck of splendid blasted expectations and ruined hopes."

According to Ralph Waldo Emerson, someone once asked Adams when he was well advanced into his seventies to reveal his formula for staying healthy and mentally sharp. There were three rules, Adams is said to have responded: "(1) Regularity, (2) Regularity, (3) Regularity." On the ivory writing brace with which he steadied his tremulous writing hand, he had inscribed the words, "Toil and Trust." Yet Adams's stoicism belied his melancholic awareness of physical decline and time's passage. "Alas! How swift the moments fly!/How flash the years along," began a poem that he wrote for his Quincy church. He began describing his birthday as "the annual warning of the shortening thread."

Arriving in New York City by train one night, he and Louisa, walking arm in arm in the dark, stepped off the four-foot-high platform. "While falling, I had the distinct idea that I was killed," wrote Adams. But he only bruised his left hip, while Louisa sprained her left wrist and bruised her chin.

On his and Louisa's forty-eighth wedding anniversary on July 26, 1845, Adams wrote, "A small remnant only can be before us. . . . We have enjoyed much. We have suffered not a little. Good and evil have followed us alternately. The thread has been of checkered yarn." His own career had been "highly auspicious," although beset by "severe vicissitudes." He had begun life with the advantages of a fine education, good character, and industry and had been more successful than he deserved. "I have enjoyed a portion of the favor of my country at least equal to my desert, but have suffered, and yet suffer, much from the slander which outvenoms all the worms of Nile."

In September 1845, Adams suffered a mild stroke. His doctor in Boston prescribed medication, Adams temporarily curtailed his morning walks, and he complained of being "very feeble." His handwriting deteriorated to the point that he was forced to rely on his granddaughter, Louisa Catherine Adams—Charles Francis's child—to help him keep up his diary and his correspondence. Old age, he gloomily observed, was "a long disease, a succession of complaints. I no longer recover from one, than I am stricken down by another."

But by late November he was feeling well enough to return to Washington and resume his congressional duties. In deference to his age and condition, Adams's colleagues assigned him the House's most accessible seat. As his recovery continued, Adams resumed his walks before breakfast, although it took him thirty minutes, instead of his former fifteen minutes, to cover a mile. He further stimulated his circulation with coldwater ablutions and vigorous massages with a horsehair strap and a mitten.

During the hot July of 1846, following his seventy-ninth birthday, Adams was "drawn by an irresistible impulse" for three mornings in a row to his old Potomac bathing spot, and he went swimming, which he had not done since his stroke. Each morning, he swam for about thirty minutes. During what would be the last swim of his life in the Potomac, the temperature dropped ten degrees, and "a brisk breeze ruffled the surface of the river, so that when I came out I shivered while dressing at my old rock." He warmed up during the half-hour walk home.

Until his seventh decade, Adams's career as a diplomat, senator, cabinet member, and president had compelled him to move from place to place without ever establishing a permanent home. But since leaving the White House, he had developed an abiding affection for the Big House in Quincy. A visit by wealthy friends who ceaselessly traveled reminded him of his strong attachment to his home place. Besides being a necessity to "profound study," he wrote in pondering this bond, a home was "the place of conjugal, parental, filial, and fraternal endearments—the place where alone we can possess and exercise the practical blessings of freedom. . . . It is a great but very common misfortune of the wealthy to lose the relish for these enjoyments."

Indeed, the Big House was often filled with grandchildren, who enjoyed visiting Adams in his library, a place described by his grandson Charles Francis Jr. as "walled in with over-loaded bookshelves." Years later, Charles wrote, "I can see him now, seated at his table . . . a very old-looking gentleman, with a bald head and white fringe of hair . . . [and] a perpetual inkstain on the forefinger and thumb of his right hand." He noted that his grandfather's disposition was not "a holiday temperament": When not working or pruning trees, he took "grave, sedate walks . . . absorbed in meditation." But while Adams might often have seemed preoccupied, he tried to be accessible to his grandchildren and to establish a connection with them. At birth, Adams gave each grandchild a Bible with a handwritten flyleaf inscription.

Charles Francis Jr.'s younger brother, Henry, recounted in *The Education of Henry Adams* the unforgettable morning when his grandfather took him in hand after five-year-old Henry threw a fit over having to attend school. "The old man slowly came down. Putting on his hat, he took the boy's hand without a word, and walked with him, paralyzed by awe, up the road to the town." Soon, Henry "found himself seated inside the school. . . . Not till then did the President release his hand and depart."

Henry Adams tried to imagine the sharply divergent perspectives that he and his grandfather brought to the "Roaring '40s," when the American industrial age of steamships, railroads, and the telegraph was hitting its stride. "For him, alone, the old universe was thrown into the ash-heap and a new one created," while for young Henry, "his new world was ready for use, and only fragments of the old met his eyes."

Advanced age deepened Adams's religious devotion and inspired him to frequently reaffirm his Christian faith. Sometimes in his diary, he enumerated his beliefs: "in the existence of a Supreme Creator of the world, of an immortal principal within myself, responsible to that Creator for my conduct upon earth, and of the divine mission of the crucified Saviour, proclaiming immortal life and preaching peace on earth, good will to men, the natural equality of all mankind, and the law, Thou shalt love thy neighbor as thyself." Every night, he recited aloud the prayer that his mother had taught him, "Now I lay me down to sleep . . ." Each day upon rising, he asked himself what good he could do, and upon retiring, what good he had done. He believed man owed God "worship, reverence, gratitude, submission, and resignation, all in sentiment-prayer and praise in action"—namely by displaying justice, charity, and mercy to others.

Yet, he could never altogether silence his "involuntary and agonizing doubts," despite having read through the Bible dozens of times and having been an avid churchgoer for decades. "I need for my own comfort to be fortified and sustained by stated and frequent opportunities of receiving religious admonition and instruction," he wrote. To inspire vigilance against temptation, he wore a signet ring bearing the figure of a rooster and the motto "Watch," the last word of Mark 13. Adams's recurring doubts centered upon the Trinity, God's will, which he too often found to be incomprehensible, and the Bible's miracles. The nature of the afterlife was an insoluble mystery, but he believed in it. These questions preoccupied Adams from the months following his father's death, when he joined the Unitarian Church of Quincy and took communion for the first time, until the end of his life.

On the rare occasions when illness kept him from Sunday services, it was a painful deprivation; religion literally sustained Adams from day to day, and week to week. When he was in Washington, he usually attended two services, one in the Capitol and the second at a church. The denomination of the church was not especially important, for he believed all Christian faiths shared the same purpose. "There is no Christian church with which I could not join in social worship," he wrote, although he preferred the simple Congregational service. He critiqued the sermons that he heard—he once described a brimstone preacher as "a chaplain to a penitentiary, discoursing to the convicts"—but he could be profoundly moved, too, as when a Bishop Hopkins of Vermont asked his listeners to consider whether their faith in Christ had banished their fear of death. "My conscience smote me, and the involuntary tear stole down my cheek," wrote Adams. "I shall remember [Bishop Hopkins] as long as any trace of memory remains upon my brain." He was moved to tears of joy another time in Quincy, when, to Adams's surprise, the minister instructed the congregation to sing a hymn that Adams had actually written, based upon the 65th Psalm. An "ecstasy of delight streamed from my eyes as the organ pealed and the choir of voices sung the praise of Almighty God from the soul of David, adapted to my native tongue by me." Later, Adams's happiness was diminished by the discovery of an "enormous blunder" made by the publisher or copyist.

Unprepossessing General Zachary Taylor, a veteran of numerous Indian wars who dressed like an old farmer, sailed with his 2,000-man "Army of Observation" to Corpus Christi, where they spent the winter of 1845–1846. At Corpus Christi was the estuary of the Nueces River, which Mexico regarded as its true boundary with Texas, whereas Texas—and President James Polk—just as adamantly regarded the Rio Grande 120 miles to the south as the border. Mexico refused to discuss the border, the sale of any of its provinces, or any other subject, until the United States compensated it for the loss of Texas. When Mexico in early 1846 spurned the diplomatic overtures by the Polk administration's envoy to Mexico, John Slidell of Louisiana, Taylor was ordered to march to the Rio Grande. To Mexico, crossing the Nueces constituted an act of war. Thousands of Mexican troops converged on the disputed region.

Adams viewed all warfare with "abhorrence" but did not believe that war was intrinsically immoral. "There are, and always have been as long as the race of men has existed, times and occasions of dire necessity for war." War in fact was "a purifier of the moral character of man," while "peace was the period of corruption to the human race." But Adams believed that every issue of war, and peace too, was a question of right and wrong: "War for the right can never be justly blamed; war for the wrong can never be justified."

Right or wrong, war with Mexico was now all but inevitable. Slidell's rejection in Mexico City, however, was not the primary reason that Taylor's army was encamped on the Rio Grande's east bank in April 1846. Rumors had reached President Polk—whose cherished secret goal was to obtain California and its magnificent Pacific ports—that England was scheming to pry California away from Mexico. The reports fanned the lurking suspicion that England wished to curtail U.S. expansion to the Pacific and thwart her Manifest Destiny. Consequently, Polk sent Taylor's army to the Rio Grande to force Mexico into negotiations or to provoke what he hoped would be a short war—and a remunerative peace treaty transferring California to the United States. As Army Lieutenant Ulysses S. Grant later described the movement in which he participated, "It became necessary for the 'invaders' to approach to within a convenient distance to be struck." Mexican President Mariano Paredes obliged by pronouncing his nation in a "defensive war" and sending troops across the Rio Grande to attack Taylor's army.

During March and April, Adams and his fellow congressmen appeared to be scarcely aware of the mounting tensions along the Rio Grande, preoccupied as they were with ending the Oregon joint occupancy agreement, as well as launching the Smithsonian Institution. Amid belligerent speeches insinuating that a third war with England would not be altogether unwelcome, Congress voted to give twelve months' notice of the cessation of the nearly twenty-year-old Oregon agreement. Polk sent it to England on April 27. At the same time, the bill establishing the Smithsonian Institution suddenly emerged from Adams's special committee. But as the Smithsonian bill edged toward a resolution, dispatches from the Rio Grande postponed final action. In an ambush on April 25, Mexican troops had killed, wounded, and captured U.S. dragoons patrolling the east side of the river.

Because it took weeks for news to travel from southern Texas to Washington, Polk and his cabinet did not yet know of the attack when John Slidell stood before them on May 8 to pronounce his mission to Mexico a failure. Impatient for action, Polk was ready to draft a war declaration to take to Congress. With one dissenting vote—Navy Secretary George Bancroft, the historian and U.S. Naval Academy founder—Polk's advisers supported the president's war proposal. Four hours later, Army Adjutant General Roger Jones handed General Zachary Taylor's report on the attack to President Polk. That evening, at a hastily convened second cabinet meeting, the vote for war was unanimous.

The United States sometimes rushes into war without due deliberation, and the House's conduct on May 11 was one of those instances. Eager to push through a war bill authorizing the president to call up 50,000 volunteers and spend $10 million, the president's floor managers limited debate to two hours and then consumed an hour and a half in reading aloud White House documents accompanying the resolution. They then deftly attached a preamble to the war bill that read, "By the act of the Republic of Mexico, a state of war exists between that government and the United States." As stunned, outmaneuvered Whigs protested, the amendment was swiftly put to a vote and approved, 123–67. Now, anyone voting against the objectionable preamble would go on record as having voted to deny materiel to Taylor's beleaguered troops on the Rio Grande. Only fourteen congressmen dared do so—Adams was one—and the bill passed, 174–14. "The Fourteen," as war hawks called Adams, Joshua Giddings, and their band, were jeered and abused. The next day, the Senate added its approval, 40–2, although John Calhoun, too, protested against the preamble, asserting that under the Constitution there could be no war unless Congress declared it. Calhoun was absent when the bill was put to a vote.

Adams expressed his extreme vexation in a letter to his old friend, eighty-five-year-old Albert Gallatin. General Zachary Taylor's presence at Corpus Christi was provocative enough, but his march to the Rio Grande, Adams wrote to the former treasury secretary and diplomat, was an act of "flagrant War. It was War unproclaimed, and the War has never to this day been declared by the Congress of the United States, according to the Constitution. It has been recognized as existing by the Act of Mexico." In giving its sanction to this "direct and notorious violation of the truth," Congress had established a precedent that it would rue. "The President of the United States has but to declare that War exists, with any Nation upon Earth, by the act of that Nation's Government, and the War is essentially declared." Since 1830, he wrote, America's "fixed purpose" had been to annex to the United States not only Texas but also several adjoining Mexican provinces, including California. Mexico, he wrote, was justified in waging a war of self-defense against the United States.

While Adams's mild stroke had not permanently impaired him, it had rapidly aged him and leached away his old stamina. He did not energetically condemn the Polk administration's conduct, as he would have a year earlier. While detesting his country's war policy, Adams dutifully supported the troops, voting to send them supplies and reinforcements. But he drew the line at emoluments or memorials celebrating the participants.

On August 8, the penultimate day of the 29th Congress's First Session, a thirty-two-year-old freshman Pennsylvania Democrat, David Wilmot, who had supported the annexation of Texas and had voted for the war, loosed a thunderbolt of an amendment barring slavery in any new territory obtained from Mexico. The so-called Wilmot Proviso was attached to a bill providing $2 million in "ready money" for the treaty negotiations with Mexico that President Polk hoped would begin any day. The "Two Million Dollar Bill" and its controversial amendment passed the House, 87–64, with Adams voting for it, but it was filibustered in the Senate and expired upon Congress's adjournment on August 10. It would resurface in early 1847, this time igniting the first exhaustive congressional debate of the institution of slavery—a debate that would spiral into bloodshed fifteen years later. While Adams would always cast his vote with Wilmot, he left it to the next generation to conduct the slavery debate that he had sought to provoke by tilting against the Gag Rule.

Believing that the final conflict between the "slave power and the puritan spirit" was now at hand, Adams at last embraced a party. As he entered his eightieth year, he began referring to himself as a "Conscience Whig," a derisive term used by Southern congressmen to describe any Northern Whig who opposed the extension of slavery. "The slave power sneers at *Conscience*, as in the days of yore our pilgrims were called *puritans* in derision," Adams wrote to John G. Palfrey, a Unitarian clergyman and historian from Boston who was running for Congress. "Let us not be ashamed of the name of Conscience Whigs but inscribe it on our banners and deserve it if need be with martyrdom and the cause of human liberty."

By mid-August, Adams was back in Quincy, groaning in his diary, "My faculties are now declining from day to day into mere helpless impotence." All of this notwithstanding, he was able to join his cousin, former Harvard President Josiah Quincy, and Quincy's son, who was Boston's mayor, in a groundbreaking ceremony for a Boston aqueduct and to turn a shovelful of dirt. Less than a week later, he was presiding over a meeting held at Faneuil Hall to protest the illegal recapture in Boston of an escaped slave and his return in chains to New Orleans. In October, Whig delegates from Massachusetts's 8th Congressional District renominated Adams to represent the district in the 30th Congress. "I accepted the nomination with grateful sentiments," reported Adams. On Election Day, he could not bring himself to vote for himself, so he removed his name from his ballot before casting it. He received 992 votes, while 341 other votes were scattered among his opponents.

Aware as he was of his physical ailments, his state of mind, and his ebbing mortality, Adams seldom remarked on the medium in which he obsessively recorded these matters—his lifelong diary. But on October 31, 1846, Adams stepped back from his daily reportage to assay the massive record he had composed. "There has perhaps not been another individual of the human race, of whose daily existence from early childhood to fourscore years has been noted down with his own hand so minutely as mine," he acknowledged, noting that he was just twelve when he began to keep a journal. Humility and a touch of self-deprecating humor tempered any pride of achievement that he felt. "If my intellectual powers had been such as have been sometimes committed by the Creator of man to single individuals of the species, my diary would have been, next to the Holy Scriptures, the most precious and valuable book ever written by human hands, and I should have been one of the greatest benefactors of my country and of mankind." But he was not so made, he concluded, nor had he bettered his portion as he might have.

NOVEMBER 20, 1846, BOSTON

Adams was staying with Charles Francis on Mount Vernon Street until his departure for Washington, where Louisa had preceded him. On this day, after rising at his usual time, between 4 A.M. and 5 A.M., he conducted his morning blood-stimulation ablutions with horsehair strap and mitten.

After breakfast, he set out with Dr. George Parkman to visit the new Harvard medical college on North Mason Street. They had not walked far when Adams suddenly fell to the ground. He had suffered a stroke—worse than the previous autumn's.

Assisted by Dr. Parkman, Adams staggered back to his son's house, where for the next several days he lay nearly immobile in bed, "with little or no pain and little exercise of intellect," as he later observed. Louisa rushed from Washington to her husband's bedside, arriving just thirty-six hours after learning that he had been stricken.

In a laboriously handwritten narrative that Adams lugubriously titled "Posthumous Memoir," he wrote of his seizure: "From that hour I date my decease, and consider myself, for every useful purpose to myself or to my fellow-creatures, dead; and hence I call this and what I may write hereafter a posthumous memoir." In his desolation, Adams, with his son's help, drew up a detailed ten-page will.

But he had not yet reached the end. Tough-minded as always, Adams willed himself back to functionality. By New Year's Day, 1847, six weeks after the stroke, he was able to ride in a carriage for an hour. Three weeks later, he was walking every day, and he had resumed his attendance at Sunday services. On February 8, the Adamses boarded a southbound train. Traveling a short distance each day, Adams and Louisa reached Washington on February 12, Louisa's seventy-second birthday.

The House rose as one to greet its patriarch when Adams slowly made his way into the chamber on February 13. The future president, Congressman Andrew Johnson of Tennessee, immediately vacated Adams's former seat, which Johnson had occupied since the session began in December. Adams thanked him and addressed his colleagues: "Had I a more powerful voice, I might respond to the congratulations of my friends, and the members of this house for the honor which has been done me. But, enfeebled as I am by disease, I beg you will excuse me." The members crowded around him, shaking his hand. Even the House's chief clerk, Benjamin French, who had once described Adams as demonic, took his hand. "I felt that a tear was gathering in my eye, & I have no doubt that many a one felt the same," he wrote. Adams, he observed, was "feeble & cannot last long. He has many failings, but he is a great & good man notwithstanding them all."

Relieved of all committee duties except oversight of the Library of Congress, Adams for the next two weeks was a silent member of Congress, observing the debates without participating. In a thin, reedy voice he cast his votes—one of them in favor of a resolution to withdraw American troops from Mexico and to refrain from demanding Mexican territory during peace talks, which failed to pass.

But on March 2, the day before the official adjournment of the 29th Congress, Adams broke his silence and delivered his only speech of the Second Session. The subject was one that no one else present knew better than he: the *Amistad*. Spain was demanding $50,000 in reparations for the vessel and the Africans, all either deceased or living in Africa. Secretary of State James Buchanan, a Northern Democrat with Southern sympathies, had proposed paying the indemnity. As Adams rose to address the House, "the members came flocking from all sides to listen to the only speech made by Mr. A this session," reported the *Congressional Globe*.

The Africans on the *Amistad*, said Adams, were freemen, and Buchanan's recommendation was totally in error and "in opposition to the findings of the Supreme Court." "There is not even the shadow of a pretense for the Spanish demand of indemnity," declared Adams, his voice stronger than it had been since his return to the House. Moreover, it wasn't Buchanan's place to unilaterally decide this question—if it actually was a legitimate one, which it was not—it was a matter for Congress to determine. "God forbid that any claim should ever be allowed by Congress which rested on such a false foundation," said Adams, warning that if it were granted, it "would be a perfect robbery committed on the people of the United States." The House defeated the amendment, 94–28.

In Quincy that summer, Adams turned eighty, and he and Louisa quietly celebrated their fiftieth wedding anniversary. A doctor gave Adams a "galvanic device" that administered small shocks, evidently to stimulate the full recovery of his still-impaired physical faculties, including his writing hand. Adams stopped the therapy upon concluding that it weakened him.

He continued to maintain his diary, although spottily, by dictating and sometimes writing in a crabbed hand. "I still struggle against my fate and force my hand to write when it has been from the 20th of last November disabled by an almighty hand forever."

On November 1, as he left Quincy to attend the 30th Congress, Adams confessed to an uneasy premonition. "It seemed to me on leaving home as if it were upon my last great journey."

Adams presented two petitions in December advocating peace with Mexico, but he no longer brought before the House hundreds of antislavery petitions; younger abolitionist congressmen had taken up this labor. After January 4, 1848, Adams's diary shows no further entries, although he continued to write letters, including one to Charles Francis in which he prayed that his son would be sustained in his "incorruptible integrity through all the trials that may be reserved for you upon earth. . . . A stout heart and a clear conscience, and never despair."

MONDAY, FEBRUARY 21, 1848, WASHINGTON

Adams appeared well enough to everyone who had seen him over the busy past four days. The previous Thursday, he had gone to a reception held by the mayor of Washington, in the company of Supreme Court Justice John McLean, Henry Clay, and several other senators. On Friday, he attended a meeting of the Library of Congress committee. Saturday, he spent three hours at an exhibit at which he spoke extemporaneously for fifteen minutes about an engraving of the death of Queen Elizabeth. That evening, Adams and Louisa hosted a reception at their home. As usual, Adams had attended two Sunday church services. And now, on Monday, he was at his desk in the House of Representatives.

At about 1:30 P.M., the new House chief clerk, Thomas Campbell of Kentucky, began reading a proposed tribute to Mexican War officers. Among the congressmen in attendance were Abraham Lincoln of Illinois and Andrew Johnson of Tennessee. Adams, who readily voted for money and materiel for the troops, but not for tributes or emoluments, was poised to vote against the measure.

Suddenly, he gripped his desk, and his temples flushed a deep shade of red. Congressman Davis Fisher of Ohio, who was seated next to Adams, caught him before he fell to the floor.

"Mr. Adams is dying!" shouted Washington Hunt of New York.

Everything stopped.

Congressmen carried the unconscious Adams to a sofa, which they moved into the rotunda, and finally into the chamber of House Speaker Robert Winthrop of Massachusetts.

The House, the Senate, and the Supreme Court immediately suspended all business. Balls and banquets that had been scheduled to commemorate George Washington's birthday were canceled, as America's last living link between the present day and the fading Revolutionary War era of Washington lay dying in the U.S. Capitol.

Adams's grandson, Henry Adams, would write, "The end of this first, or ancestral and Revolutionary, chapter came on February 21, 1848 . . . when the eighteenth century, as an actual and living companion, vanished."

Adams lingered two days. At one point, he regained consciousness long enough to ask for Henry Clay, who, weeping, came to Adams's side and clasped his hand. Adams revived a second time, reported his friend and House colleague, the Unitarian minister and historian John G. Palfrey of Boston, and was overheard to say, "This is the end of earth, but I am composed." Louisa Adams joined her husband, but he gave no sign of recognition, and she left in tears. Doctors rubbed brandy on his feet and applied suction cups to his temples, Palfrey reported in his frequent telegrams to family members in Boston. Adams remained unconscious.

On February 22, with Adams still in a coma and attended by doctors and close friends, the Senate met briefly in executive session to receive the Treaty of Guadalupe Hidalgo, the treaty signed February 2 that ended the Mexican War.

At 7:20 P.M. on Wednesday, February 23, John Quincy Adams died in the House Speaker's chamber.

Now commenced the greatest outpouring of grief for an American public figure since George Washington's death in 1799. Its equal would not be seen until Abraham Lincoln's assassination in 1865.

On February 24 and 25, fifteen thousand people filed past the bier upon which Adams's casket rested in the Capitol rotunda. The casket bore a plate inscribed with words written by Massachusetts Senator Daniel Webster:

JOHN QUINCY ADAMS

BORN
An Inhabitant of Massachusetts
July 11, 1767

DIED
A citizen of the United States, in the
Capitol, at Washington, February 23, 1848,
Having served his country for half a century,
And enjoyed its highest honors.

The fact that Adams had died in the Capitol—a rare event—while performing the public duties to which he had devoted fifty years of his life, imbued his passing with an almost sacred aura.

"He has been privileged to die at his post," said House Speaker Winthrop, during an observance in the House of Representatives attended by both senators and representatives, "to fall while in the discharge of his duties; to expire beneath the roof of the Capitol; and to have his last scene associated forever . . . with the birthday of that illustrious Patriot [Washington], whose just discernment brought him first into the service of his country."

"When a great man falls, the nation mourns," said Congressman Isaac Holmes of South Carolina. "When a patriarch is removed, the people weep. Ours, my associates, is no common bereavement. The chain which linked our hearts with the gifted spirits of former times, has been rudely snapped."

"He was the ready vessel, always under sail," said Senator Thomas Hart Benton of Missouri, noting that Adams was the oldest working member of the U.S. government. "Punctual to every duty, death found him at the post of duty . . . in the fullness of age, in the ripeness of renown, crowned with honors, surrounded by his family, his friends, and admirers, and in the very presence of the national representation."

Virginia Congressman James McDowell recalled Adams's singular presence in the House: "There he sat, with his intense eye upon everything that passed, the picturesque and rare old man; unapproachable by all others in the unity of his character and in the thousand-fold anxieties which centered upon him. No human being ever entered this hall without turning habitually and with heartfelt deference first to him."

At the service in the House chamber on February 25, a choir sang a dirge, and the House chaplain, the Reverend R. R. Gurley, took his sermon theme from Job: "And thine age shall be clearer than the noonday; thou shalt shine forth, thou shalt be as the morning."

From the Capitol, the funeral procession wound through Washington's streets, ending at the Congressional Cemetery, where Adams's casket was placed in a temporary vault for several days. Arrangements were made for thirty congressmen—one from each state and territory—to escort the remains to Boston.

Draped in black, the train chugged north to Boston, bearing the sixth president's casket and its congressional honor guard. Along the way, people lined the tracks, bowing their heads in respect as the train passed them. The mournful cavalcade paused in cities and towns along the way for local observances. At each stopping place, business was suspended, there were military and civil processions, flags flew at half-staff, bells tolled, and minute-gun salutes were fired. Never in America had there been anything like this; the haunting ritual would be repeated during Abraham Lincoln's last journey to Illinois in 1865.

Adams's remains reached Boston on March 10 in a driving rainstorm. Drenched crowds thronged the old city's twisting streets. The scheduled outdoor ceremonies were moved to Faneuil Hall. It was a fitting venue; not only had Adams often spoken there, but the "Cradle of Liberty" symbolized the early days of the war for independence, whose last living icon was now gone. At the entrance to the hall was a placard that read, "John Quincy Adams, aged 81 [*sic*]. Born a citizen of Massachusetts. Died a citizen of the United States." And on a wall between the galleries were George Washington's words from 1797: "John Quincy Adams is the most valuable character we have abroad and the ablest of all our diplomatic corps." Mayor Josiah Quincy Jr., the son of Adams's lifelong friend and cousin, found "something sublime in the scene that surrounds us. . . . One who heard the thunder of the great struggle for liberty on yonder hill, has, after a life of unparalleled usefulness and fidelity, fallen in the Capitol of the country he served."

The next day, Adams's casket was conducted in a procession to Quincy, where the Reverend William P. Lunt discoursed on Revelation 2:10, "Be thou faithful onto death, and I will give thee a crown of life." Adams's remains were placed in the family vault in the Quincy cemetery. Minute guns fired a salute from the brow of Penn's Hill, where Adams and his mother had stood on that June day in 1775, watching the Battle of Bunker Hill.

In May 1852, Louisa Catherine Adams died after suffering a stroke. Charles Francis placed her remains in a granite family crypt erected under the portal of the Unitarian church in Quincy. He then moved to the crypt the remains of his father, and of his grandparents, John and Abigail Adams.

Charles Francis penned the eloquent, moving epitaph to his parents that is inscribed on a marble tablet that adorns the church's front wall:

A

Ω

Near this place
Reposes all that could die of
JOHN QUINCY ADAMS
Son of John and Abigail [Smith] Adams
Sixth President of the United States,
Born 11 July, 1767,
Amidst the storms of Civil Commotion,
He nursed the vigor
Which nerves a Statesman and a Patriot,
And the Faith
Which inspires a Christian.
For more than half a century,
Whenever his country called for his Labors,
In either hemisphere or in any Capacity,
He never spared them in her Cause.
On the Twenty-fourth of December, 1814,
He signed the second Treaty with Great Britain,
Which restored peace within her borders;
On the Twenty-third of February, 1848,
He closed sixteen years of eloquent Defence
Of the Lessons of his Youth,
By dying at his Post,
In her Great National council.

A son, worth of his Father,
A Citizen, shedding glory on his Country,
A Scholar ambitious to advance mankind,
This Christian sought to walk humbly
In the sight of God.

———————

Beside him lies
His Partner for fifty Years,
LOUISA CATHERINE,
Daughter of Joshua and Catherine (Nuth)
Johnson,
Born, 12 February, 1775,
Married, 26 July, 1797,
Deceased, 15 May, 1852,
Aged 77.
Living through many vicissitudes, and
Under high responsibilities,
As a Daughter, Wife, and Mother,
She proved equal to all;
Dying, she left to her family and her sex
The blessed remembrance
Of a "Woman that feareth the Lord."

"Herein is that saying true, one soweth and another reapeth. I sent you to reap that wherein
ye bestowed no labor: other men labored, and ye are entered into their labors."

Epilogue

*"I have rendered to my country all the great services
which she was willing to receive at my hands,
and I have never harbored a thought
concerning her that was not divine."*
—William Seward, applying a quotation
from Cicero to John Quincy Adams

*J*ohn Quincy Adams embarked on his congressional career with no fanfare and no expectations other than to serve his constituents. He had no partisan ax to grind, no cause to champion, and nothing further to prove. For thirty-five years, with scarcely a break, he had served his country as a diplomat to Europe, a senator, secretary of state, and president.

The same deeply felt obligation to public duty that had compelled the reluctant George Washington to serve as the first president persuaded Adams to obey the summons of his friends and neighbors in the Plymouth District in 1830. It was an impulse that was fading from American public life when Adams commenced his duties at Seat 203 in the House of Representatives on December 5, 1831. At sixty-four, Adams was the oldest of the eighty-nine freshmen congressmen seated that day.

Adams probably expected that he would serve out his term in the 22nd Congress and then retire to Quincy with his family, books, diary, garden, and memories. He may have envisioned a more graceful exit than the one occasioned by his defeat by Andrew Jackson. And

253

though he never mentioned any such intention, he may also have secretly entertained hopes of avenging the abuses heaped upon him during the mudslinging 1828 presidential campaign. But never did he imagine the career that lay before him. Rather than being a museum piece from America's founding generation, Adams became Congress's conscience.

Adams's mental superstructure was an amalgam of eighteenth-century Enlightenment thought and the Calvinism of Cotton Mather. He could also be described as a Renaissance man, when one considers his literary accomplishments, his devotion to astronomy and silviculture, his commitment to establishing the Smithsonian Institution and a national observatory, and his intensive struggle to live a Christian life. Puritan self-discipline infused every facet of his life; he consistently pushed himself to rise earlier, to read and write more, to walk and swim farther and faster. In all this, he was not anomalous to American men of his generation and education. But after most of his contemporaries had passed on, Adams stood out as a rarity.

Although Adams's accomplishments greatly outweighed his failings, he nonetheless ceaselessly catalogued his shortcomings in his diary with heartfelt admonishments. At a time in life when most men of his generation were settling into retirement, Adams was pushing himself to do better, achieve more.

Although Adams was a poet, intellectual, scholar, and lifelong learner, he was no ivory-tower philosopher. He craved public life. He discovered this truth about himself only after spending decades longing for retirement among his books and plants.

As Adams found out, his congressional seat granted him a degree of freedom that he had never before enjoyed in public life. As a diplomat, he had been independent of immediate supervision, but he was tethered to U.S. policy and handcuffed by protocol. As a Massachusetts senator, he was answerable to the state General Assembly. When he was secretary of state, the president was the final arbiter. And as president, Adams, incorrigibly inept as a politician, was a leaf carried along on powerful political currents.

Now accountable to just 11,000 constituents (under the congressional apportionment ratio extant in 1830), Adams was free either to toil in anonymity as one of 213 representatives, quietly safeguarding the interests of his people, or to champion a cause. Having embarked on a wholly new public career, he learned that being a former president granted him visibility but no special privileges or advantages; some members respected his station, while others found vulnerabilities in his long public history to attack. Like all congressmen, Adams was subject to the rules of the forum, to the Speaker's authority, and to potential censure.

But Adams was no ordinary congressman; he was a statesman with a mind trained to analyze issues and take action. He made himself a master of parliamentary rules—with his near-photographic memory and encyclopedic mind, this was not particularly difficult—and consequently, he became an exceptionally effective congressman. He was so conversant in House procedures and protocol that in December 1839, when the House was unable to organize itself, his colleagues turned to him to lead them out of the morass.

Adams possessed another, incalculable advantage: a moral rudder that steered by principle and not politics. It had been an albatross when he was president, at the dawn of the second American political party system. But in Congress he could play the part of an Old Testament prophet, auguring civil war unless the United States shed its shameful legacy of slavery.

Striving, faith in God, trust in reason, a steady moral rudder, and an extraordinarily perceptive mind went into the making of "Old Man Eloquent." Four years after first taking his seat in Congress, all the ingredients were present, awaiting the pinch of yeast, the cause worthy of his talents and energy. He prayed that "a ray of light might flash upon my eyes," revealing it to him.

It came to him in December 1835. The South's suppression of the abolition societies' mass mailings and Southerners' indignant defense of their prerogatives as slaveholders had exhausted his former tolerance for the institution of slavery. Rumblings that they might next suppress the right to petition impelled him finally to act. "I have taken up the glove in the House."

With this one decision Adams changed his life, his legacy, and the course of events. "The cause is good and great," he wrote. He became expert at waging the long fight. It took eight years to rescind the Gag Rule; for nine years, he was almost single-handedly responsible for delaying the annexation of Texas. He repudiated the federal government's heartless Indian removal policy and defended women's political rights and the right of free speech. "The right of petition . . . is essential to the very existence of government; it is the right of the people over the Government; it is their right, and they may not be deprived of it." All the while, he baited and fought the slave power. Slavery was "a sin before the sight of God."

Quite by accident, Adams became more popular in his seventies than he had been as a younger man. Surprisingly, given his previous reticence, Adams found that he enjoyed the rough-and-tumble House debates, and he wore his vilification by Southerners as a badge of honor.

He not only relished the fights on the House floor but also discovered a late-blooming talent for oratory and debate. Extraordinarily skilled in marshaling facts from his near-infallible memory into cogent argument, "Old Nestor" was a formidable adversary and potent advocate.

All along, Adams intuitively knew not only that slavery was inherently evil but also that it would lead to civil war. He introduced three constitutional amendments in the House to gradually phase it out. The South, he argued, going to the heart of its objection to

emancipation, stood to gain congressional representation by transforming slaves, each counting for census purposes as three-fifths of
a white man, into citizens counting as whole men. He proposed
that all children born in the United States on or after July 4, 1842,
be free, that slavery be abolished in the District of Columbia by
1845, and that no new slave state, Florida excepted, be admitted
into the Union. As Adams expected, his attempts to amend the
Constitution died. And as Adams feared, the slavery debate, irrev-
ocably unstoppered by the Mexican War, later brought on the
deadliest war in American history.

Because historians rate American presidents on their accomplishments in office and not on their post-presidencies, John Quincy
Adams usually fares poorly. Responsibility for this assessment lies
largely with Adams; he was politically tone-deaf, almost willfully
so, at the very moment that a new political party system was rapidly taking shape in the country. He naively named Henry Clay
secretary of state, heedless of the appearance that a "corrupt bargain" had been made during the campaign. He refused to wield his
patronage or to form a party organization, and his concept of seeking office was hopelessly anachronistic. Furthermore, his administration's "Liberty with Power" program was decades ahead of its
time and out of step with public sentiment. Thus, it failed in every
respect: Few canals, bridges, or roads were built; no national university, national observatory, or U.S. naval academy was established; government research and exploration languished; Adams's
dream of a Department of the Interior would not be fulfilled until
after the Mexican War; and Congress bridled at his attempts to
foster hemispheric unity. Adams stubbornly adhered to an antiquated mode of conducting public business amid changing political realities that he refused to acknowledge.

Less to blame, but sharing some responsibility for Adams's dismal presidential legacy, is his nemesis, Andrew Jackson, who gave

his supporters free rein to vilify Adams, especially during the vicious 1828 presidential campaign. The winners write the history, and Jackson's legion of propagandists, both politicians and historians, succeeded in tagging Adams as an elitist with monarchical leanings. Perhaps this was retribution for Adams's protestations against the unsavory aspects of the Jackson program: his safeguarding of slavery, his efforts to annex Texas and thereby extend slavery, and his forced removal of the eastern Indian tribes to enable Southern slaveholders to occupy their lands. Yet Adams crossed party lines to support Jackson on nullification and French spoliations. He never forgave Old Hickory for returning his support with malignity.

Adams was skilled at agitating his political enemies—and they were legion—to the point that they tried to censure him, a decision they instantly regretted as Adams, in self-defense, proceeded to carve them up on the House floor. But in their countless attacks on Adams, never did his adversaries challenge his integrity or impugn his motives—a backhanded tribute to his high-mindedness.

Following the unsuccessful censure attempt in 1842, Adams's congressional colleagues increasingly began granting him the same iconic respect that Adams's countrymen were according him. During the Roaring '40s, the Industrial Age gained momentum in America with its steamships, railroads, the telegraph, and the penny press. As often happens in times of rapid change, there was an upwelling of nostalgia for a bygone era—in this case, the war for independence and the nation's founding, which were fading from memory. Books written about that era, such as *Washington and His Generals*, became best-sellers as people sought to learn more about American independence. Thus, it stood to reason that the public would revere the last connection with that golden age, John Quincy Adams, still serving his country fifty years after President George Washington sent him to the Netherlands.

And so, with his powers rapidly ebbing, Adams became, of all things, a living symbol. Surely, it must have made him secretly proud, and a bit amused, as would have the enormous public outpouring of emotion at his death.

William Seward, who would later become secretary of state under Abraham Lincoln, observed in his eulogy for his good friend that, like Cicero, Adams could say, "I have rendered to my country all the great services which she was willing to receive at my hands, and I have never harbored a thought concerning her that was not divine."

Adams's poem to sculptor Hiram Powers in 1837 strikes the same note of pure-heartedness. Powers had made a clay mold for a bust of Adams that now resides in the Quincy Unitarian church where Adams's remains lie. Adams's son, Charles Francis, closes his father's memoirs with the poem, whose first stanza could well serve as an epitaph for Old Man Eloquent:

> *Sculptor! thy hand has moulded into form*
> *The haggard features of a toil–worn face,*
> *And whosoever views thy work shall trace*
> *An age of sorrows, and a life of storm.*
> *And canst though mould the heart? for that is warm,*
> *Glowing with tenderness for all its race,*
> *Instinct with all the sympathies that grace*
> *The pure and artless bosoms where they swarm.*

Bibliography

BIBLIOGRAPHY

25th Congress, 3rd Session, House Executive Document 11. Correspondence, miscellany.

26th Congress, 1st Session, Serial Set No. 277. Committee Reports.

27th Congress, 2nd Session, Serial Set No. 409. Committee Reports.

28th Congress, 1st Session, House Executive Documents. Committee Reports, Vol. 2. Report No. 404.

28th Congress, 1st Session, Serial Set No. 447. Committee Reports, Vol. 3.

Abridgement of the Debates of Congress, from 1789 to 1856. New York: D. Appleton, 1861.

Adams, Charles Francis. *The Diary of Charles Francis Adams.* Cambridge: Belknap Press of Harvard University, 1964.

_____. "John Quincy Adams and Emancipation Under Martial Law." *Proceedings of the Massachusetts Historical Society.* Boston, January 1902.

Adams, Henry. *The Degradation of the Democratic Dogma.* Introduction by Brooks Adams. New York: Peter Smith, 1949. First published in 1919.

_____. *The Education of Henry Adams.* Boston: Houghton Mifflin, 1972. First published in 1918.

Adams, James Truslow. *The Adams Family.* New York: Literary Guild, 1930.

Adams, John Quincy. *An Address Delivered on the Occasion of Reading the Declaration of Independence on the 4th of July, 1821, Washington.* Washington, D.C.: Davis and Force, 1821. Courtesy of Massachusetts Historical Society.

_____. *Address of John Quincy Adams, to his Constituents of the Twelfth Congressional District, at Braintree, September 17th, 1842.* Boston: J. H. Eastburn, 1842.

_____. *An Answer to Pain's [sic] Rights of Man.* Dublin: Printed for Messrs. F. Byrne, J. Moore, and W. Jones, 1793. On microfilm, Davis Library,

University of North Carolina–Chapel Hill. First published in 1791 in the Boston *Columbian Sentinel.*

_____. *Argument of John Quincy Adams before the Supreme Court of the United States in the case of the United States, Appellants, vs. Cinque, and Others, Africans.* New York: S. W. Benedict, 1841.

_____. *Dermot MacMorrough, or the Conquest of Ireland: An Historical Tale of the Twelfth Century in Four Cantos.* Edited by Martin J. Burke, Elizabeth FitzPatrick, and Olivia Hamilton. Dublin: Maunsel, 2005.

_____. *The Diary of John Quincy Adams, 1794–1845: American Diplomacy, and Political, Social, and Intellectual Life, from Washington to Polk.* Edited by Allan Nevins. New York: Charles Scribner's Sons, 1951. First published in 1928.

_____. *The Diary of John Quincy Adams (1779–1788).* Edited by Robert J. Taylor and Marc Friedlaender. Cambridge, London: Belknap Press of Harvard University Press, 1981.

_____. *The Great Design: Two Lectures on the Smithson Bequest by John Quincy Adams.* Edited by Wilcomb E. Washburn. Washington, D.C.: Smithsonian Institution, 1965.

_____. *The Jubilee of the Constitution: A Discourse Delivered at the Request of the New-York Historical Society.* New York: Samuel Colman VIII, Astor House, 1839. Available online at Davis Library, University of North Carolina–Chapel Hill.

_____. *Lectures on Rhetoric and Oratory.* New York: Russell & Russell, 1962. First published in 1810.

_____. *Letter from John Quincy Adams Read at the Recent Celebration of West India Emancipation in Bangor, Maine* (July 4, 1843). In *Miscellaneous Works of John Quincy Adams, in Five Volumes.* Edited by Henry Adams. Vol. 1, No. 26. Courtesy Massachusetts Historical Society, Boston.

_____. *Letters from John Quincy Adams to his Constituents of the Twelfth Congressional District in Massachusetts.* Boston: Isaac Knapp, 1837. Courtesy of Massachusetts Historical Society, Boston.

_____. *Letters on the Masonic Institution.* Boston: Press of T. R. Marvin, 1847.

_____. *The Lives of James Madison and James Monroe: Fourth and Fifth Presidents of the United States.* Buffalo, New York: Geo. H. Derby, 1850.

_____. *Memoirs of John Quincy Adams, Comprising Portions of his Diary from 1795 to 1848.* Edited by Charles Francis Adams. Freeport, New York: Books for Libraries, 1969. First published 1874–1877.

_____. "Misconceptions of Shakespeare Upon the Stage." *New England Magazine,* December 1835. On microfilm, Davis Library, University of North Carolina–Chapel Hill.

_____. *An Oration Delivered before the Cincinnati Astronomical Society.* Cincinnati: Shepard, 1843.

_____. *An Oration Delivered Before the Inhabitants of Newburyport on the 61st Anniversary of the Declaration of Independence, July 4, 1837.* Newburyport: Morse and Brewster, 1837.

_____. *Parties in the United States.* New York: Greenburg, 1941.

_____. *Poems of Religion and Society.* New York: Wm. H. Graham, 1848.

_____. *Report of the Secretary of State Upon Weights and Measures.* Washington, D.C.: Gales and Seaton, 1826.

_____. "Society and Civilization." *Whig Review,* Vol. 2, No. 1 (July 1845). Courtesy of Massachusetts Historical Society, Boston.

_____. *Speech of John Quincy Adams of Massachusetts upon the Right of the People, Men and Women, to Petition.* New York: Arno Press & New York Times, 1969. First published in 1938.

_____. *Speech on the Joint Resolution for Distributing Rations to the Distressed Fugitives from Indian Hostilities in the States of Alabama and Georgia.* Speech delivered on May 25, 1836. Washington, D.C.: National Intelligencer. Courtesy Massachusetts Historical Society, Boston.

_____. *Writings of John Quincy Adams.* Edited by Worthington Chauncey Ford. New York: Greenwood Press, 1968. First published in 1913.

Adams, Louisa. *Adventures of a Nobody.* In *Microfilms of the Adams Papers,* Reel 269. Boston: Massachusetts Historical Society, 1954.

The Amistad Case: The Most Celebrated Slave Mutiny of the Nineteenth Century. New York, London: Johnson Reprint, 1968.

Bailey, Thomas A. *A Diplomatic History of the American People.* New York: Appleton-Century-Crofts, 1964.

Barber, John Warner. *A History of the Amistad Captives.* New York: Arno Press, 1969.

Barnes, Gilbert Hobbs. *The Antislavery Impulse, 1830–1844.* New York, London: D. Appleton-Century, 1933.

Bemis, Samuel Flagg. *John Quincy Adams and the Foundations of American Foreign Policy.* New York: Alfred A. Knopf, 1965. First published in 1949.

_____. *John Quincy Adams and the Union.* New York: Alfred A. Knopf, 1956.

Benton, Thomas Hart. *Thirty Years View.* New York: D. Appleton, 1856.

Biographical Dictionary of the United States Congress, 1774–1989. Washington, D.C.: Government Printing Office, 1989.

Birney, Catherine H. *The Grimké Sisters.* Boston: Lee and Shepard, 1885.

Brookhiser, Richard. *America's First Dynasty: The Adamses, 1735–1918.* New York: Free Press, 2002.

Burleigh, Nina. *The Stranger and the Statesman: James Smithson, John Quincy Adams, and the Making of America's Greatest Museum: The Smithsonian.* New York: William Morrow, 2003.

Calhoun, John C. *The Papers of John C. Calhoun.* Vol. 13. Columbia: University of South Carolina Press, 1980.

Carruth, Gorton. *What Happened When: A Chronology of Life & Events in America.* New York: Signet, 1991.

Clark, Bennett Champ. *John Quincy Adams: "Old Man Eloquent."* Boston: Little, Brown, 1932.

Concise Dictionary of American Biography. Edited by Joseph G. E. Hopkins et al. New York: Charles Scribner's Sons, 1977.

The Congressional Globe. Washington, D.C.: Blaire & Rives, 1834–1873.

The Constitution of the United States with the Declaration of Independence and the Articles of Confederation. Edited by R. B. Bernstein. New York: Barnes & Noble, 2002.

Dickens, Charles. *American Notes: A Journey.* New York: Fromm International, 1985. First published in 1842.

Documents of American History. Edited by Henry Steele Commager. New York: Appleton-Century-Crofts, 1968.

Durant, Will. *Caesar and Christ: A History of Roman Civilization and of Christianity from Their Beginning to A.D. 325.* New York: Simon and Schuster, 1944.

Earle, Jonathan H. *Jacksonian Antislavery & the Politics of Free Soil, 1824–1854.* Chapel Hill, London: University of North Carolina Press, 2004.

East, Robert A. *John Quincy Adams: The Critical Years, 1785–1794.* New York: Bookman Associates, 1962.

Emerson, Ralph Waldo. *The Journals and Miscellaneous Notebooks of Ralph Waldo Emerson.* Vol. 8. Edited by William H. Gilman and J. E. Parsons. Cambridge: Belknap Press of Harvard University Press, 1970.

Encyclopedia of American History. 1st ed. Edited by Richard B. Morris. New York: Harper & Brothers, 1953.

Encyclopedia of American History. 6th ed. Edited by Richard B. Morris. New York: Harper & Row, 1982.

Encyclopedia of the War of 1812. Edited by David S. Heidler and Jeanne T. Heidler. Denver, Santa Barbara, Oxford: ABC-CLIO, 1997.

An Encyclopaedia of World History. Edited by William L. Langer. Boston: Houghton Mifflin, 1940.

Freehling, William W. *Prelude to Civil War: The Nullification Crisis in South Carolina, 1816–1836.* New York, London: Harper & Row, 1965.

French, Benjamin Brown. *Witness to the Young Republic: A Yankee's Journal, 1828–1870.* Edited by Daniel B. Cole and John J. McDonough. Hanover, London: University Press of London, 1989.

Giddings, Joshua R. *History of the Rebellion: Its Authors and Causes.* New York: Follet, Foster, 1864.

Grant, Ulysses S. *Personal Memoirs of U. S. Grant.* Edited by E. B. Long. New York: DaCapo, 1982.

Hargreaves, Mary W. M. *The Presidency of John Quincy Adams.* Lawrence: University Press of Kansas, 1985.

Hecht, Marie. *John Quincy Adams: A Personal History of an Independent Man.* New York: Macmillan, 1972.

Historical Statistics of the United States: Colonial Times to 1970. Washington, D.C.: Bureau of the Census.

Howe, Daniel Walker. *The Political Culture of the Whigs.* Chicago, London: University of Chicago Press, 1979.

Jones, Howard. *Mutiny on the Amistad: The Saga of a Slave Revolt and Its Impact on American Abolition, Law, and Diplomacy.* New York, Oxford: Oxford University Press, 1987.

Kennedy, John F. *Profiles in Courage.* New York: Harper & Brothers, 1955.

Ketcham, Ralph. *Presidents Above Party: The First American Presidency, 1789–1829.* Chapel Hill: University of North Carolina Press, 1984.

Kunhardt, Philip B., Jr., Philip B. Kunhardt III, and Peter W. Kunhardt. *The American President.* New York: Riverhead Books, 1999.

Lipsky, George A. *John Quincy Adams: His Theory & Ideas.* New York: Thomas Y. Crowell, 1950.

Ludlum, Robert P. "The Antislavery 'Gag Rule': History and Argument." *Journal of Negro History,* Vol. 26 (April 1941). Washington, D.C.: Association for the Study of Negro Life and History.

Malone, Dumas. *Jefferson and the Rights of Man.* Boston: Little, Brown, 1951.

Marshall, Thomas F. *Speeches and Writings.* Edited by W. L. Barre. Cincinnati: Applegate, 1858.

Martin, Christopher. *The Amistad Affair.* London, New York, Toronto: Abelard-Schuman, 1970.

Massachusetts Historical Society Online, at www.masshist.org/exhibitions/jqa.cfm.

Masur, Louis P. *1831: Year of Eclipse.* New York: Hill and Wang, 2001.

May, Ernest R. *The Making of the Monroe Doctrine.* Cambridge: Harvard University Press, 1992. First published in 1975.

McCarthy, Charles. "The Antimasonic Party." *Annual Report of the American Historical Association for the Year 1902*, Vol. 1.

McPherson, James. "The Fight Against the Gag Rule: Joshua Leavitt and Antislavery Insurgency in the Whig Party, 1839–1842." *Journal of Negro History*, Vol. 48 (1962). Washington, D.C.: Association for the Study of Negro Life and History.

Messages and Papers of the Presidents, 1789–1897. Edited by James D. Richardson. Published by Authority of Congress, 1899.

Microfilms of the Adams Papers. Boston: Massachusetts Historical Society, 1954.

Miller, Douglas T. *The Birth of Modern America, 1820–1850*. Indianapolis, New York: Bobbs-Merrill, 1970.

Miller, William Lee. *Arguing About Slavery: The Great Battle in the United States Congress*. New York: Alfred A. Knopf, 1996.

Morgan, William G. "John Quincy Adams Versus Andrew Jackson: Their Biographers and the 'Corrupt Bargain' Charge." *Tennessee Historical Quarterly*, Vol. 26 (Spring 1967).

Morse, John T. *John Quincy Adams*. Boston: Houghton, Mifflin, 1884.

Musto, David F. "The Youth of John Quincy Adams." *Proceedings of the American Philosophical Society*, Vol. 113 (1969). Philadelphia: American Philosophical Society.

Nagel, Paul C. *John Quincy Adams: A Public Life, a Private Life*. New York: Alfred A. Knopf, 1997.

Oxford Companion to the Supreme Court of the United States. Edited by Kermit L. Hall. New York, Oxford: Oxford University Press, 1992.

Oxford Companion to United States History. Edited by Paul S. Boyer. Oxford, New York: Oxford University Press, 2001.

Perkins, Bradford. *Castlereagh and Adams: England and the United States, 1812–1823*. Berkeley, Los Angeles: University of California Press, 1964.

Philbrick, Nathaniel. *Mayflower: A Story of Courage, Community, and War*. New York: Viking, 2006.

Polk, James K. *The Diary of James K. Polk, During His Presidency, 1845 to 1849*. Edited by Milo Milton Quaife. Chicago: A. C. McClurg, 1910.

Portolano, Marlana. "John Quincy Adams's Promotion of Astronomy and his Neoclassical Rhetoric," *Isis Magazine*, No. 91 (2000).

Proceedings of the Massachusetts Historical Society. Boston: Massachusetts Historical Society.

Quincy, Josiah. *Memoir of the Life of John Quincy Adams*. Boston: Phillips, Sampson, 1858.

The Reader's Encyclopedia. Edited by William Rose Benét. New York: Thomas Y. Crowell, 1948.

Register of Debates in Congress. Washington, D.C.: Gales and Seaton.

Remini, Robert V. *The Election of Andrew Jackson*. Philadelphia, New York: J. B. Lippincott, 1963.

_____. *John Quincy Adams*. New York: Times Books, Henry Holt, 2002.

Richards, Leonard L. *The Life and Times of Congressman John Quincy Adams*. New York, Oxford: Oxford University Press, 1986.

Ridley, Jasper. *The Freemasons: A History of the World's Most Powerful Secret Society*. New York: Arcade, 2001.

Royall, Ann. *Sketches of History, Life, and Manners in the United States*. New York, London: Johnson Reprint, 1970. First published in 1826.

Seward, William H. *An Autobiography from 1801 to 1834, with a Memoirs of his Life, and Selections from his Letters, 1831–1846*. Edited by Frederick W. Seward. New York: Derby and Miller, 1891.

_____. *Life and Public Services of John Quincy Adams, Sixth President of the United States, with the Eulogy Delivered before the Legislature of New York*. Auburn, New York: Derby, Miller, 1851.

Shepherd, Jack. *Cannibals of the Heart: A Personal Biography of Louisa Catherine and John Quincy Adams*. New York: McGraw-Hill, 1980.

A Sketch of the Life and Services of John Q. Adams, President of the United States. Campaign pamphlet. 1827.

Story, Joseph. *Life and Letters of Joseph Story*. Edited by William W. Story. Vol. 2. Boston: Charles C. Little and James Brown, 1851.

Time Almanac 2003. Boston: Time Inc. Home Entertainment, 2002.

Tocqueville, Alexis de. *Democracy in America*. Edited by J. P. Mayer. Translated by George Lawrence. Garden City, New York: Anchor Books, Doubleday, 1969.

Token of a Nation's Sorrow: Addresses in the Congress of the United States and Funeral Solemnities on the Death of John Quincy Adams. Washington, D.C.: J. and G. S. Gideon, 1848. Courtesy of Massachusetts Historical Society.

Trollope, Frances Milton (Fanny). *Domestic Manners of the Americans*. New York: A. A. Knopf, 1949.

United States Magazine and Democratic Review, Vol. 1, No. 1 (1838). Washington, D.C.: Langtree and O'Sullivan. On microfilm at Davis Library, University of North Carolina–Chapel Hill.

Van Buren, Martin. *The Autobiography of Martin Van Buren. Annual Report of the American Historical Association*, Vol. 2 (1918).

Watson, Harry L. *Liberty and Power: The Politics of Jacksonian America.* New York: Hill and Wang, 1990.

Weld, Theodore Dwight. *American Slavery As It Is: Testimony of a Thousand Witnesses.* New York: Arno Press and New York Times, 1968. First published by the American Anti-Slavery Society in 1839.

Weld, Theodore Dwight, Angelina Grimké, and Sarah Grimké. *Letters of Theodore Dwight Weld, Angelina Grimké and Sarah Grimké, 1822–1844.* Edited by Gilbert H. Barnes and Dwight L. Dumond. New York, London: D. Appleton-Century, 1934.

Wheelan, Joseph. *Invading Mexico: Manifest Destiny and the Mexican War, 1846–1848.* New York: Carroll & Graf, 2007.

_____. *Jefferson's War: America's First War on Terror, 1801–1805.* New York: Carroll & Graf, 2003.

Whitney, David C., and Robin Vaughn Whitney. *The American Presidents.* New York: Prentice Hall, 1993.

Whittier, John Greenleaf. *Anti-Slavery Poems: Songs of Labor and Reform.* Vol. 3 of *Whittier's Poetical Works.* Boston, New York: Houghton, Mifflin, 1888.

Wilentz, Sean. *Andrew Jackson.* New York: Times Books, 2005.

Wills, Garry. *Henry Adams and the Making of America.* Boston, New York: Houghton, Mifflin, 2005.

Wood, Gary V. *Heir to the Fathers: John Quincy Adams and the Spirit of Constitutional Government.* New York: Lexington Books, 2004.

Notes

PROLOGUE

xiv   "At Davis's home" . . . John Quincy Adams, *Memoirs*, Vol. 8, pp. 239–240.

xiv   "His initial reaction" . . . Ibid., pp. 80–81.

xv   "'To say that I'" . . . Ibid., p. 241.

xv   "Accurately reading Adams's" . . . Ibid., pp. 240–241.

xv   "The *Boston Daily Courier*" . . . Bemis, *Union*, p. 206; Lincoln-Davis letter, from *Proceedings of the Massachusetts Historical Society*, Vol. 49, p. 235; JQA, *Memoirs*, Vol. 8, pp. 242–243.

xvi   "'The sun of my'" . . . JQA, *Memoirs*, Vol. 8, p. 78.

xvii   "The White House years" . . . Abigail Adams-JQA letter, May 20, 1796, *Microfilms of Adams Papers*; Shepherd, p. 262.

xvii   "Now, finally out of" . . . Hecht, p. 503; Shepherd, 332; Charles Francis Adams, *Diary*, Vol. 3, pp. 348–349.

xvii   "Their son, Charles Francis" . . . CFA, *Diary*, Vol. 3, pp. 328–329, 331.

xvii   "John Quincy Adams's eighteen-month" . . . Bemis, *Union*, p. 165; James Adams, p. 207; Richards, pp. 32–35.

xviii   "Amid the family's" . . . Hecht, p. 497; Bemis, *Union*, pp. 179, 181.

xviii   "Upon reaching Quincy" . . . Nagel, pp. 313–314; Bemis, *Union*, pp. 184–185.

xviii   "Adams compared the abrupt" . . . JQA, *Memoirs*, Vol. 8, pp. 106–107.

xix   "One satisfying task" . . . Bemis, *Union*, pp. 188–192; *JQA Digital Diaries*, No. 36, p. 278 (October 17, 1829); Hecht, p. 500; Nagel, pp. 331–332.

xix   "On the last day" . . . JQA, *Memoirs*, Vol. 8, pp. 159–160.

xix   "No matter how strenuous" . . . Ibid., p. 14.

xx   "When his would-be" . . . Ibid., pp. 245–247.

xx   "Louisa announced that" . . . CFA, *Diary*, Vol. 3, pp. 348–349.

xx "Twenty-year-old Charles" . . . Bemis, *Union*, p. 220.

xx "Adams's five presidential" . . . JQA, *Memoirs*, Vol. 8, pp. 245–246.

xxi "As he wrote" . . . Bemis, *Union*, p. 210 footnote.

CHAPTER 1: FAVORED SON OF THE REVOLUTION

2 "But the publication of, Thomas Paine's" . . . JQA, *Writings*, Vol. 1, pp. 65–66 footnote.

2 "Born July 11, 1767" . . . Morse, pp. 1–2.

2 "Adams's father and his" . . . Seward, *Life*, p. 17; Nagel, pp. 5–7, 10, 384; *Concise Dictionary*, p. 11.

2 "The Adams farm" . . . JQA, *Diary* (Taylor, ed.), Vol. 1, p. xxxxv; Nagel, pp. 3–4; Ketcham, p. 130; JQA, *Memoirs*, Vol. 8, p. 157; Bemis, *Foundations*, pp. 4, 8–9.

3 "He strolled with Sam" . . . Bemis, *Foundations*, pp. 5–6; JQA, *Memoirs*, Vol. 7, pp. 322, 325; Vol. 1, p. 5.

3 "John and Abigail Adams" . . . Nagel, p. 11.

4 "On a raw February" . . . Nagel, p. 13; Bemis, *Foundations*, p. 9.

4 "In Paris, John Adams" . . . Bemis, *Union*, pp. 10–11.

5 "On November 12, 1779" . . . JQA, *Diary* (Taylor), Vol. 1, pp. xxxii, xvii–xix, 1.

5 "Abigail continued to lecture" . . . Bemis, *Union*, p. 11; Abigail-JQA letters, January 19, 1780, and March 2, 1780, MHS online at www.masshist.org/exhibitions/jqa.cfm; Nagel, p. 16; Musto, pp. 271–281.

6 "Then in 1781" . . . JQA, *Diary* (Taylor), Vol. 1, pp. 103–151.

6 "Young Adams accompanied" . . . Ibid., p. 262; Bemis, *Foundations*, p. 14.

6 "In 1785, Adams returned" . . . East, pp. 17–18, 36, 63, 75; JQA, *Diary* (Taylor), Vol. 1, p. 317; Bemis, *Foundations*, pp. 21–22.

7 "Two years later" . . . Nagel, pp. 53–55; JQA, *Diary* (Taylor), Vol. 2, p. 428.

7 "Seeking relief from" . . . JQA, *Diary* (Taylor), Vol. 2, pp. 309, 207–208, 297–298.

7 "On his twenty-first birthday" . . . Ibid., pp. 427–428.

8 "Worries about the future" . . . Shepherd, p. 96 footnote.

8 "Adams's diary entry of" . . . JQA, *Diary* (Taylor), Vol. 2, pp. 326, 356.

8   "During a recurrence"... Nagel, pp. 60–62, 73; East, p. 88; JQA, *Diary* (Taylor), Vol. 2, pp. 456, 458–461.

8   "During his final year"... Nagel, pp. 67–69.

9   "As his courtship"... JQA, *Writings*, Vol. 1, pp. 61, 64, 44–49.

9   "Adams began to attract"... Nagel, pp. 70–73; Bemis, *Foundations*, p. 26; JQA, *Writings*, Vol. 1, pp. 50–51.

10   "In *The Rights of Man*"... *Concise Dictionary*, pp. 750–751; *Reader's Encyclopedia*, pp. 156, 928; Malone, p. 355.

11   "The publication of *The Rights of Man*"... Malone, pp. 354–357.

11   "And then in Boston's"... JQA, *Writings*, Vol. 1, pp. 65–68.

12   "Publicola sarcastically reminded"... JQA, *An Answer*; JQA, *Writings*, Vol. 1, p. 68.

12   "Flushed by Publicola's success"... East, pp. 153–156, 189; Bemis, *Foundations*, p. 28; JQA, *Writings*, Vol. 1, pp. 135–142, 126–127.

13   "Two years later"... *Encyclopedia of American History*, 1st ed., pp. 125–126; JQA, *Writings*, Vol. 1, p. 156; Bemis, *Foundations*, p. 38; Bailey, p. 89. [When France, under a new regime, sent Genêt's successor with orders to arrest him, Washington refused to hand Genêt over and thereby condemn him to almost certain death. He became a U.S. citizen, marrying a daughter of New York Governor George Clinton.]

14   "Impressed by John Quincy"... Nagel, pp. 77–82; JQA, *Writings*, Vol. 1, pp. 194–196; Bemis, *Foundations*, pp. 39–40; East, p. 193; Remini, *Adams*, p. 24.

15   "As all around him"... Nagel, pp. 89–90; JQA, *Writings*, Vol. 1, p. 425.

15   "In August 1795"... Bemis, *Foundations*, p. 79; Remini, *Adams*, pp. 26–27.

16   "For three months, Adams"... Nagel, pp. 94–95, 99–100; Remini, *Adams*, pp. 26–27.

16   "On July 26, 1797"... Nagel, pp. 111–112. [After the wedding, the Johnson family slipped out of London without paying its debts, and bill collectors accosted Adams and Louisa. President John Adams named Johnson postmaster of the District of Columbia, rescuing the family from poverty.]

16   "'At present I am'"... Bemis, *Foundations*, pp. 60–64; JQA, *Writings*, Vol. 1, pp. 354–355, 408–409.

17   "After five miscarriages, Louisa"... Shepherd, pp. 99–102; Nagel, p. 124.

17   "In Berlin, Adams fully matured" . . . Bemis, *Foundations*, pp. 90–91, 94–95, 100–101, 109–110; Wood, pp. 134–135; JQA, *Memoirs*, Vol. 12, pp. 137–138; Nagel, pp. 120–121, 125–127.

19   "After his return to America" . . . Nagel, pp. 128–135; Shepherd, pp. 96–99.

19   "Public life, Adams reasoned" . . . Nagel, pp. 133–135; JQA, *Memoirs*, Vol. 1, p. 249.

20   "Elected to the State Senate" . . . JQA, *Writings*, Vol. 3, p. 10; Kennedy, p. 38.

20   "Needing money, Adams ran" . . . Bemis, *Foundations*, pp. 113–114.

20   "The Adamses reached Washington" . . . Bemis, *Foundations*, pp. 119–124; JQA, *Memoirs*, Vol. 1, p. 371; JQA, *Parties*, p. 44; JQA, *Writings*, Vol. 3, p. 9.

21   "Even more than her husband" . . . Shepherd, pp. 3–7, 104–108; Nagel, p. 143.

21   "Every day, Adams walked" . . . Bemis, *Foundations*, pp. 129–131; JQA, *Memoirs*, Vol. 1, pp. 317, 330–331; Shepherd, pp. 113–114.

22   "Each generation, he believed" . . . Brookhiser, p. 67; Shepherd, pp. 164–165.

22   "Chronically dissatisfied with" . . . JQA, *Memoirs*, Vol. 1, pp. 425, 445; Remini, *Adams*, p. 37.

23   "In 1805, Adams broke" . . . Bemis, *Foundations*, pp. 141–142, 147, 182; *Encyclopedia of the War of 1812*, pp. 233–234; Lipsky, pp. 186–187 [Letter to Wm. Plumer, October 6, 1810]; JQA, *Memoirs*, Vol. 1, p. 380.

24   "The Federalists grumblingly" . . . Wheelan, *Jefferson's War*, pp. 334–335.

24   "Adams, who was teaching" . . . Bemis, *Foundations*, pp. 141–142; Nagel, p. 172; JQA, *Writings*, Vol. 3, p. 167; JQA, *Memoirs*, Vol. 1, p. 469.

24   "It now snapped under the strain" . . . Bemis, *Foundations*, p. 143; Remini, *Adams*, pp. 38–39.

25   "'My situation here'" . . . JQA, *Writings*, Vol. 3, p. 171; *Microfilms of Adams Papers*, Reel 118, John Adams-JQA letters, January 8 and 17, 1808.

25   "John Quincy Adams unmistakably" . . . Nagel, p. 178; Bemis, *Foundations*, pp. 145–148; *Proceedings of the MHS*, Vol. 45, pp. 358–359.

26   "Adams's abrupt departure" . . . JQA, *Writings*, Vol. 3, p. 189.

26   "In his letter of resignation" . . . Lipsky, p. 18; JQA, *Writings*, Vol. 3, p. 237; Bemis, *Foundations*, p. 149; JQA, *Memoirs*, Vol. 1, p. 536.

CHAPTER 2: THE ROAD TO THE PRESIDENCY

28   "In St. Petersburg, Europe's" . . . Shepherd, 149; *Microfilms Adams Papers*, JQA-JA letter, August 16, 1812.

28   "Adams, Albert Gallatin" . . . Perkins, pp. 159, 214, 279–280; Bemis, *Foundations*, pp. 224, 228–237.

29   "Adams's vast experience" . . . Bemis, *Foundations*, pp. 255–259; Lipsky, pp. 285–287.

29   "Adams enjoyed an excellent" . . . Remini, *Adams*, p. 51; Bemis, *Foundations*, p. 261.

30   "Adams had just departed " . . . JQA, *Digital Diaries*, No. 30, pp. 430–432; JQA, *Memoirs*, Vol. 4, pp. 157–158, 202.

30   "General Andrew Jackson had lit" . . . Perkins, pp. 285–290; Bemis, *Foundations*, pp. 313–315.

31   "During five cabinet meetings" . . . Perkins, p. 289; JQA, *Memoirs*, Vol. 4, pp. 107–114.

31   "Monroe chose the middle" . . . Bemis, *Foundations*, pp. 313–314; Perkins, p. 290; Bailey, p. 171.

31   "Jackson's invasion induced" . . . Remini, *Adams*, p. 56; Bailey, pp. 171–173; Bemis, *Foundations*, p. 327; JQA, *Memoirs*, Vol. 5, p. 473.

32   "Such an occasion arose" . . . May, p. 2; *Encyclopedia of World History*, pp. 650–651.

32   "George Canning, the British" . . . Perkins, pp. 200, 314–317, 301–302, 327; May, p. 197; Brookhiser, p. 89; JQA, *Address Washington, July 4, 1821*, p. 29 [Courtesy of Massachusetts Historical Society]; Nagel, p. 269; Bailey, p. 182; JQA, *Memoirs*, Vol. 6, pp. 177–180, 186, 194.

34   "The monumental policy" . . . Bailey, p. 183.

34   "In just three paragraphs" . . . *Documents of American History*, pp. 235–237; JQA, *Memoirs*, Vol. 12, p. 218.

34   "Reactions in Europe" . . . Perkins, pp. 337–338; Bailey, pp. 186–188.

35   "A man must fulfill'" . . . JQA, *Memoirs*, Vol. 5, p. 139.

35   "Of all of them, Adams" . . . Ibid., p. 242.

35   "In hopes of promoting" . . . Shepherd, pp. 241–242.

CHAPTER 3: AN "AGONY OF MIND"

37   "At six o'clock sharp" . . . JQA, *Diary*, January 9, 1825, from *JQA Digital Diary*, No. 36, p. 7; *Diary* No. 23, p. 403. From *MHS Online*, at www.masshist.org/exhibitions/jqa.cfm.

39   "Adams disapproved of the" . . . Lipsky, pp. 240–241, 245; Remini, *Adams*, p. 64; JQA, *Memoirs*, Vol. 4, p. 388.

39   "While Adams never organized" . . . Nagel, pp. 283–288; *Encyclopedia of the War of 1812*, pp. 132, 457.

40   "The approaching election" . . . JQA, *Memoirs*, Vol. 7, pp. 171, 195, 58; Nagel, pp. 271–273.

40   "There was no outright" . . . JQA, *Memoirs*, Vol. 7, p. 81; Bemis, *Union*, pp. 30–31.

41   "But there was never" . . . Nagel, pp. 285–286.

41   "Under the House of" . . . *Microfilms of the Adams Papers*, JQA-CFA letter, March 26, 1833; Henry Adams, *Degradation*, p. 21; Hargreaves, pp. 36–38.

41   "A few weeks after Clay" . . . Morgan, pp. 45–46; Bemis, *Union*, p. 57.

42   "The House elected Adams" . . . Van Buren, p. 152; Bemis, *Union*, pp. 31, 54.

42   "At a White House" . . . JQA, *Memoirs*, Vol. 6, pp. 508–509.

42   "The Senate sullenly approved" . . . *Register of Debates*, 19–1, March 20, 1826.

43   "The Randolph-Clay duel" . . . Hargreaves, p. 152; Remini, *The Election*, pp. 25–29.

43   "Four years later" . . . Bemis, *Union*, p. 130.

43   "Having pledged in his" . . . Remini, *Adams*, p. 88; Nagel, pp. 298–299.

43   "He firmly believed" . . . Ketcham, pp. 61–66; Lipsky, pp. 235–244.

44   "Antiquated as he was" . . . Hargreaves, pp. 311–313.

44   "Some of Adams's advisers" . . . JQA, *Memoirs*, Vol. 7, pp. 64–65.

44   "'The spirit of improvement'" . . . *Messages of the Presidents*, Vol. 2, pp. 299–317; JQA, *Memoirs*, Vol. 8, p. 233; Remini, *Adams*, p. 81.

45   "In his flattering biography" . . . Seward, *Life*, p. 374.

46   "The trouble began" . . . Hargreaves, pp. 147–152; Remini, *Adams*, pp. 81–82.

46   "From the Hermitage" . . . Remini, *Adams*, pp. 81–82.

46   "Anderson died of yellow" . . . Hargreaves, pp. 154, 162.

47   "The 'man of the'" . . . Bemis, *Union*, pp. 97–99.

47   "Crowds that gathered" . . . Remini, *Adams*, p. 101; JQA, *Memoirs*, Vol. 7, p. 332.

47   "At a Baltimore banquet" . . . JQA, *Memoirs*, Vol. 7, p. 338; Remini, *The Election*, p. 123.

48   "Adams's principled refusal" . . . Hargreaves, p. 239; Quincy, p. 148; Brookhiser, p. 94; JQA, *Memoirs*, Vol. 7, pp. 275, 536, 544; Remini, *Adams*, p. 101; Bemis, *Union*, p. 136.

49   "Vice President John C. Calhoun" . . . Hargreaves, pp. 248–249.

49   "In the House" . . . Bemis, *Union*, pp. 72–75.

49   "Even with Adams's allies" . . . Bemis, *Union*, p. 131.

50   "Adams now had the" . . . Remini, *Adams*, p. 111.

50   "Yet, he took no" . . . JQA, *Memoirs*, Vol. 7, p. 197; Henry Adams, *Degradation*, pp. 24–25 [JQA letter to Rev. Charles W. Upham, February 2, 1837].

50   "There were the ones" . . . JQA, *Memoirs*, Vol. 7, pp. 449, 366, 472 ; Vol. 8, p. 64.

51   "When Adams was informed" . . . Ibid., p. 390.

51   "Now a rising forty-six-year-old" . . . Remini, *The Election*, pp. 53–63; Earle, p. 50.

51   "Van Buren toured" . . . Whitney, p. 77; Remini, *The Election*, pp. 18–19, 63–67, 76–88; JQA, *Memoirs*, Vol. 8, p. 129.

52   "Van Buren met often" . . . JQA, *Memoirs*, Vol. 7, pp. 501, 539.

52   "While perpetually dredging" . . . Bemis, *Union*, pp. 133–134; *Historical Statistics*, Vol. 1, p. 163.

52   "Unwilling to build" . . . Hecht, p. 464; JQA, *Memoirs*, Vol. 7, p. 465.

52   "Learning that his father" . . . JQA, *Diary* (Nevins, ed.), pp. 358–361.

53   "Exhausted in the mornings" . . . Nagel, pp. 304–308, 315; JQA, *Memoirs*, Vol. 7, p. 311.

54   "From the president's room" . . . JQA, *Memoirs*, Vol. 8, p. 76.

54   ""The previous December" . . . Ibid., pp. 382–383, 520–521.

55   "'The Combination,' as Adams" . . . Remini, *Adams*, pp. 118–123; Bemis, *Union*, pp. 140–142.

56   "Lost among the slanders" . . . Hargreaves, pp. xiv, 173–178; Nagel, p. 318.

56   "Jackson attended a gala" . . . Hecht, p. 463 [JQA-CFA letter, January 29, 1828].

56   "Adams made a rare" . . . JQA, *Memoirs*, Vol. 8, pp. 49–50.

57   "Adams refused to capitalize" . . . Quincy, p. 158; Richards, pp. 44–45; Bemis, *Union*, p. 149.

57   "He resurrected an 1825" . . . Hargreaves, p. 294.

57   "'It is the transition'" . . . JQA, *Memoirs*, Vol. 7, pp. 502, 474, 525.

58 "Receiving 647,276 votes" . . . Whitney, p. 70; JQA, *Memoirs*, Vol. 8, pp. 78–79.

58 "Two years later, he" . . . JQA, *Memoirs*, Vol. 8, p. 246.

58 "The Adamses moved out" . . . JQA, *Memoirs*, Vol. 8, pp. 100–102, 105; Bemis, *Union*, p. 154; Remini, *Adams*, p. 128.

59 "Adams had pronounced, 'After the'" . . . JQA, *Memoirs*, Vol. 8, pp. 88, 98.

59 "He pessimistically believed" . . . Hecht, p. 489; JQA, *Memoirs*, Vol. 8, pp. 88, 115; Bemis, *Foundations*, pp. 174; James Adams, p. 207; *Proceedings MHS*, Vol. 45, pp. 371–372. [Adams's response was kept from the public until 1877, when his grandson, Henry Adams, published it as *Documents Relating to New England Federalism, 1800–1815*. After *Documents* appeared in print, John T. Morse, a historian grandson of one of the thirteen, wrote: "Happy were the thirteen that they one and all went down to their graves complaisantly thinking that they had had the last word in the quarrel, little suspecting how great was their obligation to Mr. Adams for having granted them that privilege."]

59 "In May 1829, George" . . . Bemis, *Union*, pp. 179–182; JQA, *Diary*, *Microfilms of the Adams Papers*, Reel 39.

60 "John Adams's depression" . . . Shepherd, p. 96 footnote; CFA, *Diary*, Vol. 2, p. 75.

60 "George's death served to" . . . Shepherd, p. 226.

61 "In Boston that summer" . . . Shepherd, pp. 283, 294–295; CFA, *Diary*, Vol. 2, pp. 375–400.

61 "In June 1829, John Quincy Adams" . . . Nagel, pp. 331–332; Bemis, *Union*, p. 188.

61 "He also tied up loose ends" . . . Nagel, pp. 331–332; *Concise Dictionary*, p. 118; Douglas T. Miller, p. 118.

62 "There were no Boston" . . . JQA, *Memoirs*, Vol. 11, p. 159; Vol. 8, pp. 150, 339–340, 347.

63 "Easily Adams's longest" . . . JQA, *Dermot*, pp. 10–19, 31, 167; JQA, *Memoirs*, Vol. 8, pp. 340, 346–347, 352.

63 "When a poem that he" . . . JQA, *Memoirs*, Vol. 10, p. 177.

64 "For his own edification" . . . Bemis, *Union*, pp. 194–195.

64 "In studying Cicero, Adams" . . . Bemis, *Union*, pp. 203–205; Nagel, p. 334; *Microfilms of the Adams Papers*, JQA-CFA letter, February 21, 1830; Durant, pp. 161–166; Seward, *Life*, pp. 397–398; JQA, *Memoirs*, Vol. 8, pp. 247–248, 243.

65　"Charles Francis, who had" . . . Bemis, *Union*, p. 211 footnote; Hecht, pp. 507–508.

65　"His son Charles Francis" . . . JQA, *Memoirs*, Vol. 8, p. 335.

CHAPTER 4: THE FRESHMAN CONGRESSMAN

67　"Thirty minutes before noon" . . . Bemis, *Union*, p. 211; JQA, *Memoirs*, Vol. 8, pp. 431, 433; Hecht, pp. 511–512; Richards, p. 57, Royall, pp. 135–136.

68　"On December 12, Adams" . . . JQA, *Memoirs*, Vol. 8, pp. 434, 449–450.

69　"Adams read the posthumously" . . . JQA, *Memoirs*, Vol. 8, pp. 270–274; 281–282.

70　"Adams also took secret" . . . Ibid., pp. 356–359, 372.

70　"And then, former Treasury" . . . Masur, p. 103; Calhoun, *Papers*, Vol. 11, pp. 159–160; JQA, *Memoirs*, Vol. 8, pp. 274–275, 405; Bemis, *Union*, p. 215.

71　"Calhoun's alienation from" . . . Calhoun, *Papers*, Vol. 11, pp. 473–474; JQA, *Memoirs*, Vol. 8, p. 331.

72　"'Go ahead! Is the'" . . . Douglas T. Miller, pp. 31–32; Tocqueville, pp. 176–177; Trollope, p. 270.

72　"'Jacksonian Democracy' would" . . . Richards, p. 28; Remini, *The Election*, p. 203.

73　"They had not spoken" . . . Bemis, *Union*, pp. 53, 128; JQA, *Memoirs*, Vol. 8, pp. 144, 484–486.

75　"Of Jackson's administration, he" . . . JQA, *Memoirs*, Vol. 7, p. 479; Vol. 8, pp. 273, 276, 546–547; Vol. 9, p. 5; Kunhardt, p. 352; Bemis, *Union*, pp. 155, 250.

76　"On his sickbed" . . . Hecht, p. 516; *Encyclopedia of American History*, 1st ed., p. 173.

76　"Adams supported the national bank" . . . Richards, pp. 76–79; JQA, *Memoirs*, Vol. 8, pp. 496–497; Bemis, *Union*, pp. 251–255; Hecht, pp. 515–516; *Register of Debates*, 22–1, Appendix, pp. 55–58.

77　"Despite the majority" . . . *Documents of American History*, pp. 270–274; Richards, pp. 79–84.

77　"Adams condemned the" . . . Richards, p. 63; Remini, *Adams*, pp. 132–137; JQA, *Memoirs*, Vol. 8, pp. 465, 476–479.

78　"So absorbed was Adams" . . . Clark, pp. 342–343; JQA, *Memoirs*, Vol. 8, p. 411; Vol. 11, p. 267.

79   "In August 1832" . . . Bemis, *Union*, p. 258; JQA, *Memoirs*, Vol. 8, pp.
      539, 533–534.

80   "In 1835, Adams forfeited" . . . Bemis, *Union*, pp. 307–317, 322–324; Van
      Buren, p. 271; JQA, *Memoirs*, Vol. 9, pp. 217, 212.

81   "Nullification's origins dated" . . . *Oxford Companion to the Supreme
      Court*, p. 139; JQA, *Memoirs*, Vol. 8, pp. 262–263; Quincy, pp. 178–179.

82   "The flashpoint was a law" . . . Bemis, *Union*, pp. 226–227, 222–223,
      237–238, 241–246, 260–265; JQA, *Memoirs*, Vol. 8, p. 200; Hecht, p. 516.

83   "Nullification was 'neither more'" . . . JQA, *Memoirs*, Vol. 8, p. 376.

83   "Thus, Adams was dismayed" . . . Ibid., p. 503.

83   "But anyone who" . . . Bemis, *Union*, pp. 228–229.

83   "On December 10" . . . *Documents of American History*, pp. 262–268.

84   "South Carolina indignantly" . . . *Documents of American History*, pp.
      268–269; *Messages of the Presidents*, Vol. 2, pp. 610–632.

84   "Adams wholeheartedly supported" . . . JQA, *Memoirs*, Vol. 10, p. 295;
      Vol. 8, pp. 512–513.

84   "A House bill proposing" . . . JQA, *Memoirs*, Vol. 8, p. 519; Bemis,
      Union, p. 266.

85   "This was too much" . . . Bemis, *Union*, pp. 266–267; JQA, *Memoirs*,
      Vol. 8, p. 515.

85   "Congress approved the tariff" . . . *Documents of American History*, pp.
      269–270; Bemis, *Union*, p. 269; Tocqueville, p. 392.

85   "Adams would later" . . . JQA, *Address at Braintree*, 1842.

86   "More than 200,000 men" . . . Richards, pp. 41–43; McCarthy, pp.
      373–374.

87   "Adams had told William" . . . JQA, *Memoirs*, Vol. 8, pp. 428, 413.

87   "He wrote letters denouncing" . . . Howe, p. 55; JQA, *Letters on the
      Masonic Institution*, pp. 110, 14–24, 281–282, 73, 246–247, 215; JQA,
      Memoirs, Vol. 8, p. 535; Vol. 9, pp. 15, 20, 33; Bemis, *Union*, pp. 298–303;
      Richards, p. 43.

88   "On March 12, 1832" . . . Hecht, p. 513; Nagel, pp. 341–342.

88   "The fifty-fourth anniversary" . . . JQA, *Memoirs*, Vol. 9, p. 12.

88   "Sometimes when Adams" . . . Ibid., pp. 13, 15, 18, 21.

89   "Reaching Washington on" . . . JQA, *Diary, Microfilms of Adams Pa-
      pers*, Reel 42; Bemis, *Union*, p. 199; Shepherd, pp. 342–343; Nagel, pp.
      346–347.

CHAPTER 5: A WORTHY CAUSE

91 "Since Haiti's black revolutionaries" . . . Richards, p. 91; Bemis, *Foundations*, p. 414; Masur, p. 35.

92 "Thomas Jefferson Randolph" . . . Masur, pp. 52–61.

92 "The American Colonization Society's" . . . Barnes, pp. 94–95; Masur, pp. 48–49; *Encyclopedia of American History*, 6th ed., p. 756.

92 "The American anti-slavery" . . . Barnes, pp. 29–31; Bemis, *Union*, pp. 332–333.

93 "The year 1830 was" . . . Barnes, pp. 3–12.

93 "Finney's prize convert" . . . *Concise Dictionary*, p. 1133; Barnes, pp. 107, 34, 134; Bemis, *Union*, pp. 81–86.

94 "It was an 'age'" . . . Barnes, p. 3.

94 "Angelina Grimké, her sister" . . . Weld, pp. 88, 26–27.

95 "Angelina Grimké described" . . . Ibid., pp. 54–56.

95 "The Grimké sisters" . . . Weld, pp. 22, 56; Barnes, pp. 153–154; Birney, p. 258.

95 "A congressman reported" . . . Weld, pp. 67–68; Trollope, p. 168; Masur, p. 35.

96 "After organizing itself" . . . Barnes, pp. 100, 104.

96 "Jackson, who owned" . . . *Messages of the Presidents*, Vol. 3, pp. 175–176.

96 "South Carolina Senator John" . . . Calhoun, *Papers*, Vol. 13, pp. 53–69; *Register of Debates*, Vol. 12, Part 4, Appendix, p. 76; Richards, p. 113; Barnes, p. 100; Freehling, pp. 347–348.

97 "Stymied by the postmasters" . . . Ludlum, p. 204; Barnes, pp. 131–132, 142–144; Bemis, *Union*, pp. 137–138; Shepherd, p. 355.

98 "During the first thirty" . . . Brookhiser, p. 103.

98 "Adams's lifelong abhorrence" . . . JQA, *Writings*, Vol. 1, p. 5.

98 "Until the debate that" . . . Bemis, *Union*, pp. 327–328.

99 "In his diary, he" . . . JQA, *Memoirs*, Vol. 5, pp. 205–211, 11–12; Vol. 4, p. 531.

99 "While Adams described" . . . Ibid., p. 531.

99 "Adams was disappointed" . . . Ibid., pp. 11–12.

100 "Adams also began to" . . . *Constitution with the Declaration of Independence*, p. 81; CFA, "John Quincy Adams and Emancipation," p. 79; JQA, *Memoirs*, Vol. 8, pp. 299–300.

100 "In the spring of" . . . *Register of Debates*, Vol. 12, Part 2, pp. 2044–2045; Burleigh, p. 235.

101 "The slave insurrection led" . . . Masur, p. 9; CFA, "John Quincy Adams and Emancipation," p. 107; JQA, *Memoirs*, Vol. 8, pp. 286–287.

101 "At the beginning" . . . JQA, *Memoirs*, Vol. 8, p. 454; Bemis, *Union*, p. 331.

102 "But Adams also bridled" . . . CFA, "John Quincy Adams and Emancipation," pp. 82–83, 101; JQA, *Memoirs*, Vol. 8, p. 269.

102 "Adams's friends counseled him" . . . *Microfilms of Adams Papers*, JQA-Nicholas Biddle letter, June 10, 1836; JQA, *Memoirs*, Vol. 9, pp. 217, 58; Hecht, p. 537.

103 "Just when Adams seemed" . . . Nagel, pp. 344–348.

104 "After days of listening" . . . Shepherd, pp. 345, 348; *Microfilms of Adams Papers*, JQA-CFA letters, December 15, 1835, May 24, 1836.

104 "The 'glove' taken up" . . . *Register of Debates*, Vol. 12, Part 2, pp. 2001–2002, 2210–2212, 2314; *Congressional Globe*, 24–1, Vol. 3, p. 161.

106 "Adams opposed the annexation" . . . Richards, pp. 156–159.

106 "Amid catcalls from" . . . JQA, *Speech on Distributing Rations*, pp. 6–7 (Courtesy of MHS); Remini, *Adams*, p. 142; *Congressional Globe*, 24–1 Appendix, pp. 434–435.

106 "The hour-long speech" . . . CFA, "John Quincy Adams and Emancipation," p. 73.

107 "Adams's speech also dissuaded" . . . Richards, pp. 160–161; CFA, "John Quincy Adams and Emancipation," pp. 72–73.

107 "The very day of" . . . *Congressional Globe*, 24–1, pp. 383, 402–403, 406–407; *Globe*, 24–1, Appendix, p. 433; JQA, *Memoirs*, Vol. 9, pp. 287–288.

108 "The House renewed the Gag" . . . Bemis, *Union*, p. 340.

108 "During the English Parliament's" . . . Barnes, pp. 116–117.

108 "The United States Congress" . . . Barnes, pp. 116–117; *Constitution with Declaration of Independence*, pp. 63, 41; McPherson, p. 178.

109 "'The right of petition'" . . . *Congressional Globe*, 26–1, Appendix, p. 747; CFA, "John Quincy Adams and Emancipation," pp. 93–94.

109 "Charles Francis worried" . . . Nagel, p. 357.

110 "It would prove to be" . . . Clark, p. 365.

110 "'This is a cause'" . . . JQA, *Memoirs*, Vol. 9, p. 298.

CHAPTER 6: ADAMS, SCIENCE,
AND THE SMITHSONIAN INSTITUTION

111   "In January 1836" . . . Bemis, *Union*, p. 501; Burleigh, pp. 168, 175, 194–196, 220, 226; JQA, *Memoirs*, Vol. 9, p. 269.

112   "Purportedly the illegitimate son" . . . Burleigh, pp. 80, 84–133, 159. [The paths of the Adamses and Percys had previously intersected tangentially. When the 1st Duke of Northumberland died in 1786, Abigail Adams visited the Percy London home where the duke's body lay in state. James Smithson's half-brother, the 2nd Duke of Northumberland, Hugh Smithson Percy, was a distinguished British officer at the Battle of Bunker Hill, seen from Penn's Hill in Braintree by Adams and Abigail. The 2nd Duke's portrait hangs in Boston Town Hall, attesting to his many American friends.]

113   "The reason for Smithson's" . . . Ibid., pp. 68, 169, 172–173.

114   "The committee's first report" . . . Quincy, pp. 264–267.

114   "He dusted off his" . . . Quincy, pp. 289–290; JQA, *Memoirs*, Vol. 10, pp. 244–251.

114   "Brooks Adams in later" . . . Henry Adams, *Degradation*, pp. 8–9, 52; Bemis, *Foundations*, p. 259.

115   "John Quincy Adams's *Report*" . . . JQA, *Weights and Measures*, pp. 48, 134; Nagel, p. 265; Bemis, *Foundations*, pp. 258–259.

116   "Adams's treatise analyzed" . . . Ibid., pp. 14, 47–48, 71.

116   "Adams rated the preservation" . . .Ibid., pp. 118, 133.

117   "Adams had begun" . . . Nagel, p. 132.

117   "But his love of" . . . JQA, *Memoirs*, Vol. 11, p. 386; Burleigh, p. 229.

117   "The spark that blazed" . . . Bemis, *Union*, pp. 122–123; JQA, *Memoirs*, Vol. 7, pp. 121, 262, 287–291, 352; Vol. 8, pp. 322–323, 544–545; CFA, *Diary*, Vol. 2, pp. 409–410; Henry Adams, *Education*, pp. 14–15; Nagel, p. 360.

119   "His passion for it" . . . *Concise Dictionary*, p. 653; JQA, *Memoirs*, Vol. 12, pp. 189, 192; Naval Observatory Web site, www.usno.navy.mil/history.shtml.

120   "When the Cincinnati" . . . Cincinnati *Post*, February 18, 1999; National Park Service Web site, www.nps.gov/history/history/online_books/butowsky5/astro41.htm; JQA, *Memoirs*, Vol. 11, p. 409.

121 "It was a triumphal passage" . . . JQA, *Memoirs*, Vol. 11, pp. 418–441; JQA, *Cincinnati Oration*, pp. 17–50, 68; JQA, *Great Design*, p. 9; Seward, *Life*, p. 324; Portolano, pp. 480–503.

122 "In May 1838" . . . Burleigh, pp. 202–203.

122 "Administration allies slipped" . . . JQA, *Great Design*, pp. 33–34; Burleigh, pp. 223–226, 232–234, 238.

123 "Adams's special House committee" . . . Burleigh, pp. 238, 246; Bemis, *Union*, pp. 513–515; *28ᵗʰ Congress, 1ˢᵗ Session, Serial Set No. 447*, Reports of Committees, Vol. 3, pp. 1–5.

124 "Adams treasured his" . . . *25th Congress, 3rd Session, House Executive Document 11* [Letter to Secretary of State John Forsyth]; Lipsky, p. 52; JQA, *Great Design*, pp. 69, 70, 73, 85, 87–88, 25; JQA, *Diary, Microfilms of Adams Papers*, Reel 45; *26th Congress, 1st Session, Serial Set No. 277*, Committee Reports, p. 20; 27th Congress, *2nd Session, Serial Set No. 409*, Committee Reports, Vol. 3, pp. 1–5.

125 "During the ten years" . . . *26th Congress, 1ˢᵗ Session*, Report #277, p. 20; Bemis, *Foundations*, p. 511.

126 "In a report on June 7, 1844" . . . JQA, *Memoirs*, Vol. 12, p. 31; *28th Congress, 1ˢᵗ Session, Serial Set No. 447*, Committee Reports, Vol. 3, pp. 1–5; Burleigh, pp. 249–250, 9–10, 14; Wheelan, *Invading Mexico*, p. 245; Remini, *Adams*, p. 144; Smithsonian Institution Web site, siarchives.si.edu/history/main.html; JQA, *Great Design*, p. 35.

CHAPTER 7: LIGHTNING ROD OF CONGRESS

129 "When Adams presented the first" . . . *Register of Debates*, Vol. 13, Part 1, pp. 1314–1321; *Congressional Globe*, 24–2, pp. 79–81; Quincy, p. 261.

130 "A month after the" . . . JQA, *Letters to his Constituents*, p. 10 (Courtesy of MHS); *Congressional Globe*, 24–2, pp. 162–165; Bemis, *Union*, pp. 344–346.

131 "'Since the existence'" . . . JQA, *Letters to his Constituents*, pp. 30, 64, 43, 50, 56–57 (Courtesy of MHS); *Congressional Globe*, 24–2, p. 165; *Register of Debates*, Vol. 13, pp. 1586–1618.

133 "To stop Adams's one-man" . . . *Register of Debates*, Vol. 13, p. 1734.

133 "Once, when the suspicious" . . . Barnes, pp. 123–124; *Congressional Globe*, 24–1, Appendix, p. 333; *United States Magazine*, pp. 78–79; JQA, *Letters to his Constituents*, p. 7 (Courtesy of MHS).

134 "'The peculiar institution'" . . . *Register of Debates*, Vol. 13, Part 2, pp. 2184–2185.

134 "Adams agreed that slavery" . . . JQA, *Newburyport Oration*, pp. 50–53; Quincy, pp. 272–274.

135 "When the 25th Congress" . . . Bemis, *Union*, pp. 362–364.

136 "American politics had changed" . . . Douglas T. Miller, pp. 155–160, 170; *United States Magazine*, pp. 78–79.

137 "Besides being arguably Congress's" . . . Seward, *Life*, p. 259; Clark, pp. 341–342; JQA, *Memoirs*, Vol. 9, p. 408; Vol. 10, p. 244.

137 "When the House dissolved" . . . Quincy, pp. 298–300; JQA, *Memoirs*, Vol. 10, pp. 143–144, 149–150, 165.

139 "As Adams's anachronistic" . . . *Congressional Globe*, Vol. 9, p. 322; Quincy, pp. 322–324; Hecht, p. 557; JQA, *Memoirs*, Vol. 10, pp. 270–271, 301; Richards, p. 135.

140 "'The most important and'" . . . Nagel, pp. 381–382; JQA, *Memoirs*, Vol. 10, pp. 338, 341–342, 533, 40; Richards, p. 87.

140 "With advancing age" . . . Shepherd, pp. 345–346; Clark, p. 341; JQA, *Memoirs*, Vol. 10, pp. 291–293.

141 "Two months later" . . . JQA, *Memoirs*, Vol. 10, pp. 332, 341.

141 "The journalist Ann Royall's" . . . Shepherd, p. 204; Royall, p. 166; Seward, *Autobiography*, pp. 204–207; CFA, *Diary*, Vol. 1, p. 365.

142 "So busy was Adams" . . . JQA, *Memoirs*, Vol. 12, p. 48; Vol. 10, pp. 269, 303, 323–324.

143 "He described Robert Barnwell Rhett" . . . Ibid., pp. 396, 399.

143 "Adams regarded Congress" . . . Ibid., p. 475.

143 "As he approached" . . . Ibid., p. 451.

CHAPTER 8: "TRUE AND HONEST HEARTS LOVE YOU"

145 "In the parlance of" . . . Emerson, *Journals*, Vol. 6, pp. 349–350.

145 "Adams's verbal marathon began" . . . JQA, *Speech on Right to Petition*, pp. 19–24; Seward, *Life*, p. 258.

147 "When a relief bill" . . . JQA, *Speech on Distributing Rations*, pp. 1, 8 (Courtesy of MHS); *Congressional Globe*, 24–1, Appendix, p. 435; Masur, pp. 117–126, 135; Remini, *Adams*, p. 100; JQA, *Memoirs*, Vol. 8, p. 486; Vol. 10, p. 256; *Oxford Companion to United States History*,

pp. 378–379. [The force-marching of the Cherokees to the West on the "Trail of Tears" resulted in 4,000 deaths.]

148   "Whenever possible, Adams denounced" . . . *28th Congress, 1st Session, House Executive Documents*, Report No. 404, p. 20; JQA, *Memoirs*, Vol. 10, pp. 331–335, 256, 492.

149   "But in the White House" . . . Bemis, *Union*, pp. 79–87; Remini, *Adams*, pp. 91–99; Hargreaves, pp. 205–207.

149   "He presented a petition" . . . Richards, pp. 149–151; JQA, *Memoirs*, Vol. 10, pp. 406, 492.

150   "Congressman Benjamin Howard" . . . JQA, *Speech on Right to Petition*, pp. 65–68, 71–80.

151   "'True and honest hearts'" . . . Bemis, *Union*, pp. 265, 372–373; Hecht, pp. 379–380, 561; JQA, *Memoirs*, Vol. 10, pp. 36–37.

152   "Ordinary people began" . . . JQA, *Memoirs*, Vol. 10, pp. 281, 340.

152   "To his surprise and" . . . JQA, *Memoirs*, Vol. 10, p. 509; Vol. 9, p. 412; Nagel, pp. 369–370, 384, 378.

154   "When a giant of" . . . Nagel, pp. 371–372.

154   "James Madison was the last" . . . JQA, *Lives*, pp. 296, 102; JQA, *Memoirs*, Vol. 9, pp. 308–309; Vol. 12, p. 229; Vol. 10, p. 181.

154   "Adams verbally besieged" . . . JQA, *Speech on Right to Petition*, pp. 83, 99, 14, 26–27, 30–33, 38–39, 44, 46–47, 52, 54–55, 58, 115, 128, 131; Nagel, pp. 346–366; Quincy, p. 287.

156   "His variegated speech" . . . Bemis, *Union*, pp. 363–364, 375–376, 348; Adams, *Address to his Constituents*, pp. 108–109, 61; CFA, "John Quincy Adams and Emancipation," p. 99; JQA, *Memoirs*, Vol. 9, p. 49.

158   "Abolitionists William Lloyd Garrison" . . . Hecht, p. 548; Shepherd, p. 368.

158   "At the same time" . . . JQA, *Memoirs*, Vol. 9, p. 365.

158   "As abolitionist newspapers laced" . . . Hecht, pp. 563–564; *Congressional Globe*, 25–3, p. 218; Bemis, *Union*, pp. 349–350, 366–367; JQA, *Memoirs*, Vol.10, pp. 43–44; Vol. 9, p. 418.

160   "Concerned that his battle" . . . Bemis, *Union*, p. 351; McPherson, p. 178; Ludlum, p. 229.

160   "The volume of petitions" . . . Shepherd, p. 355; Bemis, *Union*, p. 266; JQA, *Memoirs*, Vol. 9, p. 377.

160   "On January 22, 1840" . . . *Congressional Globe*, 26–1, pp. 150–151; Appendix, pp. 745–748; JQA, *Memoirs*, Vol. 10, p. 206.

CHAPTER 9: THE *AMISTAD*

163   "But their first choice" . . . Jones, pp. 152–154.

163   "Adams tried to turn down" . . . JQA, *Memoirs*, Vol. 10, p. 358; Weld-Grimké, *Letters*, Vol. 2, p. 856.

164   "Like his countrymen" . . . Jones, pp. 50–53.

165   "Because of the lingering" . . . Jones, pp. 55–59, 89; Martin, pp. 103, 84–86; *Amistad Case*, p. 62.

166   "Abolitionists made the most" . . . Martin, pp. 80–114; Bemis, *Union*, p. 394; Jones, p. 61.

166   "Of the U.S. government's" . . . Martin, p. 153.

167   "Kidnapped by other Africans" . . . Martin, pp. 26–40; Barber, pp. 7, 20.

168   "Now began a deadly" . . . Martin, pp. 26–54; Jones, pp. 27–28; Barber, pp. 3–4.

169   "The New London *Gazette*" . . . Martin, pp. 56–66, 118; Bemis, *Union*, p. 387; Barber, pp. 7–8, 16.

170   "The attorneys acted quickly" . . . *Amistad Case*, pp. 67–69.

170   "Lewis Tappan threw up" . . . Barber, p. 17; Jones, pp. 86–87.

171   "At a hearing before" . . . *Amistad Case*, p. 120; Barber, pp. 17–18; Martin, p. 145; Jones, pp. 43, 106–107.

171   "Early in the proceedings" . . . *Amistad Case*, pp. 39–40, 63.

172   "During the Africans' first" . . . Martin, pp. 68–73, 119, 177; Jones, p. 149.

173   "The administration withheld documents" . . . Bemis, *Union*, p. 397; *Amistad Case*, pp. 21, 27, 55–56; Jones, pp. 96, 113, 144–146; Martin, pp. 151, 161.

174   "The New Haven courtroom" . . . Jones, pp. 121–127; Barber, pp. 20–23.

175   "In January 1840" . . . Barber, pp. 23–24; Jones, pp. 130–131, 135.

176   "John Quincy Adams, who" . . . Jones, pp. 145–147; JQA, *Memoirs*, Vol. 10, p. 216.

176   "The president's management" . . . Jones, p. 156; Martin, p. 178.

177   "Oh, how shall I'" . . . Martin, pp. 184, 188; JQA, *Diary*, MHS Online, 177. 41, p. 160; JQA, *Memoirs*, Vol. 10, pp. 383, 360, 373, 406, 409.

177   "In its last days" . . . Martin, p. 190.

178   "The seven justices" . . . *Oxford Companion to the Supreme Court*, pp. 983–984, 475, 99–102.

178   "The government's attorney" . . . Jones, pp. 182–187.

179   "The defense team" . . . JQA, *Memoirs*, Vol. 10, p. 431; Jones, pp. 172–175; Martin, pp. 188–200.

179   "When Adams's turn came" . . . *Amistad Case*, pp. 3–8.

180   "The Spanish ministers' assertions" . . . Ibid., pp. 56, 74, 134.

180   "Adams mocked the demands" . . . Ibid., pp. 38–43.

180   "If the president were" . . . Ibid., pp. 16, 89.

181   "Adams, arguably the greatest" . . . Ibid., pp. 29, 38, 46–47, 84.

182   "Spain had insisted" . . . Ibid., pp. 19–20, 21, 23.

182   "Adams asked the justices" . . . Ibid., p. 22.

182   "Yet President Van Buren" . . . Ibid., pp. 79–80, 82–83.

183   "Although he had spoken" . . . JQA, *Memoirs*, Vol. 10, pp. 431–432.

183   "Adams observed that he" . . . *Amistad Case*, pp. 134–135.

184   "Justice Joseph Story, whose" . . . Jones, pp. 190–195; Martin, p. 200; Bemis, *Union*, pp. 410, 408; Story, Vol. 2, p. 348; JQA, *Memoirs*, Vol. 11, p. 248.

185   "Upon Adams's request" . . . JQA, *Memoirs*, Vol. 10, pp. 446–447; Martin, pp. 208–209.

185   "Denied legal custody" . . . Martin, p. 221; Jones, pp. 213, 218.

185   "'No one else will'" . . . JQA, *Memoirs*, Vol. 10, pp. 453–454.

CHAPTER 10: "OLD NESTOR"

187   "In June 1841, Congressman Henry" . . . JQA, *Memoirs*, Vol. 10, pp. 479–480; Vol. 11, pp. 61–62; Ludlum, pp. 241–242.

188   "In December 1841" . . . *Congressional Globe*, 27–2, pp. 2–3.

188   "At an age when" . . . *United States Magazine*, pp. 78–79; Bemis, *Union*, p. 326.

189   "Adams's sarcastic eloquence" . . . Morse, p. 231; Emerson, *Journals*, Vol. 8, p. 309; Seward, *Life*, p. 258.

189   "Wise of Virginia" . . . Richards, p. 145; French, p. 146.

190   "It would have been" . . . Van Buren, pp. 270–272.

190   "Petitioners from Massachusetts" . . . Weld-Grimké, *Letters*, pp. 899–901; *Reader's Encyclopedia*, p. 765; Giddings, p. 159; *Congressional Globe*, 27–2, pp. 158–159, 161–164, 167–168; JQA, *Memoirs*, Vol. 10, p. 515.

192 "Reports of Adams's impending" . . . *Congressional Globe*, 27–2, pp. 169–175; Weld-Grimké, *Letters*, Vol. 2, pp. 901–902.

194 "The abolitionists, in the" . . . Barnes, pp. 152, 193–194; Hecht, p. 597; Giddings, p.161; Weld-Grimké, *Letters*, Vol. 2, p. 905.

194 "The Anti-Slavery Society" . . . Barnes, pp. 193–194, 176; *Concise Dictionary*, p. 337.

195 "Theodore Weld attended" . . . Barnes, pp. 183, 195, 288 notes; McPherson, pp. 187–188; *Concise Dictionary*, p. 1133; Weld-Grimké, *Letters*, Vol. 2, pp. 885–886, 889–890.

196 "He came to meet me" . . . Weld-Grimké, *Letters*, Vol. 2, pp. 905–906.

196 "During one of their" . . . Barnes, p. 186.

196 "Each day, people filled" . . . Giddings, pp. 162–163.

197 "I defy them. I'" . . . Marshall, p. 175; *Congressional Globe*, 27–2, pp. 177, 168, 208.

197 "When it was Adams's" . . . *Congressional Globe*, 27–2, pp. 192–193.

198 "'A breathless silence'" . . . Giddings, p. 167; *Congressional Globe*, 27–2, pp. 193, 208; Giddings, p. 172.

198 "Adams turned his rhetorical" . . . *Congressional Globe*, 27–2, pp. 202, 176.

199 "Adams accused Southerners" . . . *Congressional Globe*, 27–2, Appendix, pp. 980, 173, 192; Howe, p. 61.

199 "Benjamin French, the House's" . . . French, pp. 136–137; Weld-Grimké, *Letters*, Vol. 2, p. 911.

200 "Gilmer offered to drop" . . . *Congressional Globe*, 27–2, pp. 207–208; Weld-Grimké, *Letters*, Vol. 2, p. 910.

200 "Sitting in church" . . . JQA, *Memoirs*, Vol. 11, pp. 80, 86.

200 "The next day, Congressman" . . . Giddings, p. 169; *Congressional Globe*, 27–2, pp. 214–215.

201 "'I am confident that'" . . . McPherson, pp. 191–192; Weld-Grimké, *Letters*, Vol. 2, p. 913; Giddings, p. 172.

201 "Even Adams's Southern adversaries" . . . Weld-Grimké, *Letters*, Vol. 2, pp. 909, 911; Quincy, p. 388.

201 "While Adams was undergoing" . . . Dickens, pp. 133, 119.

202 "Eight congressmen resigned" . . . JQA, *Memoirs*, Vol. 11, pp. 89, 91; JQA, *Address to his Constituents*, p. 57.

202 "Having failed to silence Adams" . . . *Encyclopedia of American History*, 6th ed., pp. 220–221; Barnes, pp. 187–190, 286–287 notes; Bemis, *Union*, pp. 413, 439; JQA, *Memoirs*, Vol. 11, p. 114; McPherson, pp. 193–194.

CHAPTER 11: TRIUMPH

205 "'My mind and body'" . . . JQA, *Memoirs*, Vol. 11, p. 241.

205 "When he walked up" . . . Ibid., p. 542; Vol. 12, pp. 97, 86.

206 "There were cash-flow" . . . Shepherd, pp. 343, 381; Nagel, p. 373; JQA, *Memoirs*, Vol. 11, p. 339.

206 "Whether he was aware" . . . JQA, *Memoirs*, Vol. 12, p. 64.

207 "'The pleasure that I'" . . . Ibid., p. 200.

207 "'The struggle,' as Adams" . . . Ibid., p. 232.

207 "Retirement was an impossibility" . . . Ibid., pp. 259, 467; Vol. 10, pp. 450–451.

207 "Adams, who despised Andrew" . . . JQA, *Memoirs*, Vol. 10, pp. 456–457; Wheelan, *Invading Mexico*, p. 20; Quincy, pp. 364–369.

208 "Thus, it was not" . . . JQA, *Memoirs*, Vol. 11, pp. 382–383.

209 "As Adams dined" . . . Ibid., pp. 521–523, 532; Vol. 12, p. 67.

209 "Adams was dismayed" . . . Howe, p. 67; JQA, *Memoirs*, Vol. 12, pp. 103–106, 168, 178; *Messages of the Presidents*, Vol. 4, pp. 373–382.

210 "His manifest discontent" . . . JQA, *Memoirs*, Vol. 11, pp. 284–285, 510–511; Vol. 12, pp. 116–117, 133.

210 "By challenging the status" . . . JQA, *Memoirs*, Vol. 10, pp. 345, 350; Nagel, p. 377.

211 "At a rally in Braintree" . . . JQA, *Address to his Constituents*, p. 55.

211 "Adams encouraged his friends" . . . Barnes, p. 125: *Congressional Globe*, 27–2, p. 267; Richards, pp. 177–178.

212 "Adams's censure ordeal" . . . Bemis, *Union*, p. 370; JQA, *Memoirs*, Vol. 11, p. 406.

213 "Louisa Adams, who had" . . . Shepherd, pp. 374, 408–409.

213 "Adams's opening salvo" . . . JQA, *Letter to be Read in Bangor*, pp. 1–6 (Courtesy MHS.)

214 "His letter was widely" . . . JQA, *Memoirs*, Vol. 11, p. 408.

214 "During a House debate" . . . Giddings, pp. 217–218.

214 "'My soul is oppressed'"... JQA, *Memoirs*, Vol. 12, p. 37; Seward, *Autobiography*, p. 672.

215 "In an 1836 speech"... CFA, "John Quincy Adams and Emancipation," pp. 76–77.

215 "Adams's popularity was at"... JQA, *Memoirs*, Vol. 11, pp. 392–400; Seward, *Life*, p. 310; Shepherd, pp. 392–394.

216 "'Old Man Eloquent'"... JQA, *Address to his Constituents*, pp. 2, 63.

216 "People accosted him"... Quincy, p. 350; Nagel, pp. 388–390, 393; JQA, *Memoirs*, Vol. 12, p. 211.

216 "In New York State"... Seward, *Life*, 316; JQA, *Memoirs*, Vol. 11, pp. 310, 328, 159, 385; Vol. 12, pp. 111–114, 126, 134.

217 "Adams had finally grasped"... JQA-William Seward letter, *Microfilms of Adams Papers*, Reel 154; Richards, p. 165; JQA, *Address to his Constituents*, p. 25.

218 "Following the family tradition"... *Concise Dictionary*, p. 3; Hecht, pp. 609–610; JQA, *Memoirs*, Vol. 11, p. 480.

218 "'They have allowed me'"... JQA-Seward letter, *Microfilms of Adams Papers*, Reel 154; JQA, *Memoirs*, Vol. 11, p. 480; *Abridgement of Debates Congress*, Vol. 15, pp. 58–59.

218 "As he prepared his"... *Congressional Globe*, 28–1, p. 878; JQA, *Memoirs*, Vol. 12, pp. 22–23, 36.

219 "Dominated as it was"... JQA-CFA letter, *Microfilms of Adams Papers*, Reel 154; *Congressional Globe*, p. 467; JQA, *Memoirs*, Vol. 12, p. 3.

219 "The report, which condemned"... Bemis, *Union*, p. 446; *28ᵗʰ Congress, 1st Session*, Report No. 404, pp. 1–20.

220 "Adams normally refused gifts"... JQA-Daniel Parker letter, *Microfilms of Adams Papers*, Reel 154; JQA, *Memoirs*, Vol. 11, p. 543; Vol. 12, p. 183.

220 "When the 28th Congress convened"... JQA, *Memoirs*, Vol. 11, pp. 450–451.

221 "To test that premise"... *Congressional Globe*, 28–1, pp. 59–62, 64–65; JQA, *Memoirs*, Vol. 11, p. 455.

222 "In a one-hour speech"... JQA, *Memoirs*, Vol. 11, p. 498.

222 "Two factors coalesced"... McPherson, p. 177.

223 "On December 3, 1844"... *Congressional Globe*, 28–2, p. 7.

223 "That night, Adams wrote"... JQA, *Memoirs*, Vol. 12, pp. 115–116, 120.

223 "Patent commissioner Ellsworth"... JQA, *Memoirs*, Vol. 12, pp. 183, 186, 15 footnote; Smithsonian Web site, www.smithsonian.org.

CHAPTER 12: A NEW WAR AND DECLINE

225 "Thus, it puzzled him" . . . JQA, *Memoirs*, Vol. 12, pp. 135–136.

225 "Adams once more angered" . . . Richards, pp. 183–185; Hecht, pp. 618–619; *Congressional Globe*, 29–1, pp. 340–342; JQA, *Memoirs*, Vol. 12, pp. 220–221.

226 "In 1844, President John Tyler" . . . Wheelan, *Invading Mexico*, pp. 20, 66; Polk, *Diary*, Vol. 1, 42 footnote.

227 "Adams's brief elation" . . . JQA, *Memoirs*, Vol. 12, pp. 49, 60.

228 "Texas, said the Democrats" . . . JQA, *Memoirs*, Vol. 11, pp. 348–349; Vol. 12, pp. 64, 78, 84, 101–102, 109; JQA, *Speech on Distributing Rations*, p. 6; Remini, *Adams*, pp. 140–141; Richards, pp. 174–175.

230 "As Adams concisely summarized" . . . JQA, *Memoirs*, Vol. 11, pp. 351, 353.

230 "As tensions increased" . . . Ibid., p. 442.

230 "Almost daily now, Democrats" . . . Ibid., Vol. 12 pp. 146–153, 171, 173, 202.

231 "John Greenleaf Whittier" . . . Whittier, p. 105.

232 "'Britain's attempted intervention" . . . JQA, *Memoirs*, Vol. 11, p. 407.

232 "Mexico declared it would never" . . . Wheelan, *Invading Mexico*, pp. 59–60.

232 "On December 9, 1845, Adams" . . . JQA, *Memoirs*, Vol. 12, pp. 219–220.

233 "The New York *American* described" . . . Barnes, p. 126; JQA, *Memoirs*, Vol. 12, p. 246; Vol. 10, p. 365.

233 "'Jackson was a hero'" . . . Nagel, p. 403; JQA, *Memoirs*, Vol. 12, pp. 210, 175; Vol. 10, p. 361.

234 "According to Ralph Waldo Emerson" . . . Emerson, *Journals*, Vol. 8, p. 353.

234 "On the ivory writing" . . . Quincy, p. 424; JQA, *Memoirs*, Vol. 10, p. 501; Vol. 12, pp. 69–71, 285–286, 205–206.

235 "In September 1845" . . . JQA, *Diary*, MHS Online, No. 45, September-November 1845; Nagel, pp. 404–405; JQA, *Diary, Microfilms of Adams Papers*, Reel 48; JQA, *Memoirs*, Vol. 12, pp. 268–269.

236 "But since leaving the" . . . JQA, *Memoirs*, Vol. 10, p. 346.

236 "Indeed, the Big House" . . . Nagel, p. 387; Henry Adams, *Education*, pp. 15, 13.

236 "Henry Adams tried to" . . . Henry Adams, *Education*, p. 5.

237 "Advanced age deepened Adams's" ... JQA, *Memoirs*, Vol. 7, pp. 147–149; Vol. 10, p. 343; Vol. 11, pp. 269–270, 341, 508; Vol. 12, pp. 200–201, 275; Bemis, *Union*, pp. 104–106; Nagel, pp. 124, 202–204, 407; Shepherd, p. 132.

238 "Unprepossessing General Zachary Taylor" ... Wheelan, *Invading Mexico*, pp. 62, 74–76.

239 "'There are, and always'" ... JQA, *Memoirs*, Vol. 12, pp. 255–266.

239 "As Army Lieutenant Ulysses S. Grant" ... Grant, *Memoirs*, p. 30.

240 "In an ambush" ... *Congressional Globe*, 29–1, pp. 791–795; Appendix, pp. 642–643; Wheelan, *Invading Mexico*, pp. 96–98.

241 "Adams expressed his extreme" ... Bemis, *Union*, pp. 499–500.

241 "While Adams's mild stroke" ... JQA, *Memoirs*, Vol. 12, p. 263; Bemis, *Union*, p. 498.

242 "On August 8, the penultimate" ... Wheelan, *Invading Mexico*, pp. 155–156, 159; *Congressional Globe*, 29–1, pp. 1215–1217.

242 "Believing that the final" ... JQA-John Palfrey letter, November 4, 1846, *Microfilms of Adams Papers*, Reel 154; *Concise Dictionary*, p. 751.

243 "By mid-August, Adams was" ... JQA, *Memoirs*, Vol. 12, pp. 272–276, 278.

243 "But on October 31, 1846" ... Ibid., pp. 276–277.

244 "Adams was staying with Charles" ... JQA, *Memoirs*, Vol. 12, pp. 279–281; Bemis, *Union*, p. 528.

245 "The House rose" ... Quincy, p. 425; French, p. 192.

245 "Relieved of all committee" ... *Congressional Globe*, 29–2, Appendix, pp. 437–438.

246 "In Quincy that summer" ... Nagel, p. 412; JQA, *Diary*, MHS Online, No. 46, p. 205.

246 "Adams presented two petitions" ... Hecht, p. 626; JQA, *Memoirs*, Vol. 12, p. 281.

247 "The previous Thursday, he" ... Bemis, *Union*, pp. 533–536; *Biographical Dictionary of Congress*, pp. 143–146; Henry Adams, *Education*, p. 20; Shepherd, pp. 402–403; Richard, pp. 202–203; Hecht, p. 626; Nagel, p. 414; JQA, *Memoirs*, Vol. 12, p. 282.

248 "On February 24 and 25" ... French, p. 200; Bemis, *Union*, p. 539.

249 "'He has been privileged'" ... *Token of a Nation's Sorrow* (Courtesy MHS), pp. 1–27; Benton, Vol. 2, p. 708.

250 "At the service" ... Nagel, pp. 415–416.

250 "Draped in black, the train" ... Seward, *Life*, p. 351.

250 "Adams's remains reached Boston" . . . Bemis, *Union*, p. 542; Seward, *Life*, p. 353.

250 "The next day, Adams's casket" . . . Bemis, *Union*, p. 543.

250 "In May 1852, Louisa" . . . JQA, *Memoirs*, Vol. 12, p. 283. [The characters "A" and "Ω" refer to the passage in Revelation 1:8, "I am Alpha and Omega, the beginning and the ending, saith the Lord."]

EPILOGUE

255 "Now accountable to just" . . . *Historical Statistics*, Vol. 2, p. 1084.

256 "'The cause is good'" . . . JQA, *Memoirs*, Vol. 9, p. 298.

256 "'The right of petition'" . . . *Congressional Globe*, 26–1, Appendix, p. 747.

259 "William Seward, who would" . . . Seward, *Life*, p. 399.

259 "Adams's poem to sculptor" . . . JQA, *Memoirs*, Vol. 12, p. 286.

Index

Acknowledgments

The friendly, helpful reference librarians at the University of North Carolina–Chapel Hill and at Duke University appreciably eased my task of bringing John Quincy Adams and his era to life.

At UNC's Davis Library, I read firsthand reports from the *Congressional Globe* during 1831–1848 about the debates of the Gag Rule and slavery, and the attempts to censure Adams in 1837 and 1842. Between the *Globe* and Davis's seemingly endless shelves of bound volumes of *House Executive Documents*, I was able to read Adams's committee reports on the Smithsonian, the Massachusetts Resolves, and the other issues examined in this book.

For my benefit, the librarians at Duke's Perkins-Bostock Library made numerous trips to retrieve many of the 608 reels of the *Microfilms of the Adams Papers*. John Quincy Adams was a prolific writer, as were his parents, his wife, their son Charles Francis, and the later Adams descendants. The *Microfilms* also contain Adams's complete *Diary*, only part of which is represented in the twelve-volume *Memoirs*.

The Massachusetts Historical Society has digitized the *Diary*, and it is searchable online. This is a terrific resource. The MHS staff was helpful and courteous when I traveled to Boston to conduct on-site research.

I am grateful to Lindsay Jones and Niki Papadopoulos at PublicAffairs for helping me to whip the book into shape, and to my agent, Ed Knappman, for his steady support.

And I am obligated to my wife, Pat, for making suggestions about the manuscript and for serving as a sounding board for my ideas.

About the Author

JOSEPH WHEELAN, a former Associated Press reporter and editor, is the author of *Invading Mexico: America's Continental Dream and the Mexican War, 1846–1848*; *Jefferson's War: America's First War on Terror, 1801–1805*; and *Jefferson's Vendetta: The Pursuit of Aaron Burr and the Judiciary*. He lives in Cary, North Carolina.

PublicAffairs is a publishing house founded in 1997. It is a tribute to the standards, values, and flair of three persons who have served as mentors to countless reporters, writers, editors, and book people of all kinds, including me.

I. F. STONE, proprietor of *I. F. Stone's Weekly*, combined a commitment to the First Amendment with entrepreneurial zeal and reporting skill and became one of the great independent journalists in American history. At the age of eighty, Izzy published *The Trial of Socrates*, which was a national bestseller. He wrote the book after he taught himself ancient Greek.

BENJAMIN C. BRADLEE was for nearly thirty years the charismatic editorial leader of *The Washington Post*. It was Ben who gave the *Post* the range and courage to pursue such historic issues as Watergate. He supported his reporters with a tenacity that made them fearless and it is no accident that so many became authors of influential, best-selling books.

ROBERT L. BERNSTEIN, the chief executive of Random House for more than a quarter century, guided one of the nation's premier publishing houses. Bob was personally responsible for many books of political dissent and argument that challenged tyranny around the globe. He is also the founder and longtime chair of Human Rights Watch, one of the most respected human rights organizations in the world.

• • •

For fifty years, the banner of Public Affairs Press was carried by its owner Morris B. Schnapper, who published Gandhi, Nasser, Toynbee, Truman, and about 1,500 other authors. In 1983, Schnapper was described by *The Washington Post* as "a redoubtable gadfly." His legacy will endure in the books to come.

Peter Osnos, *Founder and Editor-at-Large*